16

A history of

MULLION COVE

CORNWALL.

By Robert Felce BSc Hons

First Edition December 2012

Published by Robert Felce r.felce@gmail.com

ISBN 978-0-9569895-1-2

Cover photo; Net Loft and Fishing Boats in Mullion Cove 2006 Photo by author.

Produced by Westcountry Printing and Publishing, Churchtown, Mullion, Cornwall TR127HQ.

PREFACE.

In 1875 the Rev Edmund G. Harvey B.A. Vicar of Mullion and Secretary of the Mullion Lifeboat, produced his book entitled, *"Mullyon: its history scenery and antiquities"*. Since that time little has been written of the history of Mullion Cove. In the last 135 years several generations of fishermen have come and gone and listening to the dwindling numbers who are left today it was apparent that they have a wealth of information and stories, some of which have now been recorded here.

My wife and I first visited Mullion together in 1972, 40 years ago. Back then we stayed in a tiny tent at a camp site, and then called *Criggan Mill.*
Many people who live in the area have a long standing affection for the Cove. I, along with people such as local fisherman Barry Mundy, a true Cornish fisherman, a man with many stories to tell, felt that the time had come to remember and record what life used to be like, and how the picture that is the Cove, came to be painted.
Barry often begins his recollections with, *"Back in the day"*... ", *"Father used to say..."*or *"It was like this see..."* before recounting his tales. You know that there is always a smile under that beard and he`s always happy to talk to anyone who has a question.
I have come to realise that time doesn't matter too much in the Cove as long as you can get the boat safely into and out of the water. I think that is what it must have been like 150 or 250 years ago... until the shout of *"Heva, Heva"* was heard from the Hill, and there was a rush to net the shoal of Pilchards. Sadly that call is no longer heard.

Unfortunately Barry is not the best at remembering dates... but then who is anymore? It was left to me to try and put that right. After all, when we research historical information we still want to try and get our facts right... don't we?
Today, if you can use a computer, there are new tools which help us do that. The British Newspaper Archive, for example, has recently become a research tool of some importance, and information from such newspapers as the Royal Cornwall Gazette, the Cornishman, the West Briton, the Western Morning News and many others have allowed the online reader to discover details of life back 250 years ago. Many articles about Mullion Cove and Harbour have been sourced for this book and collated for the first time.
In the book we can look at the characters which made up the harbour and fishing community. This was part of the way of life, which unfortunately has almost been lost.

Among other things we can examine the details of the building of the Harbour Piers, and find out why they were built at all - surprisingly it wasn't just for the benefit of the fishermen. We can look at the old buildings, some Listed, some going back several hundred years.We can look at the individuals who have worked in the Cove and spent almost all of their life in the fishing industry.
We are in danger of losing valuable information about our past.
Knowledge is passing away with the people who have held it dear for so long. Tomorrow or next year may be too late.
I have tried to paint a picture of life in this Cornish coastal cove since the 19th century, indeed earlier in some cases, and to try to put the reader directly in touch with the Cove as it used to be.

There is always more information out there somewhere, little snippets maybe but important.
I couldn't write or record without the information provided by many elderly people living in the community, Cornish or otherwise, who would like same thing- a history to be recorded. I have lost count of the number of people who have said to me, *"I wish I had listened more to the stories my father and grandfather told".*

INTRODUCTION.

Mullion Cove (50 00`56 .64"N 5 15`26.35"W), is part of the Parish of Mullion, situated on the west coast of the Lizard Peninsula in Cornwall. It lies in an Area of Outstanding Natural Beauty (AONB). Since 1945 it has been owned and managed by the National Trust. It is a very popular visitor attraction and known the world over. The Cove is approximately 1.2 miles (1.93km) from the village church in Mullion, and is approximately 6 miles (9.66km) south of Helston. It is nearly 14 miles (22.5km) from Penzance and Newlyn, ports with which it has had traditional fishing links for hundreds of years.
The earliest known Map representation of the area is presented in the Lanhydrock Atlas but makes no mention of the Cove, and it appears to have been first recorded on an official map as Port Mellin in 1811.

Today the Cove has a Harbour enclosed by two magnificent Grade II Listed late 19[th]century granite and stone built Piers, built in two stages between 1890-1892 and 1895-1897. The Harbour encloses approximately 1 acre. It provides protection for small boats from the strong winds and tides which have regularly hit the coast over many years, helps to maintain a small fishing community with historic origins within the Mounts Bay Fishery, yet still provides a sheltered beach for summer visitors to sit or play. It has a stone and concrete slipway, which is approximately 50`(15.5m) above sea level which has been modified over several hundred years. It is regularly used to draw a small flotilla of fishing boats above the grasping fingers of the highest tides.

In the early 19th Century the river ran down the middle of the slipway with a Leat on the north side of the harbour which fed two Mills, but from 1867 its course was changed to be incorporated into an enclosed conduit, discharging onto the beach between high and low tides. Three hundred yards further inland is the site of a third Mill named either *Creggian Mill* or *"Mullion Mill"*. At the top of the slipway there is a Grade two Listed Net Loft and Winch House associated with the historic pilchard, crab, lobster and crawfish fishing and the site of old Fish Cellars. Modern rebuilding has erased some of the details of a number of Fish cellars and other buildings of interest, but the footprint of these old buildings is still very strong.

Mullion is a natural sandy Cove, originally only 40` wide and one of the few locations on the west coast capable of providing a safe berthing place. Two hundred years ago the Cove from Mullion Island to Pedngwynian, bore the name *Mullion Roads*, and could often be found full of sailing boats sheltering from the frequent easterly winds which prevented passage past the Lizard. A sudden change in wind direction often caused embayment and many lives were lost in the resultant wrecks of vessels which had been driven onto the rocks ... but yet, many lives were also saved through the bravery of the Coastguard and those who risked their lives to help.
It is not the intention of this book to delve into the distant past but to help provide an explanation for what exists today.
Lord Robartes at Lanhydrock was responsible for the upgrading of the Cove Roads, the building of the Lifeboat House and the Harbour walls and Piers in an effort not just to help local fishermen but improve trade and conditions for Victorian farmers and village businesses. There is little doubt that the Robartes were benefactors of some influence.

What of the name Mullion Cove? There has long been a connection between Cornwall and France and in particular with Breton, from where St. Mellanus is believed to originate, a name linked closely to the village Church. It was called Porth Mellon or Porth Mellin in 1840, and sometimes Porth Mellyn. The Cornish –English dictionary describes the word *melin* as meaning a Mill. There is no doubt that a fisherman returning home by sea might say that the Cliffs around the Cove look yellow for much of the year and may consider similar Cornish words such as *melyn*, meaning yellow as a source for the name, but I believe it is likely that the Grist Mills, are the real reason for it being named Porth Mellin.

Whatever the origin of the name, each year, Mullion Cove attracts thousands of people from all over the World, many of whom return every year. For some it is a pilgrimage to be able to stand again on the old stone piers and look out towards Mullion Island or The Vro, or even St. Michaels Mount and Penzance or Newlyn.
There are links to the terrible period of shipwrecks in the 19th Century and to the bravery of the Lifeboat crews and the Coastguard with their Rocket Apparatus, and the stories of the fishermen and rescues which still take place now, but with Helicopters, Cliff rescue Teams, Air Ambulance and Lifeboats.

There is the building of the Harbour Piers in the late 19th century, the Regattas which attracted thousands to cheer and watch from those piers and the cliffs , and the Mining and Quarrying which were so important in the 1700s and yet were forgotten for a long time. And two East Coast American brothers called Andrews who sailed across the Atlantic in a tiny cedar boat in 1878, trying to get to Paris, and landed in Mullion Cove. The story went around the world, but how quickly some things are forgotten.
There is the transition to, and development of Tourism and the Hotel trade in the Victorian era as well as some stories of the two World Wars.

Industry was evident in the 18th century. The Mining of Copper and the Quarrying of Soapstone to make Porcelain.

We move forward to today and the future for the Harbour and the Cove. The Piers are suffering from the rigours of time and tide.
 In 2005 the National Trust took a decision which may lead to their removal, and before we know it, the massive piers could soon be lost forever. But what else will be lost? Perhaps it is now time to reflect on the history of the Cove.
Let us try to tell their story. *"Father used to say that back in the day ..."*

ACKNOWLEDGEMENTS

I would like to thank the British Newspaper Archive for allowing me to use extracts from their records. Old news stories make excellent reading and what a fine way for someone to learn about the History of their own County or Country in their own time. Also thank you to Angela Broom at the Courtney Library, Tamsin Mallett at the County Record Offices in Truro, and the Royal Cornwall Museum Photographic section.

I also would like to thank Sarah Riddle at the National Maritime Museum, Falmouth and Dr. Joanna Bellis, the RNLI Archivist and her staff for checking their records, and likewise the Lifeboat Enthusiasts Society and also the Pilchard Works in Newlyn.

I would like to thank Barry Mundy and John Pascoe for their personal contributions and memories.

If there is anyone who knows about the workings of the Cove then it has to be Barry Mundy, a Cornish Fisherman, who is also interested in Cornish and Breton History but especially the History of the Cove. His photographs, family stories and overall knowledge have been an important contribution to the overall story. What better life could there be than putting out to sea and pulling Crab Pots for the odd Lobster, Brown Crab and Spider Crab or just fishing for Mackerel, Pollack, or Sea Bass. But I know from personal experience it can be hard and fraught with dangers.

There have been contributions and support from everyone in the Cove including Nick and Jeff Meyer, Paul & Patricia Pearson, Duncan Barron, Dorcas, Allen and Alanna.

In the village I would like to acknowledge the contributions made by Rex Bray, Lesley Thomas, and Oscar Hill and a special thanks to Agnes at Mullion Gallery. Also a special thanks to retired fisherman Geoff Wellum DFC.

Helston Museum has a number of exhibitions including Pilchard Fishing and Henry Trengrouse Rocket Apparatus. They have allowed me to publish some photos of their display, so thank you to the current staff, and one recently retired Janet Spargo.

There is always a danger that I have left someone off the list and if I have I apologise. They know who they are. Barry's wife can get her wall built, and my wife can have her table back.

Fig. 1 above, the original Silver "Mullion and Gunwalloe Challenge Cup" presented at Mullion Regatta` from 1897 - 1901. It was presented by W.Sich Esq. to John George "*Gleaner*" 1897, Sam Mundy "*Maud*" 1898, Thomas H. Downing "*Ettie*" 1899, (1900- No Regatta, due to passing of Mrs Harvey at Trenance), and Sam Mundy "*Maud*" 1901. (See Ch.14).

Photo by author 2012. Reproduced courtesy of B. Mundy.

Preface

Introduction

Acknowledgements

Contents

Appendices

    A   Mundy Memorial Church Service 1872
    B   Harbour Plans
    C   Victorian Census Records
    D   The Huers Hut
    E   1841 Tithe Map

Chapter 1 19th CENTURY MULLION COVE

In 1859 the Lloyds sub agent for the Lizard Peninsula announced that he had made an examination of all the Coves from the Lizard to Loe Bar and that "... *a boat could go to sea more frequently and with less danger than at any place inlet or Cove along the coast*". He was referring to *Porth Mellin* or Mullion Cove being one of the few locations suitable for the launch and recovery of boats on the West Lizard Coast. Mullion Cove was a fishing cove for several hundred years before the 1850s, yet that examination was necessary to find a site where a Lifeboat could be installed. It was in response to the great loss of life resulting from a series of shipwrecks experienced at that time, during a period

of increased storm activity. A later building of the Harbour and Piers in two phases between 1890-1892 and 1895-1897 changed the landscape again, and created a new chapter in its existence, one which still survives over 110 years later.

Fig.1a, left, an undated mid 19th Century Mullion Cove. Courtesy of local resident.

In the 19th Century very few people made their home in Mullion Cove. There were however, Mills, Fish Cellars and a Coastguard presence which linked it with the village, a mile away along the Nansmellyon Road. The Cove was mainly a shipping point for Minerals, Copper, Soapstone, and Fish. Until the Harbour was built the Farmers and Traders in the village were more reliant for their goods and services upon the Ports of Gweek and Porthleven, five miles away. The roads were poor, and the travel slow and arduous, so it was perhaps inevitable that modernisation should take place. Some would say it was only right and proper, and that the process of change could not have taken place without the financial help of Lord Robartes and the Lanhydrock Estate.

Thankfully, the Tithe Map of 1841 and early Victorian Photography has left us with a legacy of the mid-late 19th century landscape of the little Cove. These are the earliest scenes which we can examine in detail, and as each picture tells a story, we can try and interpret what we see today. Fig.1 tells us that the Listed Net Loft, probably the oldest building still standing in the Cove, had been extended to the North, but later part of it was removed to help construct a path to the South Pier.

Fig. 2 right, undated 19th Century Photograph Porth Mellin Cove looking west.

It also tells us that the north side of the Cove was being developed with the construction of a retaining wall. This enclosed a Leat, and through close examination of the Tithe Map we find that in 1841 the Leat connected two grist Mills. Traces of the original Mills are now long gone. The photography also shows us the protective reef stretched out to a little rock called the Var, which can still be seen today outside the West Pier, south of the large rock known as Scovern, or Ear Rock.

This reef was removed with the building of the West Pier and we know that some of the rock was used as infill for the walls. It shows us that there was a fishing industry and that the crab and lobster boats with the sails drying over the bows were hauled up out of the water to protect them from bad weather.

Fig. 2 tells us about the size of the Cove with its rocky reefs to the north and the south, both pointing out like guiding fingers towards the Serpentine of the Vro, and the ancient Pillow lavas of Mullion Island, some 700yds (670mtrs) away, with *Treguin Rock* on its north side. The Island helped to provide shelter and security for so many ships.

It shows us the fishing activities there, the resting boats, the Crab and Lobster Pots made before the start of each season by local fishermen from "*withies*". These were grown on most farms in the neighbourhood, the willow gardens helping to provide a livelihood for the fisherman. There is the hand winch made in Helston, which was needed to pull the boats and fishing gear on land to be dried, mended and barked ready for use.

Fig.3   Mullion Cove slipway & boats. After 1867.
Photograph Reproduced with The Kind Permission Of the Royal Institution of Cornwall.

When we look inland, we see the Cove as an industrious place with an active pilchard and crab fishery. We see an ordered foreshore and a small Cornish fishing community living at its own pace. We can see the labourers loading seaweed into their cart, to be pulled by two horses up the hill on the narrow winding road out of the Cove, later to be scattered onto fields as fertiliser. These are scenes which would have made a canvas for any artist of the day. We see the crab boats with their masts raised, ready to be launched and amongst them the smaller punts or followers. We see the heavy wooden seine boats, which were so important, drawn high out of the water to protect them from damage, but ready to be launched for a seasons fishing. Just behind the two seine boats, on the left, is a wooden Capstan Winch and a wooden platform, used to haul them to safety.

The remains of a Capstan still exist today sitting on a circular plinth of cemented rounded beach pebbles.

On the sloping north facing cliffside is the drying ground where the nets were laid out to dry after use before being mended and stored ready to be used again.

Directly behind the three seine boats is the Loft, now called the Winch House which was an important fish cellar, with its high stone wall to the east enclosing the "Run" to where the Pilchards were carried in gurries, "baulked" and put into wooden casks where they would be pressed to release oil and sent to the Mediterranean in their millions via Newlyn.

Behind the "Run" is a thatched cottage which census records tell us was occupied by fisherman Samuel Hichens, his wife, and family for so many years, and by its side is the "road" to Predannack Village. Perhaps the horses and cart will soon be taking the winding road to a Predannack Farm.

Fig. 4 right, Building the South Pier, began in 1895. Reproduced with permission of B. Mundy.

Between the "Run" and the Capstan was the most well known building in the Cove at that time, the Lifeboat House, built in 1867 by donation from Methodists, the RNLI and Lord Robartes. It housed a total of three lifeboats in succession until 1908, when it closed.

By 1892 the West Pier had been completed and by 1895 stonemasons and navvies were again working on the South Pier. See Fig.4

In the photograph right Fig. 5 the seine boats are on the foreshore, and behind them is the Net Loft. The Harbour is beginning to take on its modern look. By 1900 the Harbour would be immediately recognisable to many people today.

Just in view is the Pilchard Run which extended behind the Winch House. Unlike today, there are no windows facing west towards the sea. The piers were built and more buildings had been added to the North Causeway, plus a road to the village.

Note the wooden rollers, thick tree branches, used to help the boats up and down the slipway, and the little hut with an awning from where the serpentine ornaments were sold.

Fig. 5 right The Cove, c. 1900 Showing 3 Fish Cellars, Coastguard Watch House and Net Loft. Reproduced courtesy B. Mundy.

In the centre ground behind the Capstan Winch is the old Coastguard Watch House. It had a Fish cellar at the rear. Today people would recognise the SE corner of the building as the "Porthmellin Cafe".

Behind the Coastguard Watch House, damaged by fire before the First World War, and which for many years stored

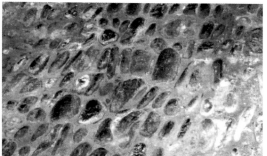

the Coastguard Rockets and other Rescue Apparatus, are the remains of a 19th century Fish Cellar.

In the mid 1900s property which had been used as fish cellars began to be converted for accomodation, a sign of changing times in the fishing industry.

Fig.6 left, Fish Cellar Floor. Photo by Author 2012.
Courtesy of P. Pearson.

Today, one remnant of the cellar still remains in situ. Part of the Cafe premises still retains the remnants of a traditional fish cellar floor, which would have run the full length of the building and would have been made from thousands of cemented pebbles. This is typical of such cellars erected throughout Cornwall.

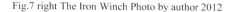

Fig.7 right The Iron Winch Photo by author 2012

Another remnant remains today, looking the worse for wear. The Iron Winch is a reminder of the thousands of times that the boats were hauled up the slipway by the fishermen after a days fishing, the end of a season, or the onset of a storm. It was made at the Toy Iron Foundary at Helston. The Winch, now missing its turning handle, is still bolted onto the slipway. It was not the only winch in regular use, and several would have been needed, and some are still visible in old photographs.

Fig. 8 right, Capstan and Plinth. Photo by author 2012

At the top of the slipway, between the Cafe and the Lifeboat House is another legacy of the 19th Century, and that is the the Capstan. It is seated on a circular plinth of cemented rounded beach pebbles and although it is beginning to show signs of serious wear and tear it provides yet another link to the hard work and manual effort required by those early fishermen to secure their boats.

When we talk of storms and sea level rises we should remember that at least once or twice every century the sea has encroached almost to the level of the Capstan, and the last time was only 20 years ago.

Chapter 2 MULLION MILLS

*"Porth Mellin Cove; A-nigh the Rustic Mill
Had I but language to portray thy charms
How would I paint the emerald of thy waves
A-twinkling `neath the glow of morning sky..."*

<u>A Brief History Of Grist Mills</u> The following article involved a study of the landscape in and around Mullion Cove, which several hundred years ago was modified by human hand to create a system which utilised an existing river to create a structured water course for three Mills. These Mills produced flour from local grain for the local community in a manner traditionally used for over a thousand years. The early relationship between the Mills in *Porth Mellin* Cove and the local community has not really been explored before, even though the very name *Porth Mellin* means *"a bay, port or harbour of the Mill or Mills"* in Cornish (1).

The Mills and their associated water management system influenced both the landscape and building in the Cove.

Water powered grain mills have existed for 2000 years. In the Doomsday Survey of 1086 there were over five thousand water grist mills recorded in England. This was the equivalent of one for every 300 inhabitants at that time.

The classic description of such a Mill is a building which uses water power to turn an external water wheel, linked to a geared drive shaft which rotates a Millstone wheel onto a fixed stone base, in a process used to grind grain to produce flour. Farmers would supply the Mill with grain which was then ground, and they would receive back the flour or meal minus the "Millers Toll".

Fig. 9 left, the remains of Mullion Mill today. Photo by author 2012.

The Mills were often built or supported by the local farming community and the villages were actually dependent upon them to provide flour for the local population to make bread and feed for cattle. They were therefore a very important local resource (1a).

The water supply was usually controlled. It fed the channel which was directly linked to an external wheel on the Mill building. The wheel was usually fixed on a vertical axis and the water could feed over the top as in an overshot wheel, (or in some cases underneath as an undershot wheel). Internally the wheel was connected to a large gear-wheel fixed on the same axle which drove a smaller gear wheel on a main driveshaft running from the top to the bottom of the Mill building. This ensured that the main shaft turned faster than the Mill wheel. Equipment such as the grindstones, usually made from Granite, usually rotating about 120 revs / minute, or lifting gear were operated off the main shaft.

A regular supply of water to the Mill was vital and it was usually supplied via a stream or river with a constant flow. Seasonal or sudden water flow changes meant that the flow had to be regulated. Often the flow was maintained by the provision of a Mill Pool, an artificial pond dug out by hand with a water channel linked directly to the Mill wheel.

The flow of water after the Mill Pool to the wheel is called the Head Race. After the Mill wheel it is called the Tail Race. A Tail race after a wheel which heads directly towards another Mill is called a Mid Race.

The water direction was provided by a man made channel or Leat. The final stage of managing the watercourse could come in the form of a mechanism to take the water to the wheel, called a Launder, often a raised wooden platform or guttering containing an open channel to carry the water. This could be turned on or off by a mechanism which could be a sluice gate, but there were alternative mechanisms. Launders were not uncommon in Cornish Water Mills.

Used water often passed back into the river or stream system, or in Mullions case, to the sea.

Mills were found in nearly every village and manor. They were valuable assets to the owners, who were frequently the Lords, rather than the community. None are mentioned locally in the Doomsday Book at Helston but they are mentioned in a Charter of 1260.

In some boroughs the inhabitants were compelled to grind their own corn in the Lords Mills and bake their own bread in the Lords ovens, but in others they were free (2).

There are records of a number of Grist Mills in Mullion Cove which date back 250 years or longer. There is evidence from as early as the 1760s in the form of a Lease for *"Ennis and the Mills in Mullion"*. It is dated 20th March 1766 (3).

Fig.10 left Mullion Mill showing overshot wheel and launder c. 1900. Courtesy D. Barron

In some villages on the Lizard Peninsula bread was a scarce commodity. Wheat was often not available and Barley was considered to be a labourers alternative. A man might have to walk for miles to buy or barter for a bag of grain, then carry it to the nearest Mill and wait for it to be milled, make payment, and then carry his milled flour home to use as needed.

Mullion Mill is situated on the south side of the Cove Road. Two hundred yards before the Harbour, are a series of farm buildings surrounding an open yard, bounded on the north side by metal gates. The single storey farm buildings were for stabling and storage and in the early 19th century there was also a Farmhouse which was rebuilt.

There is one building painted white. This is the old three storey Mill. This building is a Grade II Listed Water Mill which probably dates back to the early or mid 1800s and is made of whitewashed rubble with brick dressing, a slate roof and a reduced brick chimney. On the second floor is the gable end which has a central loading door, and an opening above.

On the ground floor is a split wooden stable door. To the rear of the building is the stone lined pit for the wheel, sadly, now gone (4). It is described as a mid 19th century Water Mill, but may have been in use earlier.

It is sometimes referred to as *Crigian, Creggian or Criggan* Mill. It was given Grade II Listing in 1980.

In 1820 there was a Sale of Land by sealed tender in the estates of Great Trenance, Trenance Vean, Ennis, Garro, and Terre Bean, involving *"...three Water Grist Mills and the Fish Cellars near Mullion Cove... in the occupation of Messrs William Thomas, and Jeremiah Jose and John Tippet etc"*.

There was no name given to these Mills in this sale (6).

These Mills were leased from Tremenhere Johns by William Thomas, Jeremiah Jose, John Tippet and others. This was probably a collective of local farmers from the area. Fig.11 right, advert dated 5th August 1820 (6).

The Mill itself had a 30` overshot wood and metal wheel, located at the rear, and probably built by Williams and Son of Lady Street, Helston (4).

ALL those valuable Freehold and Leasehold ESTATES in the Parish of Mullion in Meneage, known by the names of
GREAT TRENANCE, TRENANCE VEAN, GARRO, ENNIS, AND TERRE BEAN.
Also, Three Water Grist Mills and the Fish Cellars near Mullion Cove and Two Tenements, in Mullion Church-Town.

The whole containing about 383 Statute Acres of capital arable and pasture Land, and enclosed Crofts, now in the occupation of Messrs. William, Thomas, and Jeremiah Jose, and John Tippet, &c. The several tenants will shew the Premises, and for further information enquire of Messrs. GRYLLS, BORLASE, VIVIAN, and TREVENEN, Solicitors, Helston, where a Map of the ESTATES may be seen, and to whom the Tenders are to be made, on or before the 14th day of September next, immediately after which the most eligible Offerer will have notice thereof.
Dated 5th August, 1820.

Leading up to the wheel was a raised wooden Launder which was fed from an upstream Mill Pool. The Mill Pool, now filled in, was not operated by a sluice, but a stone plug. The Launder, as can be seen in the above photograph from the early 1900s, was a hand built raised wooden platform, an open conduit, on supporting wooden legs and brick built pillars.

A Managed Landscape. The 1841 Tithe Map (5) and the accompanying Apportionments show that there were three Mill Pools and two Mills in the valley from Porthpradnack to the Cove. A fourth Pool is indicated on the run of the mine adit below the Copper mine, running north into the valley. It appears that the water management system for the

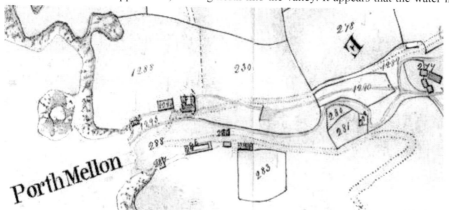

Mills commenced with the Pool at Porthpradnack, which was probably about 50 yds in length. A local resident tells me that this pool still existed in the landscape up until the 1960s.

Fig. 12 Extract from 1841 Tithe Map (5). Reproduced with permission from Cornwall Record Office. See Appendix E

The small triangular marks on the Map are Millpools on the course of a leat or artificially constructed water course. The Tithe Map 1841 shows that 170 years ago there were two Mills recorded in the Cove itself. See Appendix E, Tithe Map Apportionments 1841 Numbers *1291* and *1292* (5).

In April 1846 the three Grist Mills at Mullion were offered to be, "*Let by Tender for a Term of 7 or 14 years*", and included, "*... all those three very excellent and well accustomed Grist Mills called Crigian Mills... together with the dwelling-house, barn, outbuildings and 16 acres of Arable and Meadow Land and 18 acres of Crofts...in the occupation of John Williams*" (7).

According to a descendant of John Williams, he, his wife and his family arrived in the area about 1834.

Little information is known about these Mills, their description, or how busy they might have been, but according to the 1841 Map one was on, or adjacent to the site of the Porthmellin Cafe and the second was 100 yards to the west, on the site of what is now the North Causeway.

Leats. A Leat is an artificial watercourse, dug into the ground, especially one which supplies water to a watermill or its Mill Pond or Pool. The watercourse below the Pool is often referred to as the Tailrace They can be several hundred yards or several miles in length.

A Leat often runs along the edge or side of a valley, at a shallower slope than the main stream, the gradient determines the flow rate.

.

Fig.13 right 1846 Advert for sale of Mills then called Crigian. (7).

By the time it arrives at the Mill the difference in height between the leat and the main stream is sufficient to provide a good head of water, 5-15 feet for a watermill (8). The 1841 Tithe Map shows the course of the River, but it also shows the Leats which supplied the Mill Pools.

Their course is directly related to the supply and management of water to the Grist Mills.

Mills and Premises in Mullion.

TO be LET by TENDER, for a Term of 7 or 14 Years, from Michaelmas next, all those Three very excellent and well accustomed

Grist Mills called Crigian Mills,

In the Parish of Mullion;

Together with the Dwelling-house, Barn, Out-buildings, and about 16 Acres of Arable and Meadow Land, and 18 Acres of Crofts, as the same are now in the occupation of John Williams.

The above Mill are in a thorough state of repair, and from their situation and being supplied with a good stream of Water, command the best and most productive Grist Business in the South of Meneage.

TENDERS stating the utmost Rent that will be given (free of all outgoings), will be received by WM. JOHNS, Land-Agent, Helston, until the 9th day of May next.

Mr. JEREMIAH JOSE, of Trenance, will show the premises, and all other information may be obtained, by application to the said WM. JOHNS.

Helston, April 17th, 1846.

The course of the river running from Trenance/Tere Bean (Porthpradnack) is one which was altered prior to 1841. This appears to have been an attempt to control the flow of water leading to the Cove.

As already indicated, adverts placed in local Newspapers as early as 1820 indicated that there were 3 Water Grist Mills near the cove.

About 250 yards below the Porthpradnack pool the river branched, running along both sides of the valley. It apparently did not follow the lowest course, which may show that its course had already been altered. From this point the north tributary skirted Orchards and a Meadow before meandering around the farm buildings and joining the river below Mullion Mill.

The south branch, with a Leat joining the Mill Pool feeding Mullion Mill had been built by 1841 south of the site of the old Farmstead occupied by John Williams. The Mill Pool fed the Mill, not by a sluice, but by a stone built plug in the bottom.

A descendant of John Williams has said that when the family arrived there, intending to become Farmers and Millers the housing was in very poor condition which eventually led to a rebuilding of the Farmhouse about 1868.

Census Records. See Appendix C,

The 1851 Census Records show a dwelling called "*Mullion Mills*", occupied by 8 members of the Williams Family, a Servant and a Lodger. The dwelling and Mills were recorded under the same name.

In 1861 it was referred to as "*Creggian Mill*", occupied by John and his wife Ann Williams, their daughter, their son Andrew, described as a Miller, and their grandson John Casley aged 4 years, who later drowned in a tragic accident in the Millpool.

In 1871 the site in the census was described as "*Mill*" and as well as the Williams Family their grandson and granddaughter lived there along with one servant. By 1881 and 1891 the site was recorded in census records as "*Mullion Mills*"

Below Mullion Mill the river, the Tailrace and the Adit stream watercourses all join up in an area now covered by vegetation, but which has been manually cut out of the bedrock in the river valley. The River itself took an independent course to the Cove. Before 1841, a Leat was cut through bedrock to the north side of the valley. Part of this Leat is still visible behind Mullion Mill Cottage. The Leat ran west, parallel to the River, to a Mill Pool which was originally on land which is now the front garden of Cove Cottage. The Head race then crossed the Cove road and went on for approximately 70 yards to the site of the next Mill, at the "Porthmellin Cafe" site. It was probable, given other similar Mills in the area, that the latter part of this Headrace led to a raised Launder, which fed an overshot Mill wheel. There is certainly a sufficient drop from the site of the Millpool to this Mill.

In 1841 the "Porthmellin Cafe" site was recorded on the Tithe Map Apportionments as a Mill (1291), leased via Tremenhere John and occupied by John Williams.

Adjacent to it was the Coastguard Watch House (1293) possibly occupied by the Coastguard from the late 1820s.

There was no one recorded as living in the Coastguard Watch House in 1841, but by 1851 Thomas Sterling, RN Coastguard, was living there with his wife and three children.

Following on west from the Watch House was the Jose Fish Cellar (1294).

Perhaps surprisingly, between the Jose Fish Cellar and the sea, on what was at that time a mid race, the Tithe Map 1841 Apportionments record the existence of another Mill (1292), also leased by John Williams. After this Mill the water discharged into the Cove.

The River, however, at this time ran down the centre of the Cove over the beach and slipway, discharging directly into the sea. The current course of the waterway was engineered in 1867 with the building of the Lifeboat house.

The Mullion Cove Painting. (See page 9)

An important early 19th century painting of Mullion Cove is known to exist, but whose ownership is not currently known. It was apparently painted by an artist called Nicholas Matthew Condy 1816-1851. Condy was born in Plymouth and educated in Exeter and although he was intended to have an army career he became a successful marine painter. He exhibited at the Royal Academy. His father Nicholas Condy 1793-1857 born at Torpoint was also a landscape painter who exhibited two pictures at the Royal Academy between 1830 and 1845 (1a).

The painting is of a coastal seascape painted from the Cove looking west.

It includes features such as the Reef which were later removed from the Cove. In the foreground is a rocky reef on which are seated 3 people looking out to sea. The seine boats are at work between the Cove and Mullion Island. Behind the people are 2 fishermen talking by a boat.

The boat appears to have a sail drying over it, along with oars, which would indicate that it is a crab boat, typical of Mullion Cove. There is a similar open wooden boat towards the north side.

Fig. 14 right
Reproduction of Condy Picture showing Mullion Cove and Mill.
(Owner unknown)

The rock on which the three people are seated is part of a natural rocky outcrop, or reef, which is also seen in early photographs, and which was removed to ground level when the West Pier of the Harbour was built in 1890.

On the southern edge of the Cove, looking towards the Vro, is a boat with empty crab pots nearby, apparently being returned to the shore by half a dozen fishermen?

However the most interesting part of the painting is looking towards Scovern or Ear Rock where there is a gabled building with a chimney stack on the eastern end. By the chimney is what appears to be a split stable type door.

The building is at least two storeys high with two or more windows facing south, but on the west side is a Mill Wheel. A slight enhancement of the picture reveals an Overshot Mill Wheel with water being discharged into the Cove.

This is the Mill (Tithe Map Apportionment number 1292) indicated on the Tithe Map 1841 ... and is a very rare representation of it. It supports the existence of the Mill as recorded in 1841. Considering the subject of Condy`s other paintings this may have been painted between 1830 and 1841. By 1850 the Leat, flowing towards the sea had been altered, and the two Mills in the Cove itself had either gone or were reused.

Mullion Mill was in operation for another hundred years after the two mills in the Cove ceased operating. It was said to be much more efficient than the Cove Mills. As a central Mill for many local farmers, they brought their grain to be milled, and collected the flour mainly for animal feed but also for domestic use.

Modern times.

It was a very important operation for the community as a whole and milling operations went on until the 1950s and 1960s, run by Farmer and Miller, Hannibal Williams and his father. By now the equipment was being operated by means of an externally operated Fordson tractor with a drive belt, linked to the interior of the Mill.

As a young boy local retired fisherman John Pascoe would help with operations at the Mill. He would walk past the Mill every morning, and he remembers the icicles in winter hanging from the launder leading to the wheel.

A few lads would climb the wheel for a dare but Hannibal wouldn't be too pleased if he caught them. John recalls that the local farmers from would bring up to 20 sacks of grain on their horse and cart to be milled. Most would be left by the door to be ground down and then later collected. Hannibal was a tireless worker and would operate the Mill for many months of the year, often late into the night. John was particularly fond of the old farm horse called *Captain*, who worked the farm drawing the cart. Old *Captain* worked on until he was 25 years old and John was deeply saddened when he had to be put down. Witnessing that event left a lasting imprint on his memory.

Earlier this year two visitors who had not returned to visit the site where they camped for many years related how they were given fresh milk and eggs when arriving for their holiday late one night, but not to worry too much if they heard banging as it would only be old "Captain" kicking his stable door.

 Local Mullion resident, Oscar Hill, now in his eighties, worked at Clahar Farm as a young lad and would take a ride on the back of a horse drawn cart loaded with grain through the village and down to the Mill. He would wait his turn for it to be milled, before returning the same way to the Farm to feed the Cattle.

The Mills were some of the earliest buildings in the Cove and some of the most important for the community. The valley from Porthpradnack was transformed by the important early engineering work conducted to construct the leats and the launders, and until the mid 1800s their importance no doubt discouraged any further building activity in the locality. It has long been known that Mills existed in the Cove, but their location has not previously been fully explored. By examining the 1841 Tithe Map closely, along with the feasibility, existence and direction of the Leats, and an examination of the early 1800s painting of the Cove, a new interpretation has been presented.

Bibliography

1. http://www.howlsedhes.co.uk/cgi-bin/diskwe.pl
1a. wikipedia
2. The History of Helston. H. Spencer Toy, 1936.
3. Reversionary Lease Cornwall record Office 1766
4. http://www.britishlistedbuildings.co.uk/en-64666-criggan-mill-mullion-
5. 1841 Tithe Map (Ref TM/160) and Apportionment (X585/3), Mullion. Truro Record Office.
6. RCG 19.8.1820
7. RCG 24.4.1846
8. RCG 20.9.1861

Chapter 3 THE MULLION HARBOUR STORY

Seeking Shelter.

Mullion Cove or *Porth Mellin* lies on the west coast of the Lizard Peninsula about 5 miles (8km) north of Lizard Point. It was here, over 200 years ago, along a stretch of the coastline between Mullion Island and Pedngwynian, 2 miles to  the north, that many ships sought shelter. This stretch of coast was known as the Mullion Roads and at times of strong easterly winds, when the sailing ships and steamers could not negotiate a passage for long periods past the Lizard Point they would look to anchor for safety in the Roads. From the 1830s onwards there was a growing desire to improve conditions for all sea going vessels, their crew and passengers using Mounts Bay.

It was written that *"From Falmouth to Lands End there is no shelter but a roadstead in S or SW gales. Mounts Bay is but a man trap when the wind is from that quarter, and if a foreigner without a pilot could find Mullion Roads in a night as black as a pocket he must have uncommon good anchors to trust to for a safe lodging. There is something tragic in the thought that to a ship staggering helplessly down upon a lee shore in the darkness of the night or in a fog or in one of those storms which confounded the sky, and the sea in one abyss of cloud, the lights that twinkle from habitable homes are no better than the wandering fires that beguile the lost traveller on a morass. They seem to beckon the seaman to his fate. What a cruel irony in the welcome of those windows and hearths. Falmouth found shelter for over 300 vessels ....preserving property and lives.... This should stimulate Penzance to proceed more energetically with the great scheme for converting Mounts Bay into a harbour of refuge by the construction of a breakwater"* (1).

Thousands of sailing ships passed through Mounts Bay annually on their way around the coast and were at the mercy of the weather.

The Mullion Roads were seen as a temporary haven against the elements, but sudden changes in the wind were often catastrophic. They were the scene of many a shipwreck and amongst the inhabitants of the towns and villages there existed a growing realisation that many lives, could probably have been saved.

Mullion Cove has been a home for the Pilchard, Crawfish, Crab and Lobster fishermen, for hundreds of years. The Cove also acted as shelter for the many sailing ships against the gale force winds which regularly battered the Mounts Bay and the Lizard. At times there could be several hundred ships lying at anchor waiting for a favourable change of wind direction so that journeys could be resumed around the Lizard. What a sight that must have been.

Mounts Bay Breakwater.

In 1836 a Mounts Bay Breakwater (See Fig.15 right) was proposed by a wide deputation of MPs including Sir Charles Lemon, and a number of prominent naval men. They put their concerns and plans to the First Lord of the Admiralty who agreed to send an engineer and direct a survey. A company was formed, connected to the extension of the Railway from Truro to Penlea Point at Gwavas Lake, close to Penzance, designed to form a breakwater, ¾ of a mile out to sea, and towards St Michaels Mount, large enough to shelter 16 ships of the line and a larger number of merchant ships. The harbour at low tide at that time was unserviceable to large vessels.

It was reported in the same year that *"During the late prevailing winds from the North and North East, the Mount Bay presented a most interesting scene, being crowded with vessels of various descriptions, wind bound, no less than from 250-300 riding at anchor in the Roads, exclusive of a vast number which took shelter in the piers of Penzance and St. Michaels Mount. A sudden change in the wind direction, not an uncommon occurrence, would have left many of them stranded, but a breakwater would allow them to ride in perfect safety in any wind"* (1a).

MOUNT'S BAY BREAKWATER.

Truro, Redruth and Penzance Railway Company

In continuation of the London, Exeter and Falmouth Railway,

With a Breakwater at Penlea Point,

MOUNT'S BAY.

Capital £550,000,

In Shares of £25 each. Deposit £1 ℣ Share.

PATRON

His Most Gracious Majesty King William IV. Duke of Cornwall, &c. &c. &c. &c.

PATRONESSES

Her Royal Highness the Duchess of Kent, and Her Royal Highness the Princess Victoria.

VICE-PATRON

His Royal Highness the Duke of Sussex, K.G., P.R.S., &c. &c. &c. &c.

Around Mullion the list of stricken ships was long.

In February 1833 in Mullion Cove, a smack became embayed in Porth Pyg under Vounder Nean for several days before breaking up, and later in October of the same year a coal carrying ship, the *Bellamy* out of Padstow became stuck on the Vradden, eventually breaking up in the Vro Cove.

Shipwrecks were not restricted to the winter. The weather could change at any time, winter or summer, and wrecks occurred with great regularity.

In June 1838 the *Silus* sailing from Naples and believed to be carrying salt, became a total wreck at Pollurian after striking a rock near Mullion Cove, in a thick fog. The Captain and crew were all drowned and the bodies were later buried in Mullion Churchyard. (2) & (3).

In April 1839 three small vessels, one called the *Penrice Castle* carrying coal and the other two laden with slate were grounded between Henscath and the flagstaff. One of the slate ships ran into the *Penrice Castle* and was grounded at Pedn-y-Ke, and another at Polglas under Merres Hedge (3).

In 1849, a report was posted that *"There were now at anchor in the Mullion Roads, one hundred and twenty sail with the wind blowing very strong from the ESE"* (4).

In January 1859 an 1100 ton iron screw steamer the *Czar* carrying munitions and soldiers clothing from London to Malta foundered on the Vogue Rock half a mile off the Lizard and 18 crew were rescued. There were immediate calls for more Lifeboats including at Cadgwith and Porth Mellin.

A letter (1859) recalled that the *"Lizard is well known to be the highway of the commerce of the world, it has many miles of dangerous coast, every night there is a risk of collision, yet there is not a lifeboat on all of this coast"* (5).

In April 1859, the National Lifeboat Institution had decided to station a lifeboat at *Porth Mellin* Cove. T.J.A. Robartes Esq. MP promised £100 and the Hon. Mrs Agar £50 plus £10 per year to the undertaking.

Lloyds sub agent at Mullion said *"I would have placed one at my own expense had I been in circumstances so to do. I have carefully examined all the coves from the Lizard Head to the Loe Bar ... and I find that a boat can go to sea from Porth Mellin Cove more frequently, and with less danger, than any other place, inlet or cove on the coast"* (6).

However, changes were not immediate and more devastating losses were required before a Lifeboat station was built at Mullion. It was a fateful few days in January 1867 which began a course of events which would change the future of Mullion Cove.

The Great January Storm

On Friday 4th and Saturday 5th January 1867 there raged in Cornwall one of the most violent storms on record. The wind and rain were terrific and even snow descended in torrents. On Sunday the sun shone but on the Monday night the storm returned.

By 4pm on the Saturday afternoon the tide had risen to a great height in Mounts Bay, near to Penzance. A schooner, the *Vesper*, laden with coal, had anchored in her berth at the old pier. A second schooner similarly laden pushed in by the tide and wind cut into her moorings and both ships were forced into a collision with a third ship, the *Earl of Devon* lying close by. The 3 vessels had to be scuppered to prevent further damage. A while later a ship in distress was seen anchored between Long Rock and the Mount, and the coastguard informed. Rocket apparatus was sent and the lifeboat put to sea saving 5 men. Almost immediately the chain broke and the ship, also laden with coal, was forced onto the beach where it eventually broke up. During the course of the evening a number of ships were seen drifting the Bay towards the piers looking for shelter and there were many other incidents of both disaster and courage.

At Penzance the sea was very violent and all vessels in the harbour were placed on moorings, the sterns being held by chains and the bows by lines. Great waves were seen to pass over the Albert Pier, larger than had been seen for years, and considerable damage was done to the stonework. About half past two a coal schooner, the *Julia* successfully reached the harbour having been sheltering in Mullion Roads. The captain reported some 30 vessels in the Roads when he left. On Sunday morning a messenger was sent from Mullion to Lloyds Agents in Penzance to say that several vessels had run aground at Mullion and more were expected. A similar situation was reported throughout the Towns and Harbours of Cornwall. The lower section of Helston Town was inundated, with houses and roads flooded.

On the Lizard, an easterly wind on the Friday had prevented ships making the Channel and by Saturday evening there were 19 schooners riding at anchor to the west of Mullion Island, and though the wind was fresh overland, the high cliffs provided shelter However towards the evening the situation which was most feared occurred with the wind turning from SE to S and by 10 o'clock was blowing from South to West. Those on land knew only too well the difficulties these ships would face leaving the rocky shore. As Sunday morning dawned the disaster began to take effect.

From Gunwalloe/ Church Cove to Mullion Cliffs pieces of broken timber were strewn at intervals and there were still 5 vessels within a mile of the shore. There was no Lifeboat at Mullion at the time and messengers were sent to the Lizard for the Lifeboat. From as far away at Porthleven it could be seen that at least one of the schooners was doomed and the Lifeboat was got ready. However, the tide would not allow the Porthleven Lifeboat to launch and about 10am it was taken 10 miles by land to Gunwalloe pulled by 6 horses. As it arrived in Mullion, people attending Church were unaware of the true nature of the disaster. Rev Harvey told his Churchwarden Mr. J.B. Kempthorne that there would be no service in the Church that morning and many parishioners rushed to the cliffs at Angrouse to watch. There they found the schooner, the *Margaret* of Teignmouth in great danger and dragging her anchor towards the cliffs. The coastguard had their rocket apparatus and shot a number of rockets towards the vessel which fell short or missed before it touched the shore. During the previous night another schooner, the *Cherub* of Swansea had dragged her anchor lines over that of the *Margaret* and in the confusion one of her hands, George Mudge, had crossed over onto the *Cherub*. About 11pm the *Cherub* subsequently foundered and the crew including Mudge got into a boat and rowed for Pollurian, eventually landing on the beach and finding shelter at a cottage at La Frowder, before being taken by fishermen to Churchtown (7). So it was, on that Sunday morning that poor George Mudge was on the cliff at Angrouse watching with hundreds of people the demise of his shipmates, plainly visible, as the ship drifted slowly onto the rocks. They could not be reached by boat, or with the rocket apparatus. The captain was seen with 3 crewmen watching the hundreds of people on the cliffs and hoping for rescue. The crew thought, and hoped, that that they must be rescued. By 12 o'clock the ships stern struck the cliffs and after staying in the breakers for a minute or two, heeled over with her mast to the shore. A wave struck and two men were washed overboard and lost. Another man was carried away by the waves. A rocket line reached the rigging but was unable to be fixed. The Captain was seen to jump into the breakers, trying to swim for his life. Men with coils of rope were on the shore but could not reach him. Within the sight of the crowd the wreckage of his own ship engulfed him and so died Captain Bowden of the schooner *Margaret*. Within minutes the ship broke up and the wreckage floated away, the cargo of coals sinking to the seabed. The body of the Captain was found some 2 days later close by at Pollurian. Later on Sunday the schooner *Ebbw Vale* of Swansea which had been abandoned by its crew some time earlier dragged its anchor onto the same rocks and was destroyed, the crew previously having been taken off by another ship (3b). The Lifeboats arriving by land never got into the water. The general feeling among those present was that this was a disaster which must not be repeated.

The Public Meeting

On Monday 14th January 1867 a public meeting was convened by the Rev E.G. Harvey at the request of several of the residents (8). It was held in Mullion and attended by many local people including farmers, fishermen and the coastguard. He called attention to the main object of the meeting - that of humanity towards their fellow man. Harvey recalled his first visit to the Cove where he spoke with a fisherman saying, *"What an admirable little harbour could be formed by joining the island to the main"*. He found that this was an opinion very generally held. He was surprised also to find that there was no lifeboat stationed there although a recent attempt had been made, but refused owing to the alleged difficulties encountered by the ruggedness of the cove and the difficulty in both transporting a lifeboat, and obtaining a crew. This was regarded by many as an attack on Mullion men and also untrue. Rev E.G. Harvey supplied to the meeting an incomplete list of wrecks and incidents known to him which had occurred between 1838 and the meeting. These included the *Neapolitan* in June 1838 at Carag Luz, when 15 drowned, the Norwegian schooner the *Elizabeth* in November 1846 at Gunwalloe when 5 drowned, the Finnish Barque *Iris* in October 1847 at Poldhu when 6 drowned and 6 were saved, the *Glencoe* out of Whitby which was wrecked off Pollurian in September 1858, and in the same month and year the schooner *Chester* whose crew managed to row safely to Mullion Cove, the *Mary* of Bridgewater also in 1858, the Austrian Barque *Padre* at Poldhu in January 1862 when 13 drowned, the *Dollard* at the Rill also in January 1862, the *Arwennack* in December 1862 *at* Gunwalloe when all hands drowned, the barque *Santisto* at Gunwalloe when 17 were drowned and two saved in November 1865, in October 1862 the French Brig

Oscar, whose crew were saved using rocket apparatus at Gunwalloe ... *and only 2 months after the meeting, on 25th March 1867 the Jonkheer* at Men y Grib, when 24 drowned. He was supported by Thomas Shepperd of Tremenhee who hoped something could be done about the matter, which, he explained; he had felt strongly about for some time. Mr J.B. Kempthorne of Polhormon Farm said that the Mullion Roads provided shelter for ships in a strong easterly yet they were in imminent danger where the wind shifted to S or SW, a not infrequent occurrence, it would help to station a Lifeboat at Mullion. Mr Fred Thomas of Trevitho was keen to second such a proposal saying that it was a pressing want. He said that there were good men in Mullion, brave and active, who knew the coast well and would be best suited to man a lifeboat. Mr Curgenven of the Coastguard was asked how many ships put into the Roads and replied that he had counted 182 since he had been at the station. Mr Dionysius Williams said that he had seen 215. Several people said that they had seen 150-200 at times. Mr Fred Thomas supported the argument for a lifeboat saying that on this score alone a lifeboat would be desirable to guard the anchorage and be launched almost anywhere along the coast at Poldhu (Poljew), Gunwalloe or even Pollurian (Bollurian) if a road was available. Mr Joseph Thomas of Colroger, brought the attention of the meeting to what he regarded as even more important, that of converting Mullion Cove into a kind of Harbour of Refuge into which distressed or embayed vessels could easily run. He described a situation where the "Gap" between the island and the mainland was filled up, at once forming a harbour where ships could ride-out S or SW gales. The Chairman asked about the available depth of water in the "Gap", and Dionysius Williams replied that it was 2 fathoms at low spring tide and between the island and the beach was 6 fathoms at low spring tide. He added that there was enough shelter there for 30 ships to lie at anchor. Mr Josiah Thomas said that it would be of great use as it would not be a blind harbour, but in full sight of all ships and he proposed that an application be immediately applied for to the Government and other means to form a harbour of refuge at Mullion either by filling the gap or other measures which may be more expedient. Mr Peter Williams of Angrouse seconded the proposal but did not believe that a lifeboat could always be put out from the Cove. Mr Shepherd of Nafrego said that there would be some states of the tide when a lifeboat could not be launched unless egress could be made safer. The above proposition was carried and a committee formed to carry out the proposal (9).

After the meeting the committee contacted the RNLI. Following a visit of an RNLI Inspector an offer was made on the part of the Institution of a Lifeboat, the *Daniel J Draper.* Lord Robartes granted the ground for the boathouse and also offered pecuniary assistance for the needs of the branch. £200 was spent constructing a road to the sea. (See Ch. 4)

400-500 Vessels at anchor. It was recorded on March 15th 1867 that there had been *between "400 and 500 vessels anchoring in our roads during these last few days. All, I am glad to say, have got away safely, but yesterday 2 large barques were in a very critical position for some hours. Had it come on to blow there would have been no chance of escape for them"* (8).

On the night of 25th March 1867 another gale blew and the *Jonkheer Meester Van De Wall,* a Dutch East Indiaman, carrying coffee, sugar, spices and Tin ballast returning from the East Indies went aground and broke up on the rocks at Men y Grib between Pollurian and Poldhu with the loss of 24 men, women, a child and crew members. The only survivor was a Greek sailor Georgio Buffani, who was able to give evidence at the Inquest, held at the Old Inn in Mullion that the ship got into difficulties while tacking in Mounts Bay, and could not get out of the Bay. The ship, with all its crew on deck, could not hold and ran aground, breaking up in 20 minutes (5). The introduction of the *Daniel J. Draper* followed. The Cove entrance was widened and the beach improved. A large number of rocks which were causing obstruction to the harbour entrance were blown up and removed with the assistance of the Lifeboat Institution. The new lifeboat was successfully used in October 1867, a month after its introduction. The *Achilles* of Glasgow was carrying a load of timber and was reported in distress in thick fog off Pollurian. On that occasion the Coastguard were successful in saving the Captain and 14 hands by means of the Rocket apparatus, and the Lifeboat was able to save a further 3 men from the crew (10). Many wrecks still followed, but the most damaging for the local community was the tragic loss of a Mullion fishing boat off Porthleven in April 1872, crewed by the then Coxswain of the *Daniel J Draper*, William Mundy (58) his sons Joel (25) and Henry (13) and a friend John Henry Williams (20). (See Ch. 5)

In March 1873, again following the loss of life in wrecks, Rev. Harvey wrote to the Western Morning News in an attempt to procure *"telegraphic communication"* for Mullion. His aim was to improve the response of the Coastguard and Lifeboats by securing help for stricken vessels. It was the responsibility of the Coastguards on duty to "walk their coastal beat" which could take many hours, and something which he felt needed much better communications. He wrote that *"In 6 years and a quarter there have been 9 wrecks with the loss of 69 lives under Mullyon Cliffs on a bit of coastline not more than a mile and a half in length, and more than 100 lives lost out of thirteen wrecks in 10 years"* (See Ch. 4)

The 1868 Harbour Proposals (12).

It was reported on December 24th 1868 that the Board of Trade, or to give it the proper title, *Lords of the Committee of her Majesty's Privy Council for Trade and Foreign Plantations*, had received an application for a Provisional Order to constitute a Harbour Authority to alter deepen and improve the harbour, or cove, usually known as Mullion Cove, and to make and maintain the new works following. The improvements contemplated were sought to construct three Breakwaters, a quay or landing place and slipway. The quay or landing place was to be on the north side of the present beach or landing place and was to be about 130` long and 20` in width. The slip at the north end of the quay or landing place was to be 90` in length and 10` in width. The first Breakwater planned in 1868 was to be 630` long and to extend from the east point of Mullion Island to a detached rock near to the NE point of the Gull Rock, the second about 25` long to extend from the N. point of the Ear Rock to a central rock between it and the mainland. The third Breakwater extended from before the aforementioned Main Central Rock to the mainland being a length of about 55`. Payment for the works was to be by Mortgage of the dues (11). In accordance with the Regulations at that time they had to construct and maintain a connection with the said works, quays, wharfs, jetties, landing places, approaches, warehouses and other works and conveniences. To levy tolls, rates and duties upon or in respect of the Harbour and works, and to confer vary or extinguish exemptions from the payment of Tolls, rates or duties. To erect and maintain cranes, weighing machines, sheds and warehouses which now or may hereafter be erected, belonging to the Harbour Authority (12). Notice had to be given in the London Gazette and copies of Plans and Sections deposited with the Clerk of the Peace in Bodmin, at the Customs House in Penzance and the office of the Board of Trade in Whitehall, London. Copies of the Order could be purchased for a shilling. This Plan however did not go ahead. The proposed breakwater between Mullion Island and Gull Rock would have been a huge feat of engineering and one which, had it been completed would no doubt have created a refuge for the many ships unable to surmount the problems of the weather and tides. It would also have created a tremendous boost for the local economy.

The 1890 Harbour Proposals.

In February 1890 early plans were being put before Parliament by Lord Robartes for the construction of a Harbour of Refuge at Mullion, incorporating a pier seaward from Henscath Rock and also Mullion Island as a breakwater. The plans, it was hoped, would enclose a harbour sufficiently capacious to hold all the fishing fleets of the villages and the vessels which anchor in the Mullion Roads when easterly winds prevented them from rounding the Lizard Point.
Even in February 1890 such conditions prevailed and there were 40-50 ships seeking shelter by anchoring in the Roads. It was said that with a harbour all these ships would be able to avail themselves of supplies from the shops in Mullion Village (13).
The proposed Harbour lay between Scovarn (Ear Rock), and Henscath with the rocks now lying there being removed in the construction process.

By May 1890 new plans were prepared for the building of a Harbour at Mullion Cove. The Bill to confirm the Board of Trade Provisional Order empowering the construction of Harbour Works at Mullion Cove passed the examiner on Standing Orders in the House of Lords without opposition and went to a second reading. The original proposal was to construct two piers near to Scovarn or Ear Rock to form a Harbour (14).

Fig. 16 left the site behind Scovern originally proposed in 1868 for Mullion Harbour and initially for the 1890 Harbour.
Photo by author 2012.

<u>1890 Mullion Harbour Orders</u> (15).

The original Order of (1890-1891) authorised the following works;
1. A pier of jetty commencing at a point on the mainland opposite the rock known as Ear Rock and extending in a northerly direction 150`... together with an approach road thereto and together with all proper approaches, embankments, roads, footpaths, sewers, drains and works and sheds, buildings, landing stages, landing places and other works and conveniences for the embarking and disembarking of passengers, animals and fish, goods and merchandise of every description.
2. A pier or breakwater commencing at a point on the mainland 130`... to the westward of the northern termination of the aforementioned pier or jetty and proceeding in a southerly direction 120` or thereabouts upon or over the foreshore or bed of the sea and terminating on the north side of the Ear Rock so as to form a harbour together with all necessary openings in and all necessary and proper works aforesaid.
 There was some opposition to the plan from by the advisor William Matthews, later Sir William Matthews, KCMG, 1844-1922, born Penzance, Member of the Institute of Civil Engineers, who was vastly experienced and was responsible for building many other major harbours including Dover, Singapore and Malta. In 1906 he was appointed to a Royal Commission to investigate tidal and coastal flooding in the UK.
The initial plan was to create a small creek 180` long and 80` wide with a Quay to the east, rocks to the north and Scovern, and artificial work across the gateway to the west, with a possible extension across the rock called the Var. On close scrutiny Matthews decided that there was an almost continual heave or run of the sea within the enclosed gateway created by the initial plan which required massive and expensive engineering and structural work which would have provided minimal shelter to vessels.
He wrote in a Report in 1890 "*At low water on the 18th I carefully examined the site of the proposed works on either side of the Ear Rock. There is almost a continual heave or run, through the gateway which would render the construction of these works both difficult and costly... Upon the completion of the works as sanctioned, no shelter whatever would be afforded to the Cove, the benefits derived from the execution of the project being limited to the protection afforded to the proposed quay of about 160 feet in length during westerly winds of moderate strength only. Having carefully considered the works above described, I am unable to recommend that they be carried out...*"
The objections to this initial plan were summarised as being;
1. High Cost,
2. Lack of shelter afforded by the construction,
3. Damage to small vessels caught by heave (rhythmical rising of the sea) & swell,
4. Lack of shelter in strong or gale force SW winds requiring continual beaching of vessels for protection,
5. Vessels could lie alongside the quay in fine or moderate weather only.

He went on to consider options before concluding, *"In my opinion this can be done, most effectively certainly, and economically, by sheltering the Cove by means of short piers, or dams ... I propose to construct a west pier of 180` in length, extending from the north west horn of the cove and a south pier 130` in length starting from the first point of rock on the southern margin of the Cove. The arms have been so placed as to form a close and thoroughly sheltered harbour, having an entrance between the pier heads of 60` in width... it will be observed that the works will receive considerable protection from Mullion Island and Ear Rock during on-shore gales" The rocks within the sheltered area would be excavated so as to form a bed or laying ground of uniform declivity, the bottom along the harbour face of the west pier being throughout at the level of low water of ordinary spring tides... The quay wall on the north side ... would be 150` in length... the rocks in the harbour would be removed as required for rubble stone for the works leaving the bed alongside the quay uniform and suited for the berthing of craft alongside. The whole of the works should be completed by the end of 1891."*

Another consideration was, *"The outlay ... might be reduced to the extent of £1430 by the omission for a time of the south arm"* (16).

Fig.17. Construction of the West Pier well under way. Closer examination of the photo shows the Steam Crane in front of the Jose Fish Cellar to the right, and unusually a small boat on the notch of rock on the ledge above the junction of the West Pier and North Causeway. In addition the walled Winch House Cellar "Run" is clearly visible, along with the capstan and winch. The protective rocky reef is in the process of being removed to form the floor of the harbour. Photo courtesy B. Mundy.

<u>1891 Amendment Order.</u>

This was prepared by William Matthews and the Plan was re structured, to include;

1. A pier jetty or quay on the mainland about 150` in length, commencing at the north west corner of Mullion Cove and extending in an easterly direction along the face of the cliff forming the northern boundary of the cove together with a roadway at the back of the same, and an approach road thereto, about 70` in length.

2. A pier about 180` in length, commencing at the said north west corner of the cove by a junction of the aforementioned pier jetty or quay and extending in a southerly direction nearly at right angles to the said pier jetty or quay, which said pier jetty or quay and pier will include all proper approaches as listed above ... plus toll-houses, toll gates, buoys moorings etc.

3. The removing by dredging, digging, excavating or otherwise of any rocks sand mud or other material which it may be found necessary or convenient to remove for any purpose connected with the construction of the works aforesaid deepening of the area on either side of the piers plus removal and placing of any material outside the west pier as protection against the sea.

4. A second South Pier was planned, 130` in length from the first point of rock on the southern margin of the cove. The arms were to be placed so as form a close and thoroughly sheltered harbour having an entrance between the pier heads 60` in length. Adjustments to this gap could be made as required.

Both arms were to be of solid construction, the outer faces consisting entirely of stone and a "hearting" or middle of cement concrete with large rubble incorporated within. The rocks within the sheltered area would be excavated to form a bed which would dissipate any heave, swell or scend.

The amount of water at high water of spring tides was to be approximately 1 acre, enough to provide berthing for up to two coasting schooners and room for the seine boats and "hookers".

The bottom on the outside of the west pier being throughout at the level of low water on ordinary spring tides and the width of the surface of the West pier to be 25`, enough for cart traffic.

In addition there was to be sheltering parapet on the seaward side. Although the harbour works was limited, ample accommodation would be afforded to meet the wants of the locality, and the fishing industry long located in the cove.

It was estimated that the whole of the works would be complete by the end of 1891. In conclusion it was pointed out that the outlay in the first instance might be reduced to the extent of £1430 by omission, for a time, of the south pier. Without this arm, however the requisite degree of shelter could not be afforded and would lead to shoaling of sand in the harbour. A decision was taken that the West Pier (North Causeway and West Pier) would be the first to be built and no application to build a South Pier was made for the time being. The transport of the granite quoins for the Harbour walls created a traffic problem in the village. They had to be brought in by horse and cart and initially could not negotiate the road which then existed near the Old Vicarage.

Estimates of the cost (£) were provided as for as follows

West Pier 180 foot in length	6500
South Pier 130 foot in length	1430
Quay wall and roadway at back of same	700
Special excavation in addition to sums Included in estimates for piers, the stones Being derived from the removal of rocks on the harbour bed.	200
	8830
Contingencies 5%	442
	9272
Outlay exclusive of engineering & cost of Provisional Order	9300

As a result the road lay out had to be changed. It resulted in the current unusual layout of Nansmellyon Road as it passes the old Vicarage (L.Thomas)

In 1881 there were no more than 2 local families listing their occupation as Stone Masons. Examination of the Census records for 1891 provides some interesting results and evidence that skilled workers connected to the building of the Harbour had moved into the village as either tenants or lodgers, in some cases bringing with them their families.

The company building the Harbour were Langs of Liskeard. In Churchtown James Bidgood (56) brought his wife and family from Liskeard, including his son John (30), a Mason, along with his wife, while another son Tony Bidgood (25), a Mason, and his wife Lilly lodged at Mullion Mills with the Williams family. William Gest (60) and John Taylor (36), both "Navvies" lodged with Charles and Mary Johnson in Churchtown. Thomas Francis (35), a stone labourer, lodged with his wife and family with the Willeys at Naprego.Richard Bowden (51), a stone cutter and Thomas Frang (45), a stone labourer lodged with the Gilberts at the Vicarage. George Reynolds (34), a visiting Granite Cutter lodged at Teneriffe. Richard Bettison (39), a stone crane driver, from Liskeard lodged with his family at Trenance Vean with the Thomas family. These must have been only a few of the people employed on the building of the West Pier, and no doubt a slightly later census would be very revealing (1881 & 1891 Census Records).

Local men and lads were also employed on the building of the piers at all levels. One local lad, William John Mundy left school at 12 to work on the construction work then taking place. His job was to collect the chisels and other equipment which needed sharpening and take them up into the village blacksmith at Mullion so they could be sharpened. He would go up to the village by pony and trap and then return them to the stonemasons after they were sharpened.

Fig. 18 Left, Outer section of South Pier. Photo by author 2012.

Visitors to the Cove in August 1891 noted that satisfactory progress was being made with the construction. They were aware that throughout the site were Notices stating that when blasting was taking place they were to be aware that "*Horns would be sounded and red flags hoisted*" (17).

Fig.19 right,
Outer section of West Pier.
Photo by author 2012

The Great Blizzard.

Part of the construction of the West Pier at Mullion took place during 1891.

This also happened to be one of the worst winters within living memory in Cornwall with severe frost, snow and storms lasting for several months. On the afternoon of March 9th 1891 there was a huge snow blizzard. It was said that, *"... the weather suddenly changed and the sky became dark. Soon the air was as cold as Greenland and blinding sleet fell, while the north wind rose to hurricane force...Men and women out of doors left their work and ran for shelter... All traffic stopped on the roads and no trains ran the snow continued falling for two days... a bus with horses left Helston for Penzance and arrived five days later having been stuck between Breage and Ashton"* (18) .

It became known in Cornwall as the Great Blizzard.

Passengers in Trains were stranded for 36 hours before rescue and locally snow was reported to have been on the ground until July. However it was reported that the works at Mullyon Cove were greatly interfered with by the state of the sea, which had hardly settled down since the blizzard. It was suggested that the Harbour was unlikely to be completed for another 9 months (19).

In September a heavily laden sailing boat from Porthleven went aground off the Cove carrying 9 tons of cement. The Falmouth pilot boat, on watch in the Cove at the time, launched a cutter and rescued the crew of 2 men and 2 boys all from Porthleven, taking them ashore to the Coastguard Station where they were looked after (19a).

The winter of 1891/2 resulted in further severe weather problems including snow storms.

Work on such a scale brought a number of issues, some of which were social rather than engineering matters.

The Licensing Question

Mullion in the latter stages of the 19th Century was almost a Temperance village with the Methodists in particular opposed to alcohol.

In September 1890 there was only one Licensed House in the Parish, at the Old Inn. It was thought that the Old Inn had been built about 200-300 years earlier and was for a long time the home of the well known Mary Mundy. It had apparently outlived its usefulness and was described then as a *"relic of antiquity"*, unable to serve the needs of the village and its growing number of visitors.

It was suggested by a Mr H.M. Rogers that the investment of Lord Robartes in building the Pier and Harbour was an important example of the changes taking place in the village and a necessary requirement which would benefit visitors and the district as a whole. He therefore supported an application for a second licensed premise.

An 11 bedroom Hotel, with sitting rooms, offices and ample stabling overlooking Mounts Bay and owned by Mr Thomas Sobey of Prisk Farm was in the process of being constructed in Churchtown, Mullion.

An application was made to the Licensing Meeting at Helston before Rev. Sir Vyel Vyvyan, Baronet, H St Aubyn, M St Aubyn, Mr G Williams and Captain Rogers R.A. by a Mr Rogers to Licence the Hotel for alcohol. In support of his application he presented a petition of 100 signatures which included a number of local dignitaries, including the Mayor of Helston. The Hotel is now called the Mounts Bay Inn.

The proposal was opposed by Mr A R Thomas of Helston representing the "Mullion Band of Hope" and Messrs. Carne, Brewers and Spirit merchants of Falmouth, who had an interest in buying and updating the Old Inn. They suggested that a second licensed premise was unnecessary in such a small village of 605 inhabitants.

Mr Thomas said that he was the spokesman for the many villagers who did not want a second licensed premise and presented 2 petitions, one being signed by 140 *"Band of Hope"* members and the second by 200, all over 16 years of age, 20 out of 24 farmers in the area and the late Vicar. Mr Thomas added that of the 100 in favour of the application a great many of them were the names of Navvies engaged on the Harbour works and as such were merely passing through and not interested in the well-being and prosperity of the parish.

Evidence given by Telegram from the agent of Lord Robartes, apologising for not being able to attend the application stated that even he considered that a second licence in the village was uncalled for (20).

Construction.

The construction was a huge undertaking and was completed in 1892. The work, costing approximately £10,000 and paid for by Lord Robartes was completed by the well respected Cornish firm Messrs T. Lang and Sons of Liskeard. Lang lived in Mullion for the duration of the work and said that he had completed many contracts in Cornwall and adjoining Counties, but never had he experienced such difficulty as at that place. The bad weather seemed to concentrate in the Cove and for months together they had been unable to make any progress. On completion of the work Mr Lang said that he hoped it would fulfil the desire of those for whom he had constructed it, in furnishing protection and a means of livelihood to the fisher folk.

Mr Lang advocated the construction of a railway from Helston to the Lizard, and expressed the opinion that they would be inundated by visitors and tourists. The Engineers were Messrs S.W. Jenkin and son of Liskeard.

However, despite stories which have come down over the years the need for a harbour did not just involve the fishermen, or the seafarers. It also involved the farmers and businessmen of the parish, almost all of whom were tenants of Lord Robartes. It was known that the farmers had to convey nearly all their stores and produce by road to and from, Gweek, on the Helford River, and to and from Porthleven. It was partly this which encouraged Lord Robartes to build a pier at the Cove.

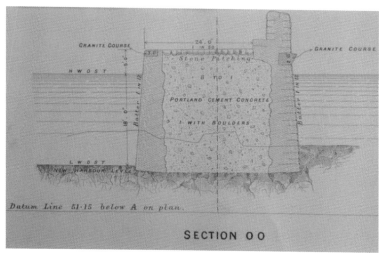

Fig.20 <u>left</u> Cross section of the construction detail of the West Pier. Plans and Sections new quay and breakwater. QSPDH/12/2 Reproduced with Permission from Cornwall Record Office (12).

Fig.21 <u>below</u>, Cross Section of the North causeway showing new harbour level and rock removed. Plans and Sections new quay and breakwater. QSPDH/12/2 Reproduced with Permission from Cornwall Record Office (12).

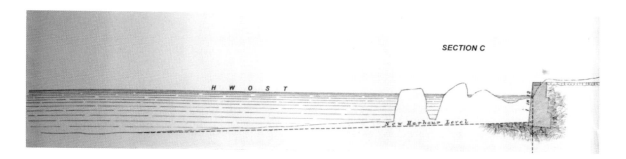

<u>Cause for Celebration</u>

After completion of the construction a grand celebration was planned for the opening of the pier. It took place in December 1892. Lord and Lady Robartes along with the Hon. Eva Robartes attended Mullion in the morning by carriage and on reaching the Square were met by a procession consisting of a large portion of the inhabitants who loudly cheered the visitors. The carriage was placed in the procession which then marched to the Cove headed by Mullion Brass Band, followed by the Parish Officials, Lord Robartes tenants and agents, the crew of the lifeboat and fishermen, schoolchildren and the local Court of Foresters (21).

On reaching the works Lord and Lady Robartes inspected the Harbour. Lady Robartes paid a visit to the Mullion Sea Caves.

Whilst down in the Cove it is said that Lord Robartes enquired of the fishermen what they thought of the new harbour and the fact that ships could now come in to load and unload.

He would undoubtedly have been taken aback by the nature of the reply he received from one fisherman who replied that *"If you bring a schooner in here, she`ll be leaving her bones behind."* Coal ships had been brought into the Cove for many years and anecdotal evidence goes that the second boat into the new harbour was a coal carrier.

It apparently took two tides to unload the coal and then quite a complicated procedure to get the boat from its mooring, under sail and out to sea again, depending on the tide. The boat had to be warped from its berth to the edge of the pier and turned to point west out to sea. In this operation there was a sea surge and the warps broke, leaving the boat struggling to get out. The boat was eventually briefly grounded below the cliffs with the Captain vowing never to bring another boat into Mullion Harbour ever again.

Following the visit to the pier the party returned to the village. A luncheon was held in the Mullion Reading Room, which was also established by Lord Robartes, and included the attendance of the Rev. Scholefield and wife, the Lord and Lady Robartes , Eva Robartes , Mr & Mrs Pearce Jenkin (his agent) and family, Messrs J Sydney Davey, S. Jenkin, E. Jenkin, F Gilbert, A.Jenkin, W. Jenkin, T.Lang , T.A.Lang, J. Postlethwaite, R. Thomas (Pollurian Hotel),W.H. Thomas, J. George, F. Thomas, Joseph Thomas, and John Thomas.

Speeches followed after which Messrs. T Shepherd Sen., D Williams and H George, three of the oldest inhabitants in the neighbourhood presented Lord Robartes with a water-colour of the Cove before the Harbour was built showing Scovern and the sandy beach, painted by local artist W.Casley.

Mr Shepherd, who made the presentation, remarked that he was the fourth generation of his family who had farmed under Lord Robartes and his predecessors. He was pleased to make the presentation as a token of their gratitude for such noble acts of generosity as had been manifested to them in Mullion.

He added that what Lord Robartes had done for them in Mullion had been from thoroughly disinterested motives, he never calculated on having big revenue from the pier but it had been done for the benefit of the fishermen and others of the neighbourhood.

Lord Robartes said that he had been glad to show what interest he could in the welfare of the district. He believed that it had been contemplated some years earlier, to build something in the shape of a pier, but it was only of late years that the plan was matured. He was aware of his fathers` interest in the earlier plans, but that would be a very difficult undertaking. He said that it might be necessary to add another arm on the other side of the cove, that seemed to be the general opinion of those best qualified to judge.

Interest was expressed on the subject of local industries including the establishment of a fish curing factory in the cove now they had facilities to land the fish.

It was further proposed to form a *"Mullyon Trading Company"*, in which it was desired to interest the farmers in the locality so that it may be a kind of co-operative concern for the benefit of those who may be able to utilise the harbour for the carriage of goods to and from the district.

The company, if formed, would probably purchase a small vessel and utilise it for the purpose. The matter was left in the hands of Mr. A H Jenkin of Redruth (21).

In October 1894 the RNLI sent a new Lifeboat to Mullion, called the *Nancy Newbon* (22).

South Pier

Following the opening of the West Pier an application was received by the Board of Trade from Lord Robartes in July 1895 for permission to construct a south pier at Mullion Harbour, something believed to be a formality (23).

The photograph below Fig. 22 (page 23) shows the South Pier almost completed.

The Steam Crane, weighing several tons, previously seen on the North Causeway a few years earlier is situated on a platform at the end of the Pier and was positioned by using by a specially constructed railway line which can be seen sloping down to the working area.

It is surprising how neat and tidy the new Harbour looks from a distance on the cliffs above the Cove and on the north causeway. The Casley Refreshment Rooms had also been built.

Fig.22 South Pier under construction. Photo c. 1897 Courtesy B. Mundy.

The Contractor, Parkinsons, began their work preparing for the construction by bringing the Plant to the Cove in November 1895.This brought between 36-40 workers onto the site as well as the engineers, which was said to have made Mullion somewhat of a more lively place. It was believed that building the south pier would be good for both tourism and business in Mullion and it would encourage visitors in the summer to consider building new "villas" and holiday residencies benefitting local people (24).

By June 1896 it was reported that the Harbour works were so far advanced that the *Cavalier*, a 250 ton schooner was able to deliver and offload a cargo of cement, entering and leaving the harbour in safety (25).

By November 1897 it was reported that Mullions new pier was now practically complete and it was hoped that Lord Robartes efforts would prove of great benefit to those who toil on the deep (26).

The Piers are still standing after 120 years creating what is now a magnet for thousands of visitors each year who benefit from free access to a monument to Victorian engineering, workmanship and skill.

What every new Harbour requires is a new Harbour Master, and the man to fulfil that role first of all was Sam Mundy. From the outset there was a mast at the end of the west pier which was in fact the lighthouse light. Initially it was an oil light, and Sam had the task of lighting it every night, and it was said that it was lit without fail by him every evening as it was getting dark.

In April 1899 electricity was introduced to the Harbour for the first time when Messrs Veale and Co. laid an electric cable from the Cove Hotel to the North and west piers and fixed an electric lamp (27) .

The task of switching on the light then fell to a member of staff at the Mullion Cove Hotel, yet was often left unlit to the annoyance of Sam. The remains of the cable are still visible cut into the surface of the cliff. From the outset essential maintenance was consistently required and was conducted by James Harry, a village stonemason whose family still live locally. His main work, was conducted in the summer, it included pointing cracks in the walls. Like all harbour walls they regularly suffered storm damage and continued to require maintenance to keep them up to standard. Since the completion of these Harbour Piers over a century of history has passed by and hundreds of thousands of visitors have walked and sat on those reminders of Victorian skill and endeavour. They are an important reminder of the difficult conditions suffered by the workers who toiled through some of the worst Cornish weather ever experienced by engineers and stonemasons.

Bibliography

1. RCG 30.11.1872
1a. West Briton 6.5.1836
2. Morning Post 5.7. 1838
3. Rev. E.G. Harvey, Mullyon. Its history, Scenery and Antiquities 1875
4. West Briton June 1849
5. RCG 28.1.1859
6. RCG 15.4.1859
7. RCG 10.1.1867
8. RCG 17.1.1867
9. RCG 24.1.1867
10. RCG 24.10.1867
11 RCG 22.12.1868
12. Cornwall Record Office Collections. QSPDH/12/1-6, Mullion Harbour Orders. Plans and Sections 1868.
13. Cornishman 13.2.1890
14. RCG 15. 5.1890
15. Cornwall Record Office Collections QSPDH/12/ 1-6 Mullion Harbour Orders 1890.
16. Cornwall Record Office Collections. CL/675 Handwritten Report and Plan of William Matthews. Mullion Harbour. 1890.
17. Cornishman 14.8.1891
18. Cornishman 6.2.1947
19. RCG 31.12.1891
19a. Cornishman 17.9.1891
20. RCG 25.9.1890
21. RCG 15.12.1892
22. RCG 11.10.1894
23. RCG 18.7.1895
24. Cornishman 21.11.1895
25. Cornishman 18.6.1896
26. Cornishman 4.11.1897
27. RCG 20.4.1899

Chapter 4 MULLION LIFEBOAT

Opened	September 1867	
Closed	July 1908	
Coxswains	William Mundy	Sept1867-April 1872
	Samuel Mundy	Oct 1876- Jan 1906
	William George	Jan 1906-July 1907
	Joseph Gilbert	July 1907-July 1908
Hon. Sec	Rev E G Harvey	1867-1884
	John H Shepherd	1884-1890
	Rev. J. H. Scholefield	1890-1908

Lifeboats *Daniel J Draper* 1867-1887 Launches 8 Lives Saved 3
Edith 1887-1894 Launches 0 Lives Saved 0
Nancy Newbon 1894-1908 Launches 6 Lives Saved 0

It was realised that a Lifeboat was required on the west coast of the Lizard Peninsula in Cornwall by the late 1850s, as a result of an increasing level of ship wrecks which were occurring during frequent storm events. In 1859 the RNLI decided to station a Lifeboat at Mullion, described then as a dangerous locality.

The Lloyds sub agent in the area said that "*The necessity of stationing a lifeboat at Porth Mellin Cove had occupied my thoughts for a long time and particularly since the wrecks in Pollurian Cove in September. I have made an examination of all the Coves in the locality from the Lizard to Loe Bar and found that a boat could go to sea from Porth Mellin Cove, more frequently and with less danger , than any other place, inlet, or cove on the Coast.*"

T.J.A. Robartes Esq., MP, had promised £100 and the Hon. Mrs Agar £50 towards the undertaking, and £10 annually towards the maintenance of any establishment (1).

However the provision of the Lifeboat at this time did not occur and it was several years, and many more shipwrecks before a Lifeboat was stationed there.

Following the Great Storm of January 1867 a public meeting was held by villagers at Mullion which concluded that a Lifeboat was an essential requirement in order to prevent further loss of life.

The Rev. E G Harvey wrote to the RNLI and Captain John Ward R.N. visited the area to make an assessment. He reported to the RNLI Committee of Management in February 1867. It was recommended that a Lifeboat station be established at Mullion, at a cost of £183-4s-0d on a site provided by T.J. Agar-Robartes of Lanhydrock (1a) (2).

Funding.

Money was raised with the help of the Weslyan Methodists, the Rev. Luke Wiseman and Mr Thomas Smith, through the medium of the *Methodist Recorder*, which helped to pay for it.

ROYAL NATIONAL LIFEBOAT INSTITUTION.
MULLION BRANCH.
PROPOSED IMPROVEMENTS AT MULLION COVE.

PERSONS desirous of CONTRACTING for the removal of certain ROCKS which now obstruct the entrance to the Cove, and for the diverting of the fresh water stream which at present has its outlet on the beach, are requested to make application to
Rev. E. G. HARVEY,
Hon. Sec. Mullion, Helston;
From whom Plans and Specifications may be obtained. All Tenders for the above Works, separately or together (the latter preferred), should be addressed to the Hon. Sec. not later than SATURDAY, 13th July instant.
N.B.—The Committee do not bind themselves to accept the lowest or any Tender.
Dated Mullion, 2nd July, 1867.

A local Appeal was launched stating that "... the *Lifeboat was supported by voluntary Subscriptions and Donations with a local Committee of Management run by The Rev. E G Harvey, Thomas Shepherd (Tremenhee), Peter Williams (Angrouse), J.B. Kempthorne (Polhormon), John Thomas (Predannack), W.Nicholas, Joseph Thomas (Colroger). The Coxswains of the Lifeboat were reported to be William Mundy and Richard George and it was hoped that annual subscriptions would meet the purely local costs of their salaries as well as costs incurred in the quarterly practice sessions. The RNLI would pay the costs of Rewards to the Crew for saving or attempting to save life, cost of repairs, painting, and replacement of gear on the Lifeboat House. The average annual expense of maintaining a lifeboat station was £50*" (3).

Fig. 23 Advert for proposed improvements to the Cove 1867.

Rev Daniel J Draper.

The Lifeboat was named after the late Rev Daniel J Draper (1810-1866) born at Wickham in Hampshire, who became a Weslyan Minister in 1834 before going to Australia in 1835 where he set up many Methodist Chapels. He returned to England in 1865 where he stayed for 12 months. On January 1866 at Plymouth, he boarded the steamship *London*, bound for Australia. The ship was caught in a severe storm in the Bay of Biscay and sank. Survivors said that he had comforted those doomed to perish with him on the sea. His memory was commemorated in every Methodist Chapel in Australia (4) (5). Fig. 24 below, *Daniel J Draper* and crew at the doors of the Lifeboat House. Photo courtesy P. Pearson.

Mullions First Lifeboat.

The *Daniel J Draper* Lifeboat, Fig. 24 above, was manufactured by Forrest of Limehouse in London and was delivered free by rail to Penzance. She was 33` in length, 8`6" wide, with a draught of 23", built of mahogany and cost £283-0-0. She had 10 oars and was built on a self righting principle and the lightness was increased by carrying on the side air boxes beneath the deck. It had 6 valves provided for the escape of water. The launching carriage cost £99-10s-0d.

The arrival and launch of the Lifeboat coincided with long awaited festivities arranged for the opening of a number of the new Public Buildings in Penzance, on Tuesday 10th September 1867, an event which had been anticipated in Penzance for 20 years.

As part of the celebrations, *The Daniel J Draper* had first been paraded on the Sennen Lifeboat carriage through the streets of Penzance. In the course of the procession there was an unfortunate delay when the carriage, ran over the legs of a woman in the crowd. About 3pm a procession was formed outside the Public Buildings and the crowd proceeded to the Western Esplanade to witness the event. There were speeches by the Rev Nye, Methodist District Chairman, and Mr Lewis, the Institute Chairman after which the Lifeboat was formerly handed over. The launch was conducted by the Lady Mayoress and it was estimated that over 10,000 people were present. Many of the crowd attending the event had been brought to Penzance by special trains of the West Cornwall Railway. One morning train contained 18 carriages and the following train had 30 with several open trucks added at Redruth.

The Mayor in a speech said that they all knew of the loss of life at Mullion some few months previously and they must thank those gentlemen who had taken so much trouble in raising the money in order to present so handsome a boat.

Many festivities had been arranged for the day including a Regatta which included a Lifeboat Race. The launch was followed about 4pm by a unique race between 6 lifeboats, the *Agar Robartes* from Porthleven, *Daniel J Draper* Mullion, *Moses* (St.Ives), *Isis* (Hayle), *Two Cousins* (Sennen), and the *Richard Lewis* (Penzance).

There had never been an occasion when so many lifeboats had met in this way around the English Coast and the race was won by the *Two Cousins* of Sennen.

It was a tragic occurrence however that during the race a member of the Porthleven crew, Edward Williams suffered a heart attack and died. He left a widow and 9 children (6) (7).

The Lifeboat was brought to Mullion on the 13th September 1867 where a Lifeboat House had been purpose built in the Cove by George & Co of Mullion. There was financial support from Lord Robartes, but the RNLI had to pay an extra £115-10s-0d (2).

To complete the installation there had to be modifications made to the Cove to take the Lifeboat. These included the removal of rocks (See Fig.23) obstructing the Cove entrance, a diversion of the stream, and the creation of an artificial water course of stone built to the north side of the Cove, which also improved safety for launching both the lifeboat and the other fishing boats (8).

Fig. 25
Daniel J Draper in the Cove.
Photo courtesy B. Mundy.

In 1807 Henry Trengrouse (1772-1854), from Helston, witnessed the wreck of HMS Anson at Loe Bar near Porthleven. As a result of that harrowing experience his thoughts turned to developing a system of firing a Rocket with a line attached from shore to ship.

At the same time in Suffolk, a man called George William Manby (1766-1854), was developing a similar system whereby a line was fired from a mortar. He went on to develop the breeches buoy and it was a system involving both methods which was eventually accepted (9).

Such was the need and desire to improve the ability to effect rescues from stricken ships that there was a third rocket system invented by John Dennett (1780-1852), which proved its worth in action on the Isle of Wight, over both the Mortar and the Trengrouse rocket and in the 1820s was approved by the forerunner of the RNLI (9a).

The Rocket Apparatus was probably the most successful piece of life-saving equipment to come to Mullion simply because its use lent itself to the geography of the area, and, with sufficient manpower could be effectively operated. Often the first warning received was after the ships had already run aground.

If the weather and sea conditions allowed, the Coastguards, the first on the scene, would fire a line to the ship in the hope it would be caught, and a hawser then pulled onto the ship and secured. From there a cradle was sent out to take passengers and crew off the ship. There were, however, problems in bad weather with the ship being tossed around by the wind and waves and the lines often became entangled.

Until 1862 Lieutenant Drew of the Mullion Coastguard had to make do with trying to shoot a line to ships using Signal Rockets and it was not until that year that the Manby Rocket apparatus was introduced to Mullion.

3 Lives Saved

About 10pm on Monday 21st October 1867, less than a month after its arrival in Mullion, the *Daniel J. Draper* was called into action at the wreck of the barque *Achilles* from Glasgow laden with timber en route from Miramichi in Canada to London. The vessel had gone aground under full sail at Pollurian and both the Coastguard and the Lifeboat called upon. The Coastguard made contact with the ship with the second Rocket and 14 hands were brought ashore using the apparatus and a further 3 were rescued by the Lifeboat on this, the occasion of her first launch.

It was recorded that *"It is gratifying to notice that whilst the Rocket apparatus was so successfully handled by the coastguard, the Mullion Lifeboat, also fulfilled her mission on this the first occasion of her putting to sea from her new station where she has been hardly more than a month and it is still further gratifying to note that on the occasion of the last wreck along this coast on 26th March last 25 lives were lost, the largest number on record, namely 18, have providentially been saved. We understand that the Mullion Lifeboat Branch...stands greatly in need of subscriptions for the annual maintenance of the station"* (10).

On 21st January 1868 an 80 ton smack, the *Marie Louisa* was wrecked at Treguin off Mullion Island but storm conditions meant that it was impossible to launch the Lifeboat (8).

On April 29th 1868, in dense fog, a vessel was heard making a signal of distress and the Lifeboat-men and launchers were called out. Shortly after the Life boat put to sea the fog lifted and the vessel which had been signalling for help was seen heading out to sea. The Lifeboat returned to the Cove (2).

Fig. 26 Coxswain Samuel Mundy alongside the *Nancy Newbon*.
Photo courtesy B. Mundy

On Friday 19th April 1872 the crew of the Lifeboat were stunned to discover that their experienced and respected Coxswain, William Mundy, two of his sons, Joel aged 25, and Henry aged 13yrs, along with a friend Henry Williams had been drowned off Porthleven in a sailing accident. Henry Williams was aged only 20, and was due to get married shortly. The accident badly affected the local community as well as the crew and a fund was started to help his wife who was left to look after 5 children.

The sea sometimes keeps its victims for many weeks or months, and it was so in this case. (See Ch. 5)

It is a fact that on the Lizard Peninsula families of sailors and fishermen, many of whom could not swim at all well, used to knit "Guernsey's" for them to wear at sea. Each family had a slightly different hand- made pattern which could identify them in the event of a tragedy.

At dawn on Saturday 23rd November 1872 the *Lochleven Flower*, a 600 ton barque with a cargo of wheat from Berdianski in the Black sea, with Captain Halywell and 13 crew was spotted 2-3 miles off Porthleven drifting eastwards in a gale. About 8am the crew were seen rowing before the wind in the direction of what they must have thought to be a sandy beach at Loe Bar. A crowd had gathered near where they were expected to beach and watched as they rowed towards what was one of the most dangerous spots on the Mounts Bay Coast. On this day the sea was breaking over the Bar, streaming across the sand towards the land locked Lake of Loe Pool. As soon as the boat had got past the last breaker it overturned and was engulfed without a chance of rescue. The boat was smashed to pieces. Although they tried in vain to make the shore, all 14 on board were drowned. A rescue attempt by those on the beach was made by a line holding hands but nothing could be done. The barque meanwhile was still drifting to the east and was seen by the Coastguard at Mullion and Gunwalloe. About the same time as the crew were drowned the *Lochleven Flower* hit the foot of the tall cliffs at Halzephron. No one was seen on board (11). The Mullion Lifeboat Crew was assembled but did not put to sea.

On the 1st March 1873 a disaster occurred below the 200 foot high cliffs off Trenance Farm at Mullion. During the previous evening, the 617 ton iron barque the *Boyne*, of Scarborough, with a 900 ton cargo of sugar from Samarang,

Indonesia was bound for Falmouth with a crew of 19. The journey from Batavia had taken about 120 days and had gone well until the vessel saw the Lizard lights about 8pm on a Friday evening. She was travelling at 8-10 knots and standing off shore. About midnight Captain Wheelan gave his orders and went below but was woken at 3am by the officer in charge and the ship was put about. The weather was described as thick, with no land visible. The crew believed they were clear of land and on route to Falmouth. One of the crew was making coffee for breakfast when suddenly and without prior warning the *Boyne* hit rocks and was thrown broadside and became helpless in the waves. The Captain immediately ordered a small rowing boat over the side and 4 men were able to get in, but they were unable to ready any more boats or take off any more of the crew. The Captain told them to pull for land but they were reluctant to do so and stayed as long as they were able before rowing to sea. A blue distress light was put up which was seen by a local farmer Thomas Jacka who informed his cousin, and together in thick fog and driving rain they crossed Pollurian valley and arrived at Merres Ledges, a renowned place for wrecks, where they heard cries for help and saw the ship on the rocks about 150 yards offshore. He immediately ran about half a mile into Mullion where, at about 6.30am, he raised the alarm with Mr White, the chief Coastguard and Samuel Mundy the Second Coxswain of the *Daniel J Draper* Lifeboat. It was 8am before the Lifeboat could be manned, launched and rowed to the scene and by then the Coastguards were in attendance with the Rocket Apparatus from Mullion. By this time the *Boyne* had parted amidships and her decks breaking up. As the tide receded the stern section fell over but still some of the crew were hanging on for their lives. On arrival White could see 7 men on various parts of the ship and almost immediately 3 men were swept overboard. One of these men was the Captain. As daylight allowed a rocket was shot 150 yards across the stem of the ship and a man caught the line and began to pull it aboard. The coastguard, Mr White, tried to make the crew understand that the line needed to be pulled aboard to secure a hawser but they seemed powerless and exhausted. The block on the line jammed and the line tangled. A man, believed to be the Captain was in the water with a lifebelt and tried to grab the line. The coastguards tried to warn him not to do so as he would be dashed against the rocks in the breakers but he fell away and was drowned. By the time that the lifeboat reached the stricken ship there were only 4 men left aboard holding on desperately to the stern. The lifeboat tried anchoring on the windward side of the ship about 60 yards away but could not do so and desperate attempts were made to throw lines to the men on board. A line was eventually caught but by now two of the remaining men had gone overboard and a second line was caught by the remaining man.

The lifeboat crew shouted to the man to secure himself to the rope and jump into the water but instead he lashed himself to the rail not seeming to understand what was being asked of him. The second man got the rope around his body but fell away and was drowned and a last survivor was carried away. A small boat with three men and a lad was seen coming into Mullion Cove. The men, William Griffiths, Joseph Parsons and Thomas Wilkinson, from Hull, and the lad, Walter Dawson, 18 yrs from Folkestone eventually made land about 9am. Having watched the Lifeboat depart from the Cove they naturally thought they could land, and on arrival they were treated for their injuries and dry clothing provided from the Vicarage. The cargo of sugar was lost and the ship broke up.

Fifteen lives were lost. It was unfortunate that further lives could not have been saved and it was believed that the length of time in the cold, wet conditions had exhausted the crew reducing their ability to help themselves, and make them understand the instructions given by the coastguard and lifeboat crew. It was described as one of the most lamentable wrecks which had ever occurred. The body of the captain was soon washed in and eventually taken to Hull. The bodies of seven crew, including two apprentices, (Alexander Clark and John Lowe Grahame), were buried in Mullion Churchyard (12) (13) (8).

Rev E.G. Harvey, who was also the Hon. Sec. of the Mullion Lifeboat Branch went on to write to a Plymouth newspaper stating that he was greatly concerned by the lack of watch kept from onboard by vessels at night and feared further similar accidents. Part of the duties of the Coastguard at this time entailed patrolling the coastline at night. On this occasion, and on this coast, the local watchman had to guard and patrol no less than 7 miles of coast, taking a total of 4 hours. He added that in 6 and a quarter years there had been nine wrecks and 69 lives lost on this stretch of coast covering only one and a half miles, and over 100 lives lost in ten years out of 13 wrecks. He also wrote to the Commanding Inspector of Coastguards expressing his views and had not got a satisfactory reply (8). The nearest telegraph at the time went straight to the Lizard. In May 1873 he also wrote to the Post Office authorities asking for telegraph to be installed at Mullion, requiring only 1 and a quarter miles of poles and 6 miles of cabling. This move was supported by many organisations locally and around Mounts Bay, including Lord Robartes, the Coastguard and the RNLI but was told that it could not be done due to cost. A similar request was made by MP John Tremayne in 1875 with a similar result (8).

Incidents continued to occur along the coast and in November 1874 there were a number of severe storms. The British Schooner *Commerce* from Newport with a cargo of Coal was forced to anchor off Mullion and the crew abandoned ship. Eventually the crew returned and she was taken to Penzance.

About 7am on 29th December 1879 a storm with thunder and lightning moved south along the west Lizard Coast forcing a 70 ton Dutch Ketch from Groningen, *Elizabeth Hendricke*, loaded with empty wine casks, went ashore at Poldhu where she was wrecked. The Lifeboat was not required to attend but the Rocket Apparatus was brought from Mullion where it was put into service rescuing Captain Hedgeman and three of the crew (14).

The British Schooner *Joseph Brindley* of Portmadoc, carrying a cargo of slates for London was involved in a collision whilst anchored in the Mullion Roads. The Mullion Lifeboat brought the crew ashore where they were able to gain assistance and the ship and crew were recovered without loss of life and taken to Penzance Harbour (15)(16).

The Rev Harvey proved to be a very capable Hon. Secretary, but in 1884 due to bad health he was forced to resign his office. He had been there since 1867 and it was chiefly down to his exertions and the assistance of Lord Robartes that the Lifeboat Station was established at Mullion. At the AGM in January 1884 a vote of thanks was passed inappreciation of his services and the Committee expressed their regret and hoped he would soon be restored to full health (17).

In addition to the RNLI Testimonial he was presented with binoculars made by Messrs Dolland and Co. Inscribed with the name and nature of the presentation together with the thanks of the Institution recorded on vellum *"To the Rev E.G. Harvey, in acknowledgement of his long and valuable co-operation as Honorary secretary of the Mullion Branch"*.

In March 1884 John H. Shepherd of Alma Cottage in Mullion took over the vacant Posts of Hon. Secretary and Treasurer (17a).

Luckily the Lifeboat was not always required, as on 5th March 1887 when a steamer, *SS Adventurer*, ran aground at Gunwalloe in thick fog. She rapidly set off distress rockets and the Coastguard and Lifeboat were informed in Mullion but the tide was coming in and she managed to reverse her engines and get off before help arrived, much to the relief of the passengers aboard (18).

Fig.27 The *Edith* in Mullion Cove.
Photo courtesy B. Mundy.

The Edith

In June 1887 a new Lifeboat was introduced to Mullion to replace the *Daniel J Draper*. It was 37 foot long and 8 feet wide rowing 12 oars, double banked. They contained all the latest fittings including water ballast fittings containing tanks amidships, one or more of which could be filled or emptied within a minute. The benefits were that it increased the ballast and immersion of the boats, and consequently their draught and their immersion, when circumstances allow without increasing the fixed weight for land carriage or draught of water when launched in very shallow water. The boat was called the *Edith*, costing £545 and was funded in the most part by a benevolent lady in London who asked that her identity should not be released (19).

A lean-to was built at the back of the Lifeboat house, at a cost of £30, in which a winch was installed to help with the recovery of the Lifeboat (2).

This would have no doubt been a very helpful innovation, given the amount of local manpower required on each occasion to haul the boat up the slipway.

RNLI Records indicate that the *Edith*, never had occasion to be launched for a rescue in the 7 years she was at Mullion, although the crew were assembled for two incidents, in November 1889 and April 1890.

On 21st April 1890 the Liverpool Steamer *Brankelow* 2344 tons went aground at Gunwalloe. It was reported that the crew were rescued by the Porthleven Lifeboat (20).

Nancy Newbon.

In 1894 the *Edith* was replaced by a new Lifeboat, the *Nancy Newbon*. She was 38` in length, 8` wide and had 12 oars and with modern features which included being fitted with three water ballast tanks and with plugs and pumps by

which water could be admitted or pumped out. It was self righting and if capsized could do so with the crew and gear aboard, mast up and sails set.

The cost was defrayed by a legacy from the late Mr R.A. Newbon of London, and the Lifeboat Station at Mullion was in the charge of the Rev J.H. Scholefield (21).

To accommodate this larger Lifeboat the boathouse at Mullion had to be altered, being extended to the rear by 12`, the floor being raised 2` 3" and the roof being raised 5`. The work was carried out by H. George and Co of Mullion and cost £245-19s-9d (2) She was launched for rescue a total on a total of 6 occasions during her service at Mullion (22).

Fig. 28 The *Nancy Newbon* being launched.
Photo courtesy B. Mundy.

The first occasion was on 2nd February 1897 to the SS *Grip* with Captain Falk and 14 hands en route from Cadiz with a cargo of salt and oranges bound for Drontheim, Norway which grounded at Gunwalloe about 11.30pm in thick fog with visibility reduced to 100 yards. Two of the crew swam ashore, while the remainder landed onshore in their own lifeboat.

The *Nancy Newbon* was launched the following morning but was unable to assist, the crew having been removed. The Captain was determined to get her afloat, and wanted to row out to get clothes for the crew but the rowlocks of his rowing boat could not be found. The steamer had remained upright but was stuck in the sands and drew the attention of a large crowd of people but was eventually got off relatively undamaged (23).

During the launch one of the helpers James Thomas was injured, later being awarded £2 in compensation plus he had his medical expenses of £3 paid for by the RNLI (2).

The nature of the coast, the isolation and the difficulties encountered by ships can be readily seen in the locality. In March 1898 a barque, the 700 ton *Abertyne* from Glasgow was en route from Caleta Buena in Cuba to Falmouth laden with Nitrate when she got into difficulties in thick fog and rain off the coast. Intelligence was received at Mullion about 11.30pm and the lifeboat launched and Rocket apparatus sent. About 1.30am the Barque ran aground off the Rill which lies between Kynance Cove and Gew Graze. Capt. Cardwell decided to order the ships lifeboat to be readied and the crew of 15, which came from many countries, to abandon ship. When the Mullion Lifeboat arrived they found no sign of the ships lifeboat with the crew or anyone onboard the vessel. It transpired that the crew had been picked up by a Falmouth pilot boat about 5am and escorted to the Sailors Home in Falmouth.

When dawn broke a local man, a Mr Thomas, living at Kynance Cove became aware of the wreck and notified Lizard Coastguard and Lifeboat which came on scene but found no trace of the crew. A crowd gathered to find the barque, which eventually broke up, jammed between rocks and still under full sail but with no signs of the crew (24).

Later that year the Lifeboat was called on to assist the French Barque, the *Antonin* in a critical position off Loe Bar, a distance of 4 miles away. The crew were called out of church and on arrival they hung on to the vessel for a short time but found that their services were not required (25).

The dangers of the Mullion Roads persisted into the 20th century. In February 1902 a 118 ton coal carrying Schooner, the *Jessie Bennett,* sailing from Newport, S.Wales was in the Mounts Bay bound for their home port of Fowey. Shortly after midnight they were approaching the Roads on a clear night. Captain Edmund Vercoe was below, and the boat in the charge of the mate, Alfred Parchard, and a boy who were on deck keeping a lookout when the light of a vessel was seen about one and a half miles away. About 15 minutes later a vessel was seen bearing down on the *Jessie Bennett* and the boy went quickly below to warn the captain and crew. They arrived on deck to see the vessel hit them amidships on the port side almost cutting them in two. The crew quickly abandoned ship in their night clothes and were immediately picked up by the vessel which hit them, which turned out to be a French brigantine *Marie Therese*. No trace of the Jessie Bennett was found. The crew were transferred to a Brixham trawler and put in at Newlyn. The French boat, in the charge of Captain Laporte, from Nantes was only slightly damaged. No explanation for the accident was known, having happened so quickly that no Lifeboat or rocket could be used (26).

The Rocket apparatus continued to be used for rescue along the coast. In March 1905 the 145 ton Boulogne Ketch *Louis,* carrying stone, was unable to deal with heavy seas and squalls in Mounts Bay on its way from Guernsey to South Wales and was driven back into Mounts Bay. The captain tried to tack back into Falmouth Bay but was unable to do so and eventually, having split a sail tried to anchor 60 yards off Poldhu. A severe squall drove her onto the cliffs at Craig a Bella between Poldhu and Church Cove and she was smashed to pieces. Three of the crew managed to jump onto a ledge and the first mate scaled the cliffs. A rope was brought by Harry Willey and with assistance from 2 members of staff from the Poldhu Hotel. One crew member was swept away while Capt. Gouyean drowned in his cabin having returned to collect his papers and valuables. The Rocket apparatus was quickly on the scene but even so it was too late to assist (27).

In November 1905 Samuel Mundy, Coxswain of the Mullion Lifeboat for 30 years sent in his resignation which the local committee accepted with regret. They recommended him to the RNLI for a Pension, normally granted to Coxswains, which was well earned and a deserved reward for his services (28).

The Lifeboat men, who were often experienced fishermen, knew only too well the tidal currents, local waters and hidden rocks. Mullion Cove was always at the mercy of the weather and storms which would regularly hit the coast from the Atlantic and this did make launching difficult. The Lifeboat crews had regular practice sessions, and every quarter these were under the supervision of RNLI Inspectors. One such session in March 1906 was conducted under the supervision of Lieut. Rowley R.N., District Inspector, who expressed himself highly pleased with the way the crew had acquitted themselves and the condition of the boathouse and gear.

A new Coxswain, Mr William "Billy" George, had been appointed to replace the retired Samuel Mundy. Lieut. Rowley was complimentary of the smart manner of the crew, who had taken only 5 minutes between the firing of the first gun and the launching of the boat (29).

On March 17th 1907 the White Star Liner *Suevic* on route from Sydney for Plymouth and London with 456 people on board under Captain Thomas Jones, went aground about 10pm off the Maenheere Rocks, near Polpeor Cove at the Lizard in bad weather and fog only a short distance from the Lizard Lighthouse. Owing to the position of the ship between rocks the *Suevic* Lifeboats could not be used. The RNLI Record for the Mullion Lifeboat shows that it was launched at 3.00am. The wind was West by South West with a long shore breeze and a rough sea and she made for the Lizard using Oars, no sail power. She was the second Lifeboat on scene and arrived by 4.25am, but had returned by 8.30am (22).

The full rescue involved Lifeboats from around the coast including Lizard (*Admiral Sir George Beck*), Porthleven (*John Francis White*), Cadgwith (*Minnie Moon*)and Coverack (*Constance Melanie*) a number of tugs from Falmouth and many local people from Lizard Village (9). All the people on board were successfully removed from the *Suevic* by the above named Lifeboats making the rescue the largest in the history of the RNLI (30).

Removal of the Lifeboat

At the RNLI Committee of Management Committee 4th June 1907 the RNLI indicated that they were concerned with the overall service record of 33 launches in 40 years, and had written to the committee saying that the Mullion Lifeboat would only be retained for another year as long as certain conditions were fulfilled (31).

In July 1907 William George retired as Coxswain and was succeeded by Joseph Gilbert.

At a meeting on 4th June 1908 it was decided to close the Lifeboat station at Mullion "... *due to altered conditions in the immediate locality, which rendered its retention no longer necessary*" (2).

In June 1908 the *Nancy Newbon* took her at Mullion on a smooth sea, under the command of Joseph Gilbert. Several people took the opportunity to take a trip in her. Signalling was gone through by Mr. Franklin Mundy and a large number of parishioners watched the launch and beaching of the lifeboat. It was feared that nothing short of a disaster would bring the lifeboat back to Mullion again (32).

The Station was formerly closed on July 3rd 1908 and the Lifeboat removed and reallocated to Sunderland Lifeboat Station where she operated until 1912. There she had one call out saving 9 lives (2) (33).

After the closure of the Lifeboat house the building was converted into a dwelling and during the course of the renovation a broken marble tablet was found under rubble. It transpired that this tablet was the very same stone which was previously found in the gable end of the entrance to the Lifeboat house. The tablet has now been restored and is visible in the wall above the seat by the Winch House in the Harbour.

The inscription reads; "*This lifeboat house was erected in the memory of the late Rev Daniel J Draper from the foundering of the steamship London in the Bay of Biscay on the 11th January 1866 and was presented to the National Lifeboat Institution by Weslyan Methodists through the medium of the Methodist Recorder Newspaper conducted by the Rev. Luke H Wiseman & Mr Thomas Smith 1867. C. H. Cooke ESO FRIBA Hon Architect*". The tablet can still be seen in the harbour.

Cooke was the Honorary Architect of many Lifeboat houses erected by the RNLI in the 19th century, symbols of a National monument to the many brave men who rowed the Lifeboats around our coasts in the storms which cost so many lives.

MULLION LIFEBOAT SERVICE RECORD

Daniel J Draper

21.10.1867	*Achilles*, Pollurian	3 Lives Saved	Alarm raised 10pm 21st Oct.
01.12.1867	Unknown Mounts Bay		Crew Assembled
01.02.1869	Brig, Predannack Head		Crew Assembled
27.02.1871	*Ernest*, Brigantine off Mullion		Assistance Declined
30.10.1872	French Schooner off Mullion		Crew Assembled
23.11.1872	*Lochleven Flower,* Off Halzephron		Crew Assembled
09.12.1872	Unknown off Mullion		Crew Assembled
19.01.1873	Unknown off Mullion		Crew Assembled
01.03.1873	*Boyne* Barque under Mullion Cliff		Put-off not able to assist
02.11.1874	*Joseph Brindley* Schooner off Mullion		Brought ashore and telegraphed
26.10.1879	*Waterloo* off Mullion		No service
29.12.1879	*Elizabeth Hendricke,* Poldhu		No Service
01.09.1882	Unknown, Predannack Cliffs		No trace of vessel
05.03.1887	*Adventurer* Gunwalloe		No service

Edith

02.11.1889	Pass by Pradam (?) Rock		Crew Assembled
21.04.1890	*SS Brankelow,* Gunwalloe		Crew Assembled

Nancy Newbon

02.02.1897	*SS Grip*, Gunwalloe,		Launched but recalled
08.05.1898	*Abertyne*, Barque Rill Head		No Service
04.12.1898	*Antonin* off Loe Bar		No Service
30.06.1899	Unknown, Vellan Head		No Service
31.12.1901	Unknown Mullion to Porthleven		Crew Assembled
26.02.1905	*Louis* Ketch Poldhu		No service
18.03.1907	*SS Suevic* Lizard Point		No Service

Bibliography

1.RCG (Royal Cornwall Gazette) 15.4.1859
1a. RCG 24.1.1867
2. Lifeboat Enthusiasts Society (J.Morris)
3. RCG 16.5.1867
4. RCG 12.9.1867
5. http://adb.anu.edu.au/biography/draper-daniel-james-1991
6. RCG 12.9.1867
7. Lanhydrock.wordpress.com/2012/06/29/the-agar-Robartes-lifeboat.
8. Rev E.Harvey, Mullyon Its History, Scenery and Antiquities. 1875 p92
9. National Maritime Museum, Falmouth. www.nmmc.co.uk
9a members.iinet.net.au/~dodd/gail/publications/trengrouse/Essay.html
10. RCG 24.10.1867
11. RCG 30.11.1872
12. North Devon Journal 6.3.1873
13. RCG 8.3.1873
14. Cornishman 1.1.1880
15. RCG 9.10.1884
16. RCG 14.11.1884
17. Cornishman 31.1.1884
17a. Cornishman 6.3.1884
18. RCG 11.3.1887
19. RCG 10.6.1887
20. Evening News 22.4.1890
21. RCG 6.10.1894
22. RNLI Records
23. Cornishman 4.2. 1897
24. Cornishman 12.5.1898.
25. Cornishman 8.12.1898
26. Cornishman 6.2.1902
27. Cornishman 2.3.1905
28. Cornishman 9.11.1905
29. Cornishman 1.3.1906
30. W. Briton. 18.3.1907
31. Cornishman 27.6.1907
32. Cornishman 25.6.1908
33. www.rnlisunderland.org

Chapter 5 THE LOSS OF WILLIAM MUNDY

About 10am on Friday April 19th 1872 a boat accident occurred off Porthleven which led to the death of four men from Mullion.

Earlier that morning William Mundy (58), an experienced sailor and the first Coxswain of the Mullion Lifeboat *The Daniel J. Draper*, along with two of his sons Joel (25) and Henry (13) and Henry John Williams (20), a carpenter

shortly to be married, had left Mullion Cove in William Mundy's 18` sailing boat in order to collect some sails made for him in Porthleven.

The weather was bright but squally from the north east. About midday the boat was seen to heel over about one mile off Porthleven Harbour.

It was noticed that those onboard were aware of danger and tried to lower the sail, which was belayed, but this could not be done. The lee bow went under water causing the boat to fill and sink.

Using a telescope from ashore witnesses saw a man struggling in the water for about two minutes, but he was lost sight of.

Three boats immediately put out from Porthleven and arrived at the scene about 10 minutes after, but there were no signs of survivors. A hat and coat were found plus 2 oars, a bag and the boats bucket with the owners name on it. The hat was sent to Mullion on a passing boat from where identification was made.

A search was made by coastguards and three other boats the following day but nothing was found.

It was reported that a gloom was cast over the village of Mullion as the deceased were all well known as steady and respectable people. In fact it was one of the greatest losses suffered by the village in its entire history.

Fig. 29 William Mundy, Coxswain of the *Daniel J Draper* Lifeboat.

The body of Joel Mundy was recovered later in June and identified by a brother Samuel Mundy who had returned from America after hearing the news. The only identification possible was from his clothing (1).

The body of William Mundy was also recovered off Gunwalloe in June (2). His place of burial is still unknown. William Mundy had spent his whole life fishing in the sea around Mullion and knew the waters well. He left behind a wife and five children.

Fig 30 & 31; A Memorial Cross located in the St. Mellanus Church in Mullion village.
Courtesy Rev S.Griffiths

A fund was started by Rev Harvey, the Hon. Secretary of the Mullion Lifeboat Branch, and adverts were placed in local newspapers. The advert read as follows;

"William Mundy, the late Coxswain of the Daniel J. Draper Mullion Lifeboat, who was unhappily drowned by the sudden sinking of his fishing boat off Porthleven on Friday 19th April, leaves a widow and five children unprovided for.

A fund has been opened for their relief, donations will be thankfully received by Messrs Vivian and Co., Union Bank Helston or by Rev. E.G. Harvey, Vicar of Mullion, the Hon Secretary of Mullion Lifeboat Branch" (3).

On the 21st April 1872 a Church Service was held in Mullion in memory of the deceased. Part of the sermon read *"William, the faithful husband, the loving father, the true brother, the steadfast friend; Joel the young man in all the strength of youth; John Henry with a career of hopeful, useful manhood, just opening before him; and Henry, the light-hearted, cheerful willing boy; gone!, taken from us in a moment" ..."The souls of the righteous are in the hands of God and there shall no torment touch them. In the sight of the unwise they seemed to die, and their departure is taken for misery, and their going from us utter destruction, but they are in peace. Amen." WHOSE TURN NEXT?*

A copy of the 1872 Memorial Booklet (4) can be found at the rear in the Appendix A. Courtesy of B. Mundy.

Bibliography
1. RCG 1.6.1872
2. RCG 15.6.1872
3. RCG 27.4.1872
4. Memorial Booklet of Church Service

Chapter 6 A HISTORY OF MULLION COASTGUARD

Park Lough, Predannack Head.

Just over a mile to the south of Mullion Cove lies Predannack Head. The highest point on the West Lizard Coast it was a "Mark" for fishing boats returning to the Cove. It is in the Parish of Mullion and also lies on the boundary between Predannack Wartha and Predannack Wollas. Today all that is visible is a nearby Triangulation Point in a stone wall and a mark on an Ordnance Survey Map. This piece of headland also holds a secret which is unlocked on the 1841 Tithe Map (1).

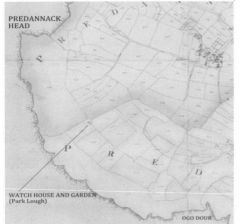

Fig. 32 Mullion Tithe Map 1841. Extract showing location of Park Lough. Predannack Head Reproduced with permission from Cornwall Record Office. Ref. TM/160

About 100 yards inland from the cliff edge, 50 yards South of the Triangulation Point sit the faint remains of a building which was of great importance to the safety of both Cornwall and England in the late 18th and early 19th centuries. In a tiny square of land between *Peden Menor, Park an Lock, and Park Menor,* surrounded by nothing but fields, lies a reference in the Apportionment Record called simply *"Watch House and Garden"* (Tithe Map Apportionments. Ref. 1318).

Such a building would have been very isolated and had it still existed today many people would say that it would have provided one of the best views of Mounts Bay and the South West approaches. In the late 18th Century England was at War with France and in the 1790s the French had successfully invaded a number of European Countries. There was a serious threat of invasion from across the English Channel and the Government and the Admiralty were keen to ensure that the England was protected. In the winter of 1796, and in support of an Irish rebellion against English rule, the French attempted a seaborne invasion of Ireland called the *"Expedition d'Irlande".* They were hoping that by doing so they could rely on the further support of 250,000 Irishmen in support of their invasion of England. It was a seaborne invasion involving 14,000 French troops intended to gain a foothold in Ireland and then a springboard for an invasion of England. They managed to elude the Royal Navy but by the time they got to Bantry Bay they were caught in a storm and lost many men and ships.

A LIST OF OFFICERS EMPLOYED AT SIGNAL STATIONS,

With the Dates of their Appointments.

STATION.	Lieutenants.	Apptd.	STATIONS.	Lieutenants.	Apptd.
DEVONSHIRE.					
Maker Church, Plymouth	John Hiatt	9July11	Lizard Point, Park Braws, Helston	Hugh Tredwin	10Oct11
CORNWALL.					
Penhale, East Looe	Perkins Prynn	21June	Park Lough, Helston ..	Degory King	31May05
Nealand, Polpero	Wm. Tucker	18Dec.07	Tregonning Hill, do.	George George	2July11
Deadman's Point, Mevagissey	Ar. Stapledon	7Mar.10	Tetterdieu, Penzance ..	George Grant	31May05
Greber Head, Tregony	Charles Adams	6Dec.15	St. Levan's Point, do. ..	Richard Jones	7Mar.07
St. Anthony's Head, St. Mawes	Thomas Wilks	31May05	Land's End, do. ..	Thomas Ratsey	10July09
Manacle Point, Helston	Jos. Withers	do.	Inspector of Telegraphs	G. Roebuck, Admiralty Office	
Black Head, do. ..	Samuel Cock	do.	Do. In the Islands of Guernsey, Jersey, &c.	— Mulgrave	

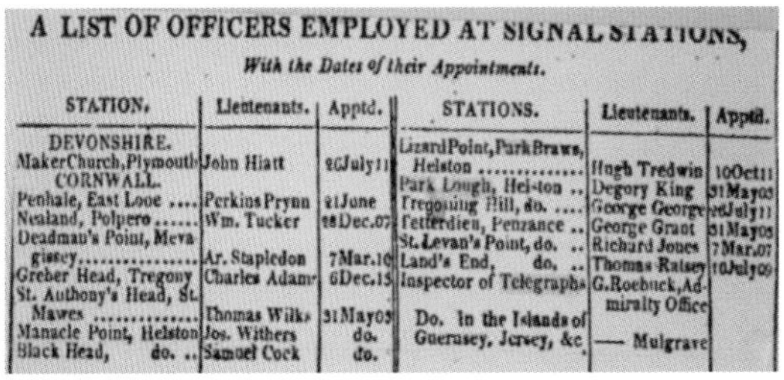

Fig.33 Navy-List of SW Signal Stations.

In the invasion attempt of 1796 it also became known that the French had plans to invade England through Cornwall. The plan included creating an army of 2000 from criminals let out of prison and conscripted. The plan was for them to invade Cornwall in October 1796 as a distraction to the main invasion elsewhere along the coast, but create a beach head for future invasion plan.

The plan was subsequently revised and an army of more than 15,000 men was prepared, to be led by General Hoche from the French Port of Brest. A large body of men and the entire French Atlantic Fleet were put at his disposal. Despite problems with ship building, and an army of unreliable soldiers, many of whom deserted; in August 1796 the French initiated a practice voyage of the Cornish invasion fleet towards England. It proved to be a total failure owing to the inability of many small French sailing craft to operate on the open sea and the soldiers were either drafted into the Irish invasion attempt or returned to prison. The French tried two further attempts to invade, at Fishguard in 1797 and again, with 2000 men in August 1798 but again failed to gain a foothold. As in 1939, the security of the nation was at stake. In May 1798 Admiral Sir Home Riggs Popham created an Order in Council which set up a little known organisation called the Sea-Fencibles to act as an anti- invasion force in coastal waters. It mainly included naval officers and volunteering seafaring men (2). It included all fishermen, and other persons occupied in ports and on the coast, and included relief from the *"press gang"* or enforced naval enlistment.

Smugglers, many of whom were trading with France were often keen to volunteer as it exempted all seamen.

The Sea-Fencibles were divided into districts covering a stretch of coast each under the command of a post- captain, assisted by 3-6 lieutenants, depending on the size of his command. The men received payment and were trained in the use of arms.

They manned the signal towers and with telescopes also looked for messages from other towers and signals from and between ships at sea. Also available were a small fleet of gunboats, armed cruisers, and small ships such as colliers and coastal vessels which would be armed.

The Government would fund the use of the boats as long as the boat owners paid for the gun fittings. In return for helping the Government and country they were allowed compensation and also salvage rights.

The signal towers or *"Watch Towers"* formed the all important communication link. There were a series of Towers along the Devon and Cornwall coast, and importantly each one had to be visible to the next in order to pass and receive messages.

The list of Cornish Towers was as follows, Plymouth (Devon),East Looe, Polperro, Mevagissey,Tregony, St. Anthonys Head, St.Mawes, Manacle Point, Helston, Black Head, Helston, Lizard Point, Park Braws**,** Park Lough, Helston, Tregonning Hill, Tetterdieu, Penzance, St.Levans Point, Penzance, Lands End ,Penzance (3).

There is now no building left at the site of Park Lough (*Park-an-Lock*), and no visible sign of its past existence as a Watch Tower. It was removed at the end of the Napoleonic War.

The French threat in the Channel was never far away. Armed French ships were known to have hijacked fishing boats and other small craft, taking away the crew for questioning about the activities and whereabouts of the Royal Navy. Unfortunately having let go many of the crew this often worked to their disadvantage and sought only to provide information of their own activities.

In March 1802 the *Peace of Amiens* was signed ending the hostilities between France and England and the need for the Sea-Fencibles, which were disbanded, but in May 1803 hostilities were resumed by England and they were recalled.

Fig. 34 Original Telescope used by the Coastguards in Mullion in the early 1800s. Courtesy J. Meyer. Photo by author 2012.

One of the first orders from the Admiralty to each district was to carry out a survey of the coast for areas which might be exposed to enemy landings, and to provide details of how tides, currents, surf etc might affect a landing, plus details of any creeks or rivers.

How did they signal between towers? There was a code of signals using flags and balls depended upon each flag representing a number, and a combination of flags could indicate a series of numbers which was the entire message in code. The system had obvious difficulties in adverse weather, rain or fog for example, and it would negate the possibility of any messages being passed at night. Continuous observation by the operatives in the watch tower and a good understanding of the signal code was imperative, as well as, good telescopes. There was also a need for vigilance to protect against French attack and particularly the theft of the code books. The Sea-Fencibles were however reasonably well armed. In practice there were difficulties between the Navy signal books and the Merchant Navy signal books. They had different codes and this had to be resolved. A better telegraph book was introduced in 1803 (4).

Each volunteer was paid a shilling a day when required for service and the main incentive appeared to be the immunity from service in both the militia and navy press gang. Naval officers received full pay for their services, as against half pay when they were unemployed.

Part of an advertisement in newspapers of the time said that, *"As the situation of the country requires the service of every person on the sea coast, no seafaring man, fisherman or other person, whose occupation or calling may be, or has been, to work in vessels, or boats or otherwise, nor any of those who have received regular protections, such as pilots ,fishermen, masters of barges, or who are protected by being in the service of the Excise, Customs, or Post Office will be exempted from the impress, unless enrolled in the Sea-Fencibles ... and those who shall enrol themselves, and perform properly, the services required, will be protected from being impressed."*

Anyone doubting the importance of the Sea-Fencibles may be surprised by the fact that in 1798 Napoleon had his first *"Army of England"* waiting in France to invade. Luckily this did not materialise. By 1803 they had reorganised and had 100,000 men trained and waiting at Calais to invade in specially built barges. They were called the *"Armee des cotes de l`ocean".* By 1805 numbers had risen to 200,000. Again... the invasion did not take place.

Smuggling or *"Free Trading"* between England and France was a massive business at this time and one which was never fully controlled. It was estimated that a third of all brandy entering the country was smuggled, avoiding a massive amount of tax revenue. Towards the end of the Napoleonic Wars, Napoleon allowed English smugglers free entry into the Ports of Dunkirk and Gravelines.

Whatever the English sailors took to France, they returned with vast amounts of textiles, silk, tea, brandy and gin.

At its peak the Sea-Fencibles employed over 30,000 men nationally, but it became costly to run, and by 1810 it was disbanded. After the end of the Napoleonic Wars some 300,000 soldiers and sailors were discharged, many of whom were recruited around the country into smuggling in order to make a living.

The problem with smuggling meant that security had to be tightened and the preventative forces, the Preventative Water Guard had to be strengthened and reorganised. It was divided into 31 districts, made responsible to the Treasury and worked in coastal waters. Preventative Cruisers were under the responsibility of the Admiralty and Riding Officers responsibility of the Customs.

H.M Coastguard. H.M. Coastguard came about as a result of reorganisation of other existing services used to combat smuggling. By 1809 the "Preventative Water Guard" was formed to operate in local coastal waters. The prime objective of the Preventative Water Guard was to catch Smugglers, but for the first time they were instructed to help at ship wrecks, so often a problem in parts of Cornwall (5). They were based in Watch Houses around the coast and boat crews operated their stretch of allotted coast at night. At the same time there were a number of Cruisers around the Coast operating off shore.

In 1822 they were all placed under the authority of the Board of Customs, renamed, and became the Coastguard, and later H.M Coastguard so well known today.

In 1829 the first instructions were issued stating that when a shipwreck took place the Coastguards were responsible for tasking all possible action to save lives, to take charge of the vessel and to protect property. By 1831 the Coastguard Service became a Reserve force for the Royal Navy. Coastguards were nearly always posted away from home for fear of collaboration with smugglers.

Each station had a Chief Officer who was an RN Lieutenant and beneath him were Chief Boatman, Commissioned  Boatman and Boatman Ranks. The Board of Customs continued to be in charge of the Coastguard until 1856 when the Admiralty Board took over, and associations with the smugglers had begun to disappear. Duties and responsibilities involving ship wrecks salvage and rescues had begun to be more common place. In 1866 Coastguards were informed that they had to take a more active role in the workings of a Lifeboat.

Fig.35 left 1890s Coastguard Night Watch man with Tuck stick (5a).

Learning the art of Signalling became a priority and was regularly practiced, using semaphore and telegraphy, with the use of flashing lamps at night. Wireless telegraphy eventually followed when the need for communication between Lifeboat Stations and Signal Stations was pointed out by the RNLI. A substantial Coastguard Watch House was known to exist in 1840 in the Cove as part of the "Porthmellin Cafe" complex. By 1848 two further Coastguard Houses were built near the Cove, and by 1900, seven Coastguard Houses were built behind the Cove Hotel. The most senior officer lived in the tallest house to the west. Other houses were also built in the Village. It is thought that the Watch House, in Mullion Cove, and mentioned in the 1840 Tithe Map may have existed there in the 1820s. Evidence of other Watch Buildings exists along the coast. There are the remains of later observation posts or "Flank Stations", last used in the 1960s at Pedngwynian, called Mullion North, Men-te-huel, called Mullion South and the main Mullion Station which was within 30 yards of the edge of the cliffs, slightly to the north of the Mullion Cove Hotel. Although now covered in thick vegetation remains, including the old fireplace can still be found.

Fig 36 right, representation of a Coastguard Watch Room c.1890s (5a).

Fishermen who became Coastguard watch men, such as William John Mundy had to walk night time coastal beats between Stations with "Tuck Sticks" during their period of duty, and hold at least two "conferences" per shift with the flankers.

Tuck Sticks were made of oak and the holder could withdraw from it a blade of steel, they were in fact sword sticks. They were not used for defence against attack but merely for prodding suspicious articles, bales or piles of old sails on a boat- hiding places for contraband.

Protection was provided by a hand held blue light which could be stuck into the ground. It contained a detonator which, when pressed, burst into flame and burnt for 6 minutes.

One retired Coastguard recalled that in poor visibility the early Coastguards in Mullion used to have what were called "Fog Bellows", sounded by them to warn vessels of their location in foggy conditions, something only too common even now. These were a set of hand bellows similar to those used to build a fire, on the end was attached a large brass trumpet. They were often also used by ships to warn of their presence in the days of sailing ships.

In 1923 responsibility was given to the Board of Trade and since 1939 by a succession of 7 further bodies including the Ministry of Shipping (1939-40), Admiralty 1940-1945), Ministry of (War) Transport 1945-1964, Department of Trade (1964-1983), Department of Transport (1983-1997), DETR (1997-2001) and Department of Transport from 2002 (6).

Fig. 37 Coastguard Houses behind the Cove Hotel built about 1900. Photo by author 2012

The Rocket Apparatus

There were many shipwrecks around the coast of Great Britain and it seemed that little was being done to help save the lives of the poor individuals. From the early 1800s there were attempts to manufacture the means to help shipwrecked sailors for the first time.

One of the items brought into use around the Country by the Coastguard was known as the Manby Mortar, invented by Capt. George William Manby and developed whilst he was barrack master at Great Yarmouth. During the Napoleonic war the French had developed ships, called Bomb Ketches, which carried a series of mortars and which were fired at the English ships in battle. The British Navy copied the idea, but they were never really effective. However, the idea led to the invention of important Life Saving equipment. His system was first trialled in 1807 in Suffolk. It originally utilised an iron launching mortar and was used at a rescue on the *Elizabeth* of Plymouth, wrecked on the beach at Great Yarmouth in February 1808.

The system was later trialled there before a Naval Committee at Woolwich in October 1808 before an Admiralty Committee and in May 1809, and was in regular use before 1810 (7) (8) (9) (10).

The mortar fired out a line to the stricken ship. It was tied to a hawser which was pulled onboard. A cradle was attached which ferried the shipwrecked survivors to land and safety. While this system was used around the coast, especially in

East Anglia, it was not the only system successfully trialled and coincidentally another system which had its origins in Cornwall was trialled a few years later.

Fig. 38 left Trengrouse Rocket Apparatus displayed at Helston Museum. Photo by author 2012. Courtesy Helston Museum

HMS Anson

On Christmas Eve 1807 the Frigate *HMS Anson*, a 64 gun British warship, captained by Charles Lydiard, left Falmouth heading towards the French coast at Ushant where there was an ongoing blockade of the French Fleet lying in Brest harbour. On reaching the French Coast a storm developed which became so bad that the Captain was forced to put about and return to Falmouth. It was reported that the ship was caught in a storm off Lands End which they had mistakenly believed to be The Lizard. Rather than returning to the shelter of Falmouth they were in fact heading straight towards Loe Bar, south of Porthleven. On the look- out seeing breakers ahead the bow anchor was quickly despatched. It held fast for some time but eventually broke away. The sheet anchor was then despatched and also held for an hour or so but the force of the storm caused the second cable and anchor to part from the ship. The storm, with waves running above the masts, forced the *Anson* to ground the ship on Loe Bar about 8am. The fallen masts managed to form a makeshift bridge to the shore allowing some survivors to reach land while local villagers helped with the rescue.

During this subsequent rescue attempt a group of rescuers including a Methodist Preacher were seen to wade into the surf and climb aboard to look for more survivors. A group of men, women and children were found still sheltering below deck and the Preacher and his helpers managed to help effect the rescue of some men and women. The children however were lost. About 2pm, some 6 hours after the grounding the ship began to break up. Other men, still clapped in irons below deck were found and one was saved but by 3pm the ship had virtually disintegrated. It was reported that many people lost their lives in the tragedy. The loss of the ship and the difficulties of the rescue left many distressed. One of the crowd of people to witness the ship wreck and the rescue attempts of the crew was a local man living at Helston called Henry Trengrouse 1772-1854. He was deeply affected by the loss of life and took it upon himself to investigate ways of improving the available methods of rescue. His plan was to fire a rocket and line from a safe location onto the stricken boat and the subject brought to land via a chair, rather than a cradle.

This plan had several advantages over the Manby mortar. Firstly it could be fired from a musket. To the musket was fitted a cylinder which to which was attached the bayonet mounting. The rocket with a line attached was placed into the cylinder and on firing the musket the line could extend cleanly as the velocity of the shot increased in a gradual process rather than the explosive release from the Mortar.

The whole system could be loaded into a chest, was light and portable, and there was less chance of the line breaking. It could be used from ships to land, as well as from land to sea.

It was in 1818 that Trengrouse, who had not patented his system, was able to test it in front of a Government committee. It was established as being superior to the Manby Mortar. However, rather than allow Trengrouse to manufacture it, the Government had the apparatus constructed by the Ordnance Department, while Trengrouse only received a small cash donation of £50 for his trouble. The 1818 letters were printed in the Royal Cornwall Gazette of 1839, twenty years after the Trengrouse Rocket system was first developed (11). There is little doubt that given the widespread use of such a device both from land and from ships at sea that it was a clever invention and one which saved many lives, with the inventor deserving of far greater recognition than he actually received.

Fig. 39 Right A Copy of Letter 1818 showing test results for Trengrouse Rocket System.

" Woolwich, 2nd March, 1818.

Sir,

In reference to your communication, • • • Mr. Trengrouse exhibited his apparatus, consisting of a section of a cylinder, which is fitted to the barrel of a (small) musket by a bayonet socket. A rocket with a line attached to its stick is so placed in it that its priming receives fire immediately from its barrel — The following experiments were made:—

1st. A small rocket of 8 oz. fixed as described, was fired to the distance of 180 yards.

2nd. A pound rocket was fired in the same manner, which ranged 450 yards; the line broke at 150 yards, owing to a knot in it.

3rd. A pound rocket was fired from a wooden frame at an elevation of 50°, and ranged 212 yards. The line used with the above three rounds was a mackerel-line.

4th. A 4 oz. rocket was then fired from the musket to the distance of 112 yards with a line called a mackerel-snood.

I have the honour to report that the committee are of opinion that Mr. Trengrouse appears to them to be the best mode of gaining a communication with the shore for the purpose of saving lives from shipwreck that has been suggested, as well as to communicate between ships in heavy gales of wind, and that the experiments they have witnessed have fully succeeded.

I have the honour to be, &c. &c.

(Signed)   John Ramsey."

Prior to the introduction of the Rocket Apparatus and the Lifeboat there was a high degree of improvisation and courage shown by rescuers.

The summer of 1858 had been a hot and sunny one, but in September it gave way to fog and then severe storms.

The gales arrived from the SE and ESE and sailing ships unable to negotiate the Lizard ran for cover to Mullion and Penzance. Four arrived in Mullion but the wind drifted around to the WSW and WNW and while two escaped the cliffs, the other two, *Glencoe* and *Mary* met trouble and were driven towards the coast.

The *Glencoe*, a brig skippered by William Hill was running her 240 ton cargo of coal from Swansea to Rouen when she met with the gale and was forced towards cliffs when her anchor rope parted. Fearing the inevitable, the crew made for the sandy beach at Pollurian, and by 6pm were aground. They could make no contact until 2 or 3 o'clock the following morning. Rescuers were led by Coastguard man Lieut. Drew who had the idea of firing a signal rocket with a light fishing line attached, but the ship was too far offshore and the Coastguard cutter was sent for. At the same time the *Mary*, carrying bricks and mortar, which had also anchored in Mullion Cove and found her anchor chain parted in the gale was also driven ashore at Polbream Point on the north corner of Pollurian towards the evening. At first watchers thought that she was deserted but the crew came onto deck and almost everyone ran towards her leaving the crew of the Glencoe still in the rigging thinking they had been abandoned.

Signal Rockets were fired towards the *Mary* to secure a line and a hauser. The landward end of the hauser slipped away and it was then that John Mundy, the brother of Mary Mundy, dived into the waves at risk to his life, to retrieve it. The hauser was made fast between the mast head and land and the coastguard man John Williams constructed a sling by which a rescue was made.

The Captain, mate and one other made the transfer to land, the mate having been clinging onto the rope for an hour, and as the ship repeatedly rolled from side to side he was being repeatedly thrown into the air and ducked under the waves, narrowly missing the rocks.

The ships boy, 14 years old, only known as Frederick, had only joined the ship a short while earlier at Bridgwater. Being the last one left onboard, he could not be convinced to cross over and was drowned when the ship broke up, still clinging to one of the last surviving masts in the twilight. His body was recovered and buried in Mullion Churchyard. The last signal rocket was then fired to the Glencoe but failed to reach its mark. As the tide was now almost out, a crew member tried to swim 200 yards to shore carrying a line. A hawser was drawn aboard and several of the crew including the captain made shore. By now W. Nicholas, the Lloyds agent, and the Coastguard had brought a boat over from Mullion but they were too late to affect any rescue (12) (13).

One incident occurred in January 1862 at Poldhu. The *Padre*, an Austrian barque from Trieste, was en route to Falmouth with a cargo of grain. Captain Bogdanovitch, and crew plus the Captains wife and child were on board when it ran aground just after dawn. Coastguard man Mr Isaac Goldsack was on his own and without assistance could do nothing to help so he ran a mile and a half obtaining help from fisherman Henry George, Messrs Williams, Kempthorne, Wilcock, Cuttance, Sheppard, and their neighbours managed to save 4 Italian members of the crew. The Captain, his wife, child and ten of the crew perished. The captain, his wife and 2 of the crew were washed up the following day at Gunwalloe where they were interred in the churchyard.

A letter from a Mr William Nicholas, Mullion Village Draper and Agent to the Shipwrecked Fishermen and Mariners Royal Benevolent Society was full of praise for the bravery of the rescuers and special praise was pointed towards Coastguard men Mr Isaac Goldsack, Row and Willcock, as well as Mr Williams who was officer in charge of the Mullion Coastguard Station. Those involved in the rescue had showed the utmost courage and put their own lives at great risk as they were under a cliff and had themselves been washed into the water several times. Mr Nicholas wished the names of the Coastguard *"... be kindly noticed, as it might stimulate others to do the like when such awful disasters occur"* (14). The incident showed the limitations of those who wished to help shipwrecked sailors and the lack of equipment available at the time. For their gallant efforts and bravery Isaac Goldsack and Henry George received the Humane Society's Medal for their brave conduct.

Fig. 40, left, Certificate of Enrolment for HMC Life Saving Corps.

A Manby Rocket Apparatus, with its "car" was sent to Mullion Coastguard Station in 1862, and later a Trengrouse system. Between 1862 and 1875 it had helped save at least 30 lives (13).

Lord Robartes enquired whether a Lifeboat would be feasible but was advised by the Parish that, at that time, there were too many rocks in Mullion Cove which required removal before a Lifeboat could be considered.

In stormy weather during the early morning of Tuesday 8th December 1874, the 535 ton Austrian Barque *Diana* carrying a cargo of wheat left Falmouth for Dublin. Near Wolf Rock she met with a strengthening south westerly gale and she sustained damage to sails which required her to return to Falmouth, but, like so many ships she could not clear the Lizard. About 3pm she was spotted off Mullion Cliff and then lost sight of, before being spotted again off Mullion Island. She was seen to "wear ship" (turn her stern to the wind so that the wind turns from one side of the boat to the other) which was an unusual manoeuvre, and likely to cause her to run aground. She took about 4 minutes to reach Poldhu and then grounded stern first on the sand about 3.30pm at Gunwalloe/Church Cove. The Rocket Apparatus and the Lifeboat crew were readied but it was the Rocket Apparatus which was used. The Coastguard under Mr Harris fired the first rocket which missed. A second shot was successful but tangled in the rigging before a third shot was caught and a hauser run out. The cradle was added and brought off the Captains wife followed by an exhausted Captain. The remainder of the crew were also removed and all looked after by local residents of both Gunwalloe and Mullion Churchtown. The Coastguard in this case were able to effect a marvellous rescue during which, for once, all went well, and it was a grand example of a system working well. Over the next three weeks the cargo was removed, but eventually she broke up on the beach (13).

There were several occasions when the Lifeboat could not be launched due to the weather and other occasions when the Lifeboat could not get close enough to a wreck or survivors. The Lifeboat was sent away in 1908, but the Rocket Apparatus remained in use. Rocket Parties comprised many men. Quarterly practice involving the Rocket Apparatus took place at locations such as Poldhu Beach.

In the late 1800s when a practice party assembled the men with white bands around their waist were volunteers, fishermen etc. They also had a badge on their left arm. Each man had to give their name to the Chief Officer and receive a ticket. This was apparently to prevent those who had never lent a hand from making claims for saving life and property. No ticket, no claim.

In practice there were limits to the operation of the Rocket Apparatus governed, not by the distance achievable by the rocket but the length of the hauser subsequently used after the rocket line had reached a stricken ship. The longest hausers were limited to 120 fathoms (240 yards), with 20-30 yards allowed for Veer and haul on. The hawsers couldn't be kept too tight as they would break with the roll of the ship. Over 200 yards long and there was a risk that the rescued crew would be drowned. This was about the maximum limit for rescue. The Rocket Apparatus was used in Mullion until well after the Second World War and overall was responsible for saving many lives. For many years the Rocket Apparatus was stationed in the village in a building adjacent to the Old Vicarage and, such was its importance that it was regularly used for practice. During the war years this was in fields on the Nansmellyon Road, near to Trenance Farm. One village resident Rex Bray recalls that in the Second World War his father, William Bray, see Fig. 40 was a crew member and he sometimes took him along in the back of the lorry and he remembers the thrill of sitting alongside the rocket apparatus (15).

21st Century

The Government delegated responsibility for civilian maritime search and rescue to HM Coastguard- part of the Maritime and Coastguard Agency. HM Coastguard coordinate maritime search and rescue within the UK using a number of resources at their disposal whether the emergency is at sea, or on the coast and coastline. HM Coastguard also has a voluntary service which comprises teams of volunteers who can respond to land based emergencies such as cliff rescues, mud rescues or searches for missing people. Other organisations involved include Coastguard Rescue Teams, RNLI Lifeboats, First Response Paramedics, Land Ambulance, RNAS (Culdrose) and RAF Search and Rescue Helicopters (16). A long haul has been made since those early days in the 1800s.

LOCAL RESCUES OVER THE YEARS

Local Fisherman helps to save Ship of the Line On the morning of 12th May 1857 HMS Exmouth, a 91 gun Albion Class ship of the Line with auxiliary Steam, captained by Mr Harry Eyres and with 800 men aboard was en route back from the Mediterranean when she went aground on the rocks at Gew Graze (Soapy Cove) in a worsening fog. The ship had lost its course and was travelling along the Lizard Coast. They hailed a fisherman who shouted to them that they were heading straight for land and he waved his hat, but almost immediately they hit the rocks. About the same time two Mullion fishermen Richard George and Frank Harris were out at Pigeon Ogo, just south of Gew Graze, tending to their crab pots when they became aware of a large ship running in before a light SSW wind in foggy weather right towards the cliffs. She came to a sudden stop just after passing them and they realised she had gone aground. Henry George and Samuel Hichens, also Mullion Crabbers, were at the time off Vellan Head when they heard a gun fire, a recognised distress signal. They made for the ship where Sam Hichens was taken on board. He advised them what they needed to do and exactly where they were, Gew Graze with Pengersick Point on the starboard bow. The Captain got up steam and two hours later as a result of the help they were given, and minus their anchor, 90 foot of chain, part of their keel and copper sheathing, were able to get off the bottom. Sam Hichens was given a certificate of service for his help before leaving in his own boat. After 3 months Sam Hichens had received nothing by way of remuneration and with the help of the Coastguard he appeared before the Inspecting- Commander to relate his story and as a result he was given a £5 reward for helping to extricate one of her Majesty's ships from a position of very great danger (13).

Fishermen and Firemen Not all the dangers were out to sea. In January 1901while a south westerly gale was blowing, a serious fire started in the engine house at the Pollurian Hotel, less than half a mile to the north east of the Cove Hotel. In a short while flames were seen coming out of the windows and all hands were needed to help stop it spreading. The fire began to spread to the accommodation. The nearest Fire Station was at Helston and the Engine was wired for, but there was no such thing as a fast response even a hundred years ago as the horses had to be found first. Luckily the Cove fishermen had not put to sea because of the gale and soon attended. Along with the Coastguard they provided assistance and helped to prevent the fire from spreading (17). The Polurrian Hotel, the first of the big hotels built along the Mullion Cliffs in 1899, suffered a second fire in May 1909, but this time the building and contents were totally destroyed. No one was killed but several were injured and the cost of the damage was put in excess of £12000, a huge sum of money now by modern standards (18).

The Fishy Tale of the Barry Ketch. On 9th June 1906 a 20 ton ketch called "*Breeze*" of Gloucester, owned by a William Morgan, was reported missing from Barry Harbour in South Wales. There were reports that a similar vessel had been seen near Lundy Island and later seen anchored at Padstow where 2 men had been spotted leaving the vessel in a rowing boat and then acting suspiciously there. They were challenged but one man was seen to return to the vessel anchored offshore (20).

On the following Sunday morning some Mullion Fishermen noticed a vessel circling Mullion Island before finally running ashore on the rocks. A fisherman called Downing was placed in charge of going out to the Island by Mr Linke, the Coastguard. On reaching the Island they approached the boat to find a solitary occupant, who turned out to be a German man who appeared unable to speak a word of English. He was in an exhausted state and apparently he had not eaten for 3 days.

Fig.41, left, Mullion Island. Photo by author 2011.

The boat, although not seaworthy was taken in and moored in the Harbour and the man was taken ashore to the nearby Coastguard Station where he was given food and water by Chief Boatman Groggett and detained for further enquiries.

It was found that the name of the Ketch had been covered in tar to hide her identity and also cut out of the Tiller with a knife (21). It was established that the vessel was the missing ketch "*Breeze*" of Gloucester.

The man was believed to be a German sailor called Paul Maier and was taken by PC Ede to Helston Police Station and detained pending transportation back to South Wales.

On the Monday Maier was escorted back to South Wales where he was charged with theft of the Ketch and remanded in Custody. Through an interpreter he told the Court that just before he reached Mullion there were 3 men on the boat and two had disappeared shortly before his capture. He explained that they were not carrying a mast light which had been broken (22). His story subsequently changed when he gave a further statement to the Court in Wales declaring that he had deserted a Scandinavian steamer "*Dorgen*" at Calais and then signed on the *Breeze*.

The captain and one other crew member had left the *Breeze* off Lands End in a punt, taking all provisions, leaving him without food or water. He later found his way to Mullion, saying that he had never been to Barry (23) (24).

Evidence was given at Court that it was believed that the Ketch had travelled via Lundy Island where the vessel had been ordered by HMS *Duncan* and other Admiralty boats to display a mast light. They were not located again at that time and it was suspected that they had been reconnoitring in connection with manoeuvres (25).

Airship in the Cove In the 1st World War a number of local fishermen joined the Royal Navy, and some went to the trenches. In the Western Approaches the German submarines began attacking the British Shipping and in one day 4 ships were sunk near the Scillies.

The Government decided to set up a series of coastal RNAS Stations to counteract the problem, one of which was RNAS Mullion at Bonython. Balloon patrols began in 1916. The first balloon at Mullion was the C9 which began patrolling in July 1916. They were filled with hydrogen manufactured on the airfield site, had 5 crew members and

supported a gondola made from two joined aircraft fuselages (26). Research by a Lieutenant Struthers suggests that the C9 was the airship pictured here and occurred on the 23rd July 1916 after the C9 was on patrol over Jersey when it was accidentally fired upon by British troops there damaging the envelope. It managed to get back to Mullion Harbour where it probably couldn't gain enough height to reach Bonython.

It was apparently rescued and carefully walked up the Cove Road minus its gondola, narrowly missing the houses in the process.

After repairs it was apparently flying again in 3 weeks (27).

They were not very fast but occasionally they were able to surprise German submarines on the surface.

In September 1916 the C10 was patrolling off the Lizard with the Destroyer HMS Foyle when she spotted two burning ships which had come under attack from a German submarine. The submarine was still on the surface and they were able to attack but it got away before they were able to bomb it (28).

The Night of the Flood. The elements have always had a big influence on life in Mullion and occasionally a weather event took place which left an indelible mark on the community. In May 1877 the road in the Cove was washed away by the sea after a storm and had to be rebuilt. It was decided to make a new road further inland (29). During the evening of Sunday 17th October 1920 a violent thunderstorm left its mark on the area. About 7pm fierce lightning accompanied by heavy thunder began. Torrential Rain lasted from 7pm until about 10pm and every gulley, drain and stream was quickly overflowing. Congregations at Church and Chapel were forced either to stay where they were or to wade knee deep through the streets. Houses in the village and outlying hamlets were flooded, with furniture washing around in rooms. All the streams were flooded, and each side of the river banks were inundated.

Fig. 43 Flood damage in the Cove, 1920

Boulders were washed down towards the Cove along with the remains of hedges. Down in the Cove a local fisherman John Pascoe remembers being told about the floods. He recalls being told that the floods were a disaster for many people and the surface of the stone lined culvert of the north pier was forced upwards and breached by the volume of water and blockages caused by trees and debris backing up. The result was that the stone blocks covering the walkway were forced up and houses there were flooded. In some cases people struggled to get out safely. Some houses in the Cove were damaged but according to information provided by local residents of the time the old Coastguard Watch House in the photo were already in the process of renovation, following a fire. One of Johns relatives lost a sturdy chest which contained all his personal papers and documents, along with other property, and was last seen floating away out of the Cove in the floodwaters, never to be recovered.

Two young girls, whose family are still associated with the Cove, were forced out of their home. Two Fishing boats in the Cove belonging to fisherman Mr John Bray were washed away, and the (north) Pier badly damaged. The cost of the damage was put at over £200 and it was described as the worst flood for over 50 years (30).

The photograph from the damage site, presents a scene of devastation reminiscent of other more recent coastal flooding events. The fill from the culvert under the north pier was removed and restructuring of the drainage system was necessary.

Mullion Mill is a good guide for the amount of water flowing down the valley at the time of the flood. The front door has a small square hole about 3 foot from the ground, and the Farmer of the time stated that the flood water reached and almost covered this hole in the door.

The rain was not confined to Mullion and badly affected other Towns and villages in the region. In Redruth water was seen coming out of kitchen windows of some properties. Streets and buildings, including a school there took months to repair. Also after the flooding the underground section of stream culvert was repaired and the section of damaged walkway on the north pier was replaced. As a result of the flooding an overflow channel was constructed at the top of the foreshore. This still exists today.

Wartime Rescue

The Harbour at Mullion Cove has always been a magnet for visitors and locals alike but the weather can turn the sea into a maelstrom and even the stone piers into dangerous places. Care has to be taken at all times when the weather is rough. Back in February 1946 two waitresses from the Mullion Cove Hotel were walking on the pier in a gale when a huge wave washed them into the sea. Luckily two servicemen were in the vicinity and rushed to help. Flt/Lt.. Smith, RAF Officer from Predannack and an airman named Stapley were walking along the cliffs and saw what happened.

They ran down to the Cove and plunged into the surf to rescue the girls who were taken to a nearby house and given medical aid and by the following day had made a good recovery (19) .

A Fishermans Story

The winter of 1963 was remembered by many for the cold, frosty weather which numbed the fingers and kept people indoors away from the freezing temperatures. One family had decided that they wanted to visit the Cove on a wild day with the waves sweeping over the pier, and into the Harbour. One of the children ran towards the end of the west pier followed by his parents and family when a big wave came over the wall and caught them. While the parents were able to keep hold of the nearest offspring the child in front took the full force of the water and was thrown off the pier into the icy waters below. At the time there was no one around to help, but a local fisherman, John Pascoe, had heard their cries and realised the danger. Without hesitation he took off his shirt and shoes, dived into the sea and was immediately

hit by a wall of freezing water which took his breath away. He swam out to the boy who appeared to be gripped by the cold and was at risk of being pushed out of the harbour entrance by the tide. By the time he got to the boy the lad had almost lost consciousness and took hold of him pulling him back into the harbour towards the outlet of the stream. What he didn't know was that 2 other local men had seen what was taking place and had managed to launch a punt and were heading towards them. With the intense cold now affecting them both they were each hauled into the punt and the boy returned to a grateful set of parents. What the two rescuers didn't realise was that the boat they borrowed didn't have a "bung" to keep out the water and during their rescue it also became very wet! There would have been no time to call the rescue services and only a quick selfless decision kept this young disabled visitor from drowning. A Queens Commendation was awarded to John for his heroic act.

Fig. 44 *Patrice,* PZ125 on the slip at Mullion. Photo by author 2003.

John has now retired and the name *Patrice* is not seen in the Harbour any longer. *Patrice* is a name associated with the Cove and used by several generations of the Pascoe family who have been fishermen in the Cove. About 25 years ago the owner had an unfortunate accident off Mullion when out baiting his crab pots with his brother. Coming to the end of a long session of re-baiting his pots John Pascoe saw a trawler a few hundred yards away heading in their direction. He recognised the boat and mentioned it to Jimmy. Thinking they might be coming over to talk he continued working but as the trawler bore down on them, it seemed neither to change course nor speed. Realising, but not really believing, what was about to take place he said to Jimmy not to move until he said jump. The reason was that Jimmy wasn't a good swimmer, and he was wearing waders. Just before the collision occurred John shouted "Jump" and the two men suddenly found themselves in the cold water as the Trawler hit their boat. He hadn't time to take them off. The crabber, *Patrice* sank straight away. John helped Jimmy stay afloat, and though he is somewhat reluctant to say how hard he worked to make sure that both men survived, the truth is likely that he saved his brother from drowning before being picked up by the trawler. The two men were taken to Newlyn, surprisingly uninjured. The fisherman involved in both these stories is a modest man, who, like several generations before him have spent their lives working in Mullion Cove and knows that fishermen often have to rely on each other when they are out at sea. The boat was eventually located upright on the sea bed and with the help of two Cadgwith divers they cleared the Pots from the deck and put inflatable bags around it. The boat was lifted from the bottom although just under water with the weight of seawater inside it was towed slowly around to Cadgwith and beached. They spent a long time pumping the water out and the local boat mechanic soon got the engine working again despite the immersion. Although she was taken for renovation John was not able to resume crabbing in her again.

The late Jim Downing, long time Mullion Harbourmaster was also congratulated for a Rescue in the Cove in 1963.

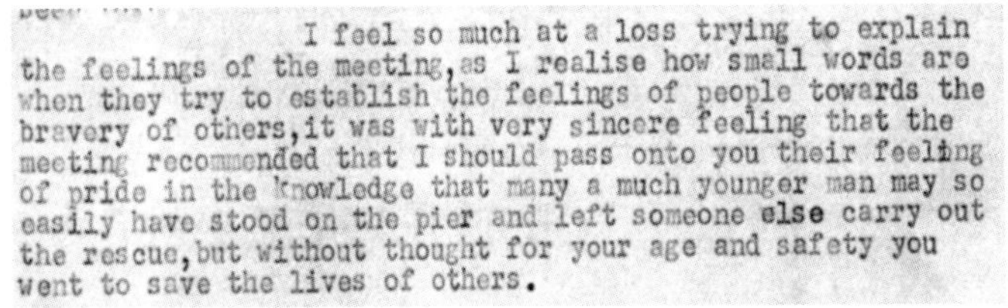

I feel so much at a loss trying to explain the feelings of the meeting, as I realise how small words are when they try to establish the feelings of people towards the bravery of others, it was with very sincere feeling that the meeting recommended that I should pass onto you their feeling of pride in the knowledge that many a much younger man may so easily have stood on the pier and left someone else carry out the rescue, but without thought for your age and safety you went to save the lives of others.

Fig. 45 Extract from Letter dated 20.3.1963 from Parish Clerk Reg Curtis to Jim Downing. Letter courtesy James Anderton.

There were other rescues in the locality and the local Parish Council sent letters of appreciation. In 1963 Jim Downing, a long time harbourmaster and retired fisherman was involved, with another, in a rescue and received such a letter. Part of the letter has been reproduced above. There have always been a need for effective rescue services on the Cornish Coast and every year there are more calls for the services of trained personnel. In Mullion today there are for example First Responders to ambulance calls, Ambulance, Fire Service, Cliff Rescue, Lifeguards, Inshore Lifeboats, RNLI Lifeboats, Coastguard, Cornwall Air Ambulance, RNAS Culdrose... the List goes on. All involved in these organisations do a wonderful and necessary job.

Bibliography

1. 1841 Tithe Map & Apportionments.TM/160,X585/3 Truro Record Office.
2 http://en.wikipedia.org/wiki/Sea_Fencibles 3.http://books.google.co.uk/books?id=0xYYAAAAMAAJ&pg=RA1-PA76&lpg=RA1-PA76&dq=a+list+of+officers+employed+at+signal+stations&source=bl&ots=r59GWlARv2&sig=_QXfzJaG11bpPsWid7SaXuT0yu0&hl=en&sa=X&ei=wspyUNLxNYOr0QWll4DYBg&ved=0CCEQ6AEwAA#v=onepage&q=a%20list%20of%20officers%20employed%20at%20signal%20stations&f=false (The Navy List Gt. Britain Admiralty)
4. http://www.pbenyon.plus.com/RN/Signal_Stations.html
5. http://www.hm-waterguard.org.uk/History.htm
5a Graphic 18.6.1892
6. www.dft.gov.uk/mca/mcga07-home)
7. Ipswich Journal 27.2.1808
8. Norfolk Chronicle 15.10.1808
9. Kentish Gazette 5.5.1809
10. Norfolk Chronicle 24.11.1810
11. RCG 1839
12. RCG 24.9.1858,
13. Rev E.G.Harvey Mullyon, its History, scenery and antiquities. 1875p57-9
14. RCG 7.2.1862 , Letter.
15. Local Resident
16. http://www.dft.gov.uk/mca/mcga07-home/emergencyresponse/mcga-searchandrescue/mcga-theroleofhmcoasguard.htm
17. Cornishman 10.10.1901
18. Cornishman 20.5.1909
19. Cornishman 7.2.1946
20. Cornishman 19.6.1906
21. Cornishman 28.6.1906
22. Cornishman 21.6.1906
23. Western Times 28.6.1906
24. Cornishman 5.7.1906
25. Gloucester Citizen 18.6.1906
26. http://www.mycornwall.tv/pdf/MC03-p42-45.pdf
27. Local Resident
28. WMN 9.1.35
29. RCG 18.5.187
30. Cornishman 20.10.1920

Chapter 7 SMUGGLERS AND WRECKERS ABOUND

The subject of Smuggling or "Free Trading" in the South West has been given a lot of attention in recent years. The wealth of information and research on the subject has however shown that Revenue evasion was not exclusively a Cornish occupation but was carried on right around the country!

No true Cornishman would ever admit that smuggling or *"Free Trade"* was wrong. If anything were wrong, it was the harsh law which prevented men from earning an honest living.

However, saying that, an 18th century visitor to the west coast of the Lizard Peninsula could be forgiven for thinking they had entered a land devoid of morality and religion, but the way of life was hard and harsh for many. Of the Mounts Bay, it was written in 1753 that *"The coasts here swarm with smugglers from the Lands End to the Lizard"* (1). In 1817 the Rev George C. Smith, known as "Bosun Smith" wrote of the coastal occupants at Predannack a short distance from Mullion Cove that, *"There is no preaching whatever in this village and there are some who cannot walk far out of it. The neighbourhood is sadly infested with the wreckers. When the news of a wreck flies around the coast, thousands of people are instantly connected near the fatal spot, pick-axes, hatchets, crow bars and ropes, are their usual implements for breaking up and carrying off whatever they can. The moment a vessel touches the shore she is considered fair plunder, and men women and children are working on her to break her up, night and day....."* (2)(3).

The vast growth in international and local trade by sea in the 18th and 19th centuries brought thousands of sailing ships and steam ships from all countries past the Cornish coast, travelling by day and night; often through fearsome storms they were looking for landmarks which ensured that they were on a correct course for their destination. The coast around the Lizard was littered with wave battered ships, all of which were trying to reach landfall before life was lost and they broke into ten thousand pieces.

But although some consider that the act of wanton wrecking may have been exaggerated the removal of goods from wrecks which turned up on a beach was rife and accounts indicate that on occasions in Cornwall several thousand local people could be present at a wreck in the hope of gaining at least some "useful" item from the site.

Part of the problem, it has been argued, may have arisen from within in the complex subject of "Right of Wreck" possessed by the Manorial Lords in Cornwall for centuries around the Cornish Coast, as much as poor social and financial conditions experienced by the majority in the Duchy at the time.

Smuggling of goods which evaded revenue was a huge problem for the Government and was recognised as a reason for the loss of thousands of pounds in tax revenue- which they could use to fund a war! The Board of Excise was set up in 1643 to collect duty on imported goods of all types, but generally operated within Ports, which left vast areas of coastline for the "Free Traders" to operate.

Many Incidents of smuggling and also stealing from wrecks were reported over the centuries. In February 1733 the *Betty Galley* from Malaga carrying wine was wrecked at Gunwalloe in a storm and Edward Penrose Esq. had to call in troops from Penzance to deal with the *"country people"* who were taking the pipes of wine from the wreck. He said that he *"ran much hazzard among these rude inhuman people, who dreaded the sight of a bayonet screwed onto the end of a musket"* (3a). (A pipe was 120 gallons). In 1739 a large ship called *Naboths Vineyard* carrying a cargo of wine from Bayonne was wrecked at Mullion and part of the cargo, 190 hogsheads, was recovered by soldiers then quartered there. It should be remembered that, at that time, there would be no coastguards or local customs men available here to preserve the cargo of a shipwrecked vessel. By 1748 the soldiers had been removed from West Cornwall (4).

In fact over 120 years later the whole force from Porthleven to the Lizard was only one officer and six men (3).

In 1786 it was said by the Customs Collector at Penzance that " ... *the whole coast is principally inhabited by a lot of smugglers, under the domination of fishermen, it is next to an impossibility for the officers of the Revenue to intercept any of these goods after they are landed, unless by chance a trifling matter...*". Captain Pellew however, working out of Falmouth, took his post so seriously that for a long time kept his two Revenue Cutters, the *Hawk* with 14 guns, and the *Lark* with 12 guns constantly at sea. A notorious smuggler was Thomas Welland who had an armed lugger called *"Happy-go-Lucky"*, with 14 guns and a crew of 30. He had vowed that he would never be taken alive. In April 1786 he was surprised by the Revenue Cutters Hawk and Lark at anchor near to Mullion Island. She cut her cable and sailed away to the west, closely followed by the Cutters. They soon caught up and fired grape shot and canister killing Welland and wounding 12 of his crew, resulting in their surrender. On boarding the prize they found what Welland had been smuggling fighting cocks. The deck was awash with Cocks fighting each other, their cages having been destroyed in the skirmish (5).

The Rev C.A. Johns, who was a regular visitor to the Lizard for 20 years, recounted in his book *"A week at the Lizard"* in 1848 that few Mullion families were not engaged in smuggling. In fact one veteran in particular, who had since dropped his profession as a smuggler told him how "... *on many occasions he risked his life in an effort to save shipwrecked vessels, but on many occasions could tell a tale of being chased by a kings boat, of his having thrown himself overboard, of having swum for his life, of having eluded, by diving, blows dealt by an oar or a cutlass and had escaped to land".*

An incident was relayed to Johns by Rev Gregory which apparently took place in the early 1800s when a Mounts Bay Boat owned by a man known as *Billy the Praow* came onshore at Mullion Cove with barrels of French brandy. He was seen by the Preventative Cutter, the *Hecate*, and captured. People in the neighbourhood became aware of the incident and quickly offered their own resistance by collecting in large numbers and breaking into the Armoury of Militiamen at Trenance, armed themselves with guns and ammunition and fired on the preventative men from rocks causing them to give up their captured barrels of brandy and return to their ship. Many local people were threatened with prosecution but the matter was hushed up (2) (6).

The truth of the matter was probably that there was smuggling activity ongoing at or near Mullion Cove for a long time after these incidents.

On the 17 April 1840 a smuggling vessel attempted to run her cargo in at Mullion.

A fight took place between the smugglers and the coastguard, in which several persons were wounded on both sides. The goods were sunk, but it was reported that the *Dove* cutter, one of two coastguard boats out of Falmouth was looking for the smugglers (7).

In March 1850 a large fishing boat called the *Talbot*, out of Plymouth was detained by Revenue officers in Mounts Bay on suspicion that her illicit cargo had been sunk off Mullion. Mr Forward, commander of the Revenue Cutter *Sylvia* was able to recover 60 tubs of spirits, which together with the craft was returned to the custom house at Penzance (8).

It is hard to say whether there was a rapport between the smuggler and the coastguard. In some cases there may have been a mutual respect, but in many cases there was collaboration. Certainly there are cases where some of the coastguard men would turn a blind eye, but this may well have been out of fear for themselves. In March 1769 William Odgers, an Officer, stationed at Porthleven was murdered while trying to seize smuggled goods. The Coroner named one of the murderers and many of those involved fled the area. Some even sought refuge underground in tin workings where they remained for a year. Agents for the murderers offered money to a witness to leave the country and eventually, to the amazement of many, when suspects were put on trial at Bodmin they were acquitted, only later to be seen drinking with members of the Jury (9).

Fig. 46 Sandy Vro, Mullion Cove. Photo by author 2011

One local smuggler, Henry George, was known as *"Spotsman"*. The role of a Spotsman was to find a safe place for the contraband to be landed and he was a target of the local Coastguards. The coast around Mullion had many locations where this could be achieved. He possessed stealth and guile, and an ability to avoid capture in the cliffs and caves on the blackest of nights. On one occasion the Preventative men discovered that he had taken a trip to France and took steps to strengthen their defences using the Revenue cutter to patrol the Mullion coast. He returned at night but despite a keen lookout being kept, he landed his cargo of brandy at *The Chair*, about half a mile south of Mullion Cove. He sent the boat away with two hands and went to meet his "friends" nearby at Predannack.

With the enemy not far away he located the men lighting a fire, a signal to warn of the presence of the enemy. With the Brandy onshore, they were able to hear the sound of the Revenue cutter as it approached their empty boat, detaining the

two crew members left on board. Quietly they collected some of the barrels and hid them in a nearby mine shaft.
The preventative men were unable to find the remaining barrels and returned empty handed. The smugglers then collected all but two of the remaining barrels and in the early light saw the cutter anchored offshore. Not wishing to miss out on an opportunity, a fishing boat was later sent out on a "long lining" trip around the Cove to drag the bottom and collect the two remaining barrels and while doing so held a friendly conversation with the men on the revenue

cutter, oblivious to their true role, about the fishing. They had been duped again. On another night he was challenged by a member of his own group and failed to respond, was fired upon, and received a wound to his thumb (2).

Fig. 47 "Smugglers Cave" near Sandy Vro, Mullion Cove, originally a Soapstone Tunnel. Photo by author 2011.

The caves were not used solely by seagoing smugglers and many a stolen sheep or cow found its way into the secluded ones to be cut up. In the 18th and 19th century many cliffside caves which today seem impossible to reach had elaborately engineered paths leading to their entrances.

One night Lieutenant Drew of the Coastguard suspected that a "run" would be made one dark night at Sandy Vro in Mullion Cove. With his men he discovered a party of smugglers awaiting the arrival of their boat. The smugglers fired, narrowly missing Drew. A rope was found which was hauled in and found to be tied to no less than a hundred barrels of spirits. All this was watched by the *Spotsman* who had hidden rather than run off. He was forced to watch as each barrel was chalked up to the coastguards and hauled to the top of the cliff (2).

To the north east of the sandy beach are caves which are in fact 18th Century Soapstone mining levels cut through the serpentine headland ... no doubt ideal hiding places. The old path down to the beach has now gone and access is by sea only. On one occasion, so the story is told, two Prussia Cove (Mounts Bay) smugglers, well known for the exploits of John, Harry and Charles Carter, were returning home from Roscoff with a small sailing boat laden with contraband. The wind had dropped and they were forced to row from a good way off the Lizard.

To save the last few miles they decided to put in at Mullion, but on arrival found two Excise men waiting on the beach. Somewhat exhausted they offered the excise men five pounds each to be allowed to land but it did not work and they were forced to continue rowing to Prussia Cove.

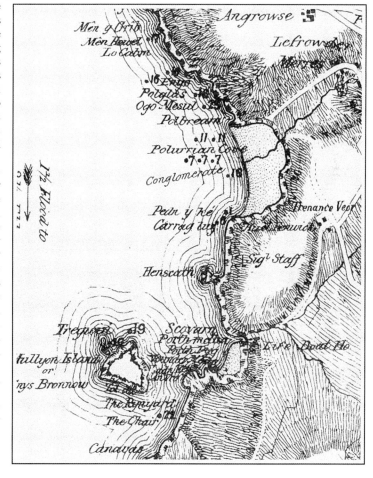

In the meantime the two officers mounted their horses and kept pace with them on the cliffs. Just short of the Cove the smugglers passed out of sight of the excise men behind a headland where they found a crabber hauling his pots. They quickly swapped cargoes returned the pots to the seabed and rowed on their way. Shortly before arriving at the Cove they were joined by the excise men on horseback and immediately on landing their boat was searched. Nothing untoward was found. A few hours later the crab fisherman returned to the shore and unloaded his newly caught cargo. It was a fine deception.

Prussia Cove was renowned for its smugglers, but St Keverne had Tobias Johns and Harry Cuttins. Johns was apparently a man of moderate height but great strength. He had a large pale face and black hair. Like Henry Carter he had religious doubts and later became a preacher. There were few Preventative men on the Lizard, there being only two west of Falmouth, and they were at Mullion.

It was said of Johns that in one altercation he caught them, tied their hands and carried them to the sea and they would have been drowned if they had not been able to free themselves from the ropes with their teeth.

The brandy tubs in use cost £2 a pair and were sold for £7. About five trips were run each year. Customers included Farmers, Publicans and gentry. A good cargo was about 200 tubs or barrels of brandy holding about 4 gallons each, and tied in pairs by Lanyards so one could be carried on a man's back and one on his chest. The tubs were tied to a long rope called a stray line so that if the barrels were sunk they could be found with a grapnel hook. When the cargo was landed each man had 2 tubs slung on his shoulders and once landed they would head off to local wooded areas. On one occasion the Preventative men came across them and were captured by Tobias Johns, placing them under guard until the cargo had been disposed of. The Keverne men were not afraid to attack the Preventative men. Cuttins was eventually arrested an put on a Man-of-war where he worked for several years as an Able seaman (10).

 It is said that some of the customers were local, and some of the cargo often found its way over towards Mullion via secluded footpaths (10a.).

The Rev E. Harvey wrote in 1875 after walking to Mullion Cove along the Cliff, from Predannack," *Here below is Canavas and the Chair, the Rinyard and Vro Sand, where before now, hundreds perhaps thousands, of kegs, that never saw the Customs, have been landed"* (3).

Bibliography

1. Borlase G. The Lanisley Letters, Journal Royal. Inst. Cornwall XXIII 1753
2. The Wreckers, or a tour of benevolence from St Michaels Mount to the Lizard Point, Rev R.C. Smith 1817 ,
3. Rev E.G. Harvey Mullion, Its Histories, Scenery and Antiquities. 1875
3a Derby Mercury 28.2.1733.
4. Cornishman 19.3.1931
5. Edward Osler The Life of Admiral Viscount Falmouth 1835
6. A week at the Lizard, Rev. Johns 1848
7. Hull Packet 24.4.1840
8. RCG 22.3.1850
9. http://smugglers.oldcornwall.org/cornish_jury.htm
10. Cornishman 15.4.1937
10a. Anecdotal evidence from local resident.

Chapter 8 MULLION PILCHARDS, CRABS AND LOBSTERS

"And note you, man, low seated on the verge
Of the green hill awaiting the pilchard- shoals
He is the Huer, and on their approach,
Discerned by ruddy tint upon the wave,
He heralds the glad sight with hue and cry,
From his long sounding trumpet horn, and lo!
`Tis echoed loudly from the hill to coast,
And all the land is soon alive with men;-
Seine boats are manned and launched, and heva shout
Tells the waiting ones "The fish has come"!

Mullion Cove was part of the Mounts Bay Pilchard Fishery, but like other fisheries it also had a longstanding Crab, Lobster and Crawfish Fishing Industry. The Pilchards are no longer caught in large numbers nor are the Crawfish but the crab and lobster fishery still survives today.

History.

Sea fishing has been at the very centre of the Cornish way of life for centuries. As early as the 13th century King John had granted licences to French merchants to fish in the English Channel for as long as they brought salt and materials for making nets.

For centuries fishermen have sailed hundreds of miles in order to catch fish. Only 30 years after Columbus visited the American continent in the 1490s the fishermen of Devon and Cornwall were fishing the western Atlantic at Newfoundland. The fishing boats caught so many fish that they could only bring back a small proportion in their boats (1).

In 1584 the twenty year war with Spain began. Cornwall was the nearest point to Spain and suffered from seaborne attacks. In 1588 the Spanish Armada attempted to invade England. In 1594 the Spanish *"Men of War"* were chasing the Devon fishing vessels back from Newfoundland as far as Dartmouth and in 1595 four Spanish galleys attacked and burned an unarmed population of Mousehole, and Paul in Mounts Bay killing an estimated 200 occupants and later attacked Newlyn and parts of Penzance (2).

By the early 17th century there were over 200 West Country fishing vessels engaged in the Newfoundland trade including boats from Fowey, Falmouth, Penzance, St Keverne, St Ives and Padstow. It was reported that fishermen in Mounts Bay were sometimes subjected to kidnapping by Spanish or French vessels, their Captains trying to gain intelligence on British Ship movements. In the 1600s and 1700s Turks and Moors made regular visits to Mounts Bay in search of slaves and plunder both at sea and on land (1).

An extract from a letter from Mounts Bay published in 1753, dated March 7th, *"Several French vessels have lately put into this bay, & Falmouth, and prevailed on the fishermen to sell them considerable quantities of fresh pilchards, which are salted on board and carried off. They first sell their cargoes of Brandy, Tea &c along the coast: for which reason, some people, who encourage smuggling, have taken pains to favour this scheme; which; should it be suffered to go on, the curing &c by which many thousands are supported, will be entirely lost to the nation"* (3).

An extract of a letter from Mounts Bay in December 1754 shows a healthy industry, *"Since my last we have had one of the most pleasing sights ever beheld in these parts, near twenty seines down at one time which has surrounded, upon the best calculation 17 or 1800 hogsheads, the largest quantity ever enclosed in this place at one time in the memory of man."*

A letter written from a gentleman at Penzance, to a friend in London, dated June 14th 1776, *"Thursday last, from a garret window in this place, I saw an action, within half a league from shore, between a French Privateer called the Magdalena Henrietta, mounting 22 carriage guns ,eight pounders ,with swivels ,commanded by Captain Anthony and the Lark, Customs House cutter, of Falmouth mounting eight guns, six pounders with swivels. The Frenchman had 55 men, the Lark only 19. The engagement was very hot on both sides and lasted upwards of an hour, when the French Vessel "struck". The crew of the Privateer acknowledged their intention was to have set fire to Mounts-Bay, and plunder the place, and several small vessels lying there, but they were luckily disappointed"* (4).

A letter from Falmouth, 3rd September 1779, *"Two fishermen who have just come in here say that a vessel of force is on shore in Mounts Bay, that they spoke with a fishing boat off Mounts Bay, who told them that the ship had gone ashore about an hour before, but he believed her to be a foreign vessel, though he could not distinguish them very well as it blowed hard, he judged her to be a Moorish ship. The people of this toen have caught the news, some say it is an Algerine,... that they have brought the plague others believe her to be an American privateer... this season... we have been at some places in want of casks to pack them* (pilchards) *up in, and have actually let the fish lie on the ground and rot, after drawing the oil from them"* (5).

Piracy

Problems with piracy of boats and kidnapping of sailors had persisted from an early time and there must have been a fear amongst the fishermen that their activities might be interrupted. A keen eye and recognition of foreign boats would have been essential. Domestic State Papers at the time of Charles I, dating from the 1630s indicated that there were about 60 fishing vessels and 200 men without employment as a result of Turkish activities. In 1640 a petition was sent to the King asking for help after Pirates took 60 men women and children from their houses at night in Mounts Bay near to Penzance. A further petition in the same year asked the King to help after 3000 were reported in captivity, undergoing hardships such as rowing in galleys, drawing carts, grinding in mills, suffering much hunger and beatings by which cruelty many, not being able to undergo it have been forced to turn Mohammedans. In 1636 the ships known as Corsairs (Barbary Pirates) were watching the coast so hard... that fishermen were forced to refrain from their occupation for fear of being made prisoners. Their activities in some countries led to small coastal villages being abandoned.

It was said that the Turks show themselves daily at St.Keverne, Mounts Bay and other places that the poor fishermen are fearful not only to go to sea but that the Turks would come and take them from their houses (5a).

Among the minor duties of the 17th century Mayor of Helston was to send local news to the *London Gazette*. Shortly after the Restoration the editor got in touch with officials at leading seaports of the country plus other places in order to obtain accurate information. In return for information, copies of the *Gazette* were sent out. The Mayor of Helston was on the list, the information being sent to Helford Creek. (Gweek).

In the calendar of state papers for 1636-7 is a record which reads *"At St. Keverne and Helford Creek seven more fisher boats were taken by the Turks... The seven were made up of three fisher boats belonging to St. Keverne, three others of Helston and one more of* Mollan, *(Mullion) and about 50 men in them"* (6).

As well as the awful information about the taking of a Mullion fishing boat and crew by the Turks, this information of course, shows that there was a fishing industry in Mullion back in the early 17th century. No local information about this incident exists, but looking through Parish Records of the time makes the reader wonder who was taken away?.

The first recorded exports of pilchards were from Looe in East Cornwall in 1555 with the main buyers being Italy. An industry peak was reached in 1871 (7). The transport of Pilchards in the 17th Century was largely in the hands of the Dutch but later in the 18th century the British and Cornish vessels were exclusively involved.

A large fleet of vessels was required to transport the fish in a successful season. An average cargo was 5-6000 hogsheads, about 100-120 tons. Few sailing ships were able to make more than one trip a year but by 1859 steam ships began to transport catches. For Mounts Bay Fisheries it became easier to transport catches to Newlyn or Penzance to be cured and shipped (8).

Catches of pilchards varied year on year. Hostilities between nations, in particular the wars with France often interfered with both the operations of the fishermen and their ability to sell their catch.

Salt was obtained from France and Spain. It was a commodity which the Cornish fishing industry relied upon, but the main market for the cured pilchards was not in England, Wales or Ireland, but in Italy. The quantities of pilchards taken in 1790 and 1796 were so great that ships had to be despatched to France to buy extra salt.

Catches of Pilchards at the Mullion Fishery varied through the years. Fortescue Hitchins and Samuel Drew wrote in 1824 that the industry began in the early 1700s recording that catches could be as high as 1000-1500 Hogsheads per year to a low where the catches were unable to meet the cost of expenses. They also say that there were between 6 and 14 seines employed annually in the early 19th century and that it was necessary to take the catch to Newlyn to be cured as there were no fish cellars erected in Mullion for the purpose (9). However the Royal Cornwall Gazette of 2nd April 1814, and 9th September 1820 contain adverts showing there were definitely fish cellars at Mullion by then. The Jose fish cellars for example may date back to the 1700s.

BUILDINGS LINKED TO FISHING IN THE COVE

Many of the original Net Lofts and Fish Cellars associated with the industry are still present, but they have all been rebuilt or modified in some way. They do however still retain the footprint and character which epitomizes a Cornish Pilchard Fishing Harbour. The Pilchard fishing has long since died out in Mullion Cove and, most of Cornwall, apart from a recent small revival in Newlyn, but Crab and Lobster fishing is still carried on with methods almost unchanged from those employed back in the day. The association with fishing in the Cove can be seen in a number of buildings.

1.Net Loft (Fig. 48, below)
This building was listed in 1984 by English Heritage as Harbour Cottage Fishermans Net Store or Net Loft (10). The

Net Loft is believed to have been built in the 1700s and with a backdrop of some of the finest coastal scenery anywhere in Cornwall is reputed to be one of the most frequently photographed buildings in the whole Country. It was recorded in 1841 as being owned by John Shepherd, and described as being *"Rubble stone built with a scantle slate roof, one storey, with 6 stone steps leading to a doorway in the east side with the north gable end facing the harbour... and a square red brick chimney on the south gable end"*.
The site is cut into the north facing bedrock of the cliffside, adjacent to a raised path which now leads to the South Pier. Today it measures 24` in length and 17` in width. It has been modified over the years and late 19th century photographs show that the north gable end extended some 14` to the edge of the Harbour. This extension was for net storage, although French fishermen have been known to use it when the weather has been too bad to cross the channel to home waters. It also had a double wooden door facing east. Remnants of this early extension can still be seen at ground level. The steep sloping cliff side to the south, behind the net store was often used to dry out seine nets after use and before storage.

2. The Winch House. (Fig. 49, below left)
The Winch House was listed by English Heritage in 1984. In the English Heritage Listing and a National Trust Survey (12) it is described as *"...constructed of serpentine stone rubble with large rubble quoins and timber lintels to openings... two storeys, asymmetrical... stone steps on the east side lead up to the south pier.... On the first floor, [is a] central casement window with lapped glass"* (11). There is a working winch on the ground floor which came from an ocean going sailing ship of the late 19th century and later converted in to be operated by electricity. The first floor, with a chimney on the east side, is still used as a net store.

This building was shown on the 1841 Tithe map as part of a much larger stone built Fish Cellar which was owned and used by the Pilchard Merchant, Thomas Leah of Newlyn.

Some 19th Century photographs indicate that the rear of the Fish cellar extended eastwards with an enclosed rectangular walled "Run", which at one time had a sloping roof along its length, see Fig. 50, right
The southern boundary of the rectangular "Run" can still be seen today as a garden wall at Harbour House but is reduced in height by 2-3`. The path to the south side leads to the South Pier.
The Winch House measures 27` from west to east, by 20` north to south. The run measures a further 50` in length by 25` in width. The total length from west to east is 70`. The E-W wall had a series of rectangular holes which held long wooden posts.

On the posts were attached large granite or stone boulders used to press down on the pilchard casks to remove the oil which was collected when it drained into the run.

It was also the wall which supported a roof. The size and proportions of this roof changed in the late 19th century, at one stage covering the whole "Run". Within the enclosed area was the working floor of the fish cellar. It would have had a sloping pebbled floor made of thousands of serpentine beach pebbles collected locally and cemented to the ground. On the northern wall was a set of double wooden access doors, which, in Victorian photographs is adjacent to the large Capstan winding gear and winch used to haul the seine and crab boats up the slipway out of the way of high tides. Within the "Run" was a square brick boiler, fuelled by wood and with a brick chimney which was used to boil water, and cutch, used to treat the nets before use.

3.Jose Fish Cellar. See Fig. 51, below

On the northern side of the harbour was the Jose Fish Cellar now known as "Cellar House". It was recorded on the 1841 Map, situated just to the north of the Mill Leat. In 1841 the building was owned by Tremenhere Johns of Helston and leased to Jose and Company.

This Cellar consisted of a substantial stone built building, with two sections, one having a pyramidal roof and an upper storey. This taller section had upper storey windows facing south, but little else is known about it until it was converted to a dwelling in the 1930s. An assumption might be that this was used to store nets and fishing gear as well as process pilchards and other fish. Some of its original stone foundations can still be seen in the current building.

4. Coastguard Watch House & Fish Cellar   Fig. 52 right

To the east of "Jose Fish Cellar" is the first large building approached on the northern side of the valley. Today this building includes the Porthmellin Cafe and Island View Flats but in 1841 it was a "U" shaped structure recorded on the Tithe map. Where the Cafe is now situated it was recorded as a "Mill" leased by John Williams, from Tremenhere Johns, and next to it was the Coastguard Watch House believed to have been used from the 1820s. Part of this building was occupied by Coastguard families after 1841 and it also stored the Coastguard Cutter, a boat used by the Coastguard for patrols, and storage of Rockets and other equipment. The rear section became a Fish Cellar. In the 20th Century many Crab Pots were also made there.

Following a fire in the early 1900s it was renovated and the current ground floor later became the Harbour Masters office and home. The current cafe site was also occupied in the 20th century. In fact Barry Mundy`s parents and his grandfather William John lived there for many years before moving up to the village in the 1930s.

The Cafe, originally on the first floor was later moved downstairs. The building has since undergone renovation.

5.Capstan Plinth and Garages.

The Photo above right shows this building after 1897. The long Fish cellar can just be seen to the rear and in front are Seine Boats, and Crabbers. In front of the building is the Capstan, used for hauling the heavy seine boats and other boats up the slipway using wooden rollers. This operation is still done today, but with a motorised winch, smaller boats and fewer men.

To the east of Harbour House (The old Lifeboat House) is an attached garage and private car park, and to the south of that is a boat house/garage. The latter is the site of the old thatched cottage occupied in the 19th century by fisherman Sam Hichens and his family.

Fig. 53 right Reproduction of the Mullion engraving.
In a Victorian book entitled *"Our Own Country"* from the 1870s is an engraving of Mullion Cove which appears to show the site of these two thatched cottages in the middle foreground.
(The reproduction of the engraving is well circulated and often sold separately now). To the left on this engraving, on the south side of the valley is the Hichens cottage. The second cottage is believed to have been occupied in 1841 by Michael Williams.
On the Cliffside above the cottage site today can be seen the remains of an enclosure, or small reclaimed field which would have been used by the occupants.

THE SEINE FISHERY

Seine fishing for Pilchards or *"Fairmaids"* was a way of life involving thousands of people in Cornwall and Devon and several books have been written covering the subject (8).

Only a few have recorded any information about Mullion. Pilchard fishing was conducted by either Seine Netting in shallow coastal waters, or Drift Netting in deeper water.

Seine netting required water no deeper than the depth of the nets and preferably a sandy sea floor. They were caught in their millions, taken ashore, processed and preserved in the Cornish fish cellars or "Pilchard palaces" which grew up in the harbours, villages and towns around the coast.

Many Pilchards were traded abroad, in France and Spain but most were sent by sea to Catholic Italy where they were consumed as an alternative to meat. William Borlase wrote in 1758 that in the 10 years from 1747-1756 the quantity of pilchards despatched from the 4 principal Cornish ports of Fowey, Falmouth, Penzance, and St.Ives averaged almost 30,000 Hogsheads or 90 million fish annually (13).

In 1796 the number of fish caught outpaced available salt, and ships had to be sent to France for extra salt to cure all the fish taken (1).

However in some years the catch was almost nil and the Pilchard fishery failed. Rev. E. Harvey recorded in the 1870s that at Mullion *"The Pilchard Fishery, here, although of no extensive scale has been at most times attended with fair profits to the adventurers, excepting in the seasons between 1859 and 1864 during which time not a single fish was taken"* (14).

This was in fact a generalisation but catches were extremely low and varied widely in number around the Mounts Bay Fishery.

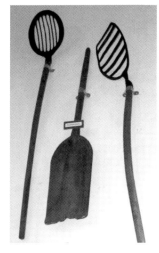

Fig. 54 right, A Maglen and pilchard shovel. Courtesy of Helston Museum.

Richard Carew wrote of Pilchards in 1602 as being, "*the least in bigness, greatest for gaine, and most in number*". In Carews time a "*sayne*" consisted of 3 or 4 boats carrying about 6 men apiece "*with which, when the season of the year and weather serveth, they lie hovering upon the coast, and are directed in their works by a baulker or huer, who standeth on the cliffe side and and from thence best discerneth the quantitie and course of the pilchard, according whereunto they cundeth the master of each boate by crying with a lowd voice, whistling through his fingers, and wheezing certain diversified and significant signs with a bush which he holdeth in his hand. At his appointment the sayners in the boats cast out their net, drawing it round to either hand as the schoell lyeth, beating with their oars to keep in the fish and at last either close and tuck it up and draw the same on land* (1).

Pilchard Processing

Historically they were processed using one of three methods. Carew described these as being, "*fuming, pressing, or pickling.... they are first salted and piled up row by row in square heaps on the ground in some cellar, which they term bulking, where they remain for ten days until the superfluous moisture and blood be soaked from them. .. they then rip the baulk and save the residue of the salt for another like service*". He wrote that those to be sold in France were "*packed in staunch hogsheads, to keep them in their pickle*". Those for hotter countries, such as Spain or Italy were first smoked on long sticks to dry them after which they retained the name Fumadoes. This method was later superseded as follows; The pilchards were taken from the "bulk", washed and packed into Hogsheads which were purposely made to leak, with gaps between the slats, after which they were pressed with large stones which removed more blood and water. This ran along the ground in the cellars or the "run", being collected in a trap or vessel away from the casks.

The Pilchard Count in Cornwall is both unusual and the origins interesting. It varied in different Fishing Ports.

One way of counting by the Cornish is interesting. In some areas they were not known to consecutively count above the number 30. For a hundred they would count three consecutive thirties, add nine and one for a hundred, and so forth and to any higher number. The numbers from one to ten were counted as, on-den-trez-payer-pymp-whetz- seith-eith- naw-deig (15).

It was estimated that to cure a hogshead of pilchards required 2-3 bushels of salt (16-24 gallons).

Fig. 55 right, A stone "Bully" with metal hook used to press the pilchard casks. Courtesy of Helston Museum.

The preferred Cornish source of salt was France or Spain. Attempts by the British Government to get the fishermen to use English salt failed miserably. The merchants made efforts to secure the quality prior to transportation as bad curing practice would lead to serious complaints and loss of trade. Such complaints were made in 1827 when some attempt at standardisation was made at a meeting of seine owners and merchants in Falmouth. At that time, for example, it was intended for each hogshead to weigh at least 476lbs. In 1871 a year when huge quantities of Pilchards were caught, quantities of substandard fish were sold to the Italian market creating a disaster for future sales.

Ships which traded pilchards were expected to bring back Mediterranean wood to replace that used in the traded casks and fishing ports often had cask makers. In a good fishing season 20-40,000 hogsheads would be required for exports in addition to casks for oil and "dregs" (8). The value of the pilchard fishery was well known. It was in Elizabethan times when an Act of Parliament containing the following clause was passed "*Statute 35th Elizabeth: No stranger shall transport beyond the seas any pilchard in cask unless he did bring into the realm for every 6 tunnes two hundred of clapboard, fit to make cask, upon payne of forfeiting the sayd pilchards*".

Cornwall was a county without a great quantity of wood resources (16).

Most of the Pilchards traded by Merchants from Cornwall, including those from Mullion, found their way to Italy. For example from 1833-1848 the main importers of Pilchards were Genoa, Leghorn, Civita Vecchia, Naples, Ancona, Venice Trieste and to a lesser extent Malta (17).

Left; looking south towards the Vro.

Photo by author September 2012.

Below; looking west across the Harbour.

Photo by author September 2012.

Above; Mullion Harbour looking inland to the east. Photo by author 2012.

Above; Modern view of the buildings in the Harbour area. Photo by author 2012

Right; A summer Lobster from the Pots for local fisherman Barry Mundy. Photo by author June 2012.

Below; A sunny panorama of the Cove and Harbour. Photo by author May 2012.

Left; Waves hit the West Pier in December 2011

Photo by author.

Right; Modern Rescue in action in the Cove with the Cornwall Air Ambulance. Photo by author July 2012.

Below; A fine sunset. Photo by author September 2009

There were three main areas around Cornwall where the Pilchard was found at different times of year. These were effectively the north coast of Cornwall to Lands End centred on St. Ives, between the east Lizard coast to south west Devon and the area south of Lands End to the west coast of the Lizard, this latter area being known as the Mounts Bay Fishery. The Mounts Bay Fishery was based around Newlyn with the largest fleets, merchants and pilchard cellars to be found at that location. Within this area were a number of smaller seine fisheries at Porthleven, Gunwalloe, Lizard, and Mullion Cove.

In 1827 there were 5 seines at Mullion and 2 at Gunwalloe (18).

In 1835 there were 10 seines at Mullion, but it was reported of that "*not one have been wet for the season*" (19).

In 1838 the number of seines between Lizard and Lands End was 34, but by 1850 it was only 15. Eight were at Newlyn, and the rest at Porthleven, Mullion, Gunwalloe, and the "Mount" (20).

In the 18th and early 19th centuries the fish made their appearance in large shoals in deeper water around July and came into shallow water by August being caught in seine nets until November or December. These seasons, however, changed and the summer fishery was dispensed with well before 1850.

In 1806 or 1807 at Mullion as many as 7000 hogsheads of summer pilchards were taken and cured, being shipped to the Mediterranean in the autumn. By about 1830 winter fish were being taken and gradually summer fishing declined (21).

Despite the tough existence fishermen would class themselves as being "god-fearing". They certainly preserved the no fishing rule on Sunday. An old Porthleven fishermen, when interviewed in 1946, recalled the time when Mullion Boats used to come to Porthleven for St. Peters Day, June 29th (22).

Sailing ships would often observe large shoals in deeper water and pass the information to the fishing boats. While the Drift fishermen, who operated in deeper water could take these shoals with their nets the Seine fishermen had to wait until the Pilchards reached shallow water.

There was often a great diversity of opinion between the two types of pilchard fishermen, and the Seiners argued for stricter control of the Drifters who, they argued, were affecting their catches and split the shoals. The Pilchards could remain in deeper water for several weeks and without prior warning they would often appear close to the shore, hence the need for observation by the "Huers" who were based on the cliffs or coastal areas bound by the fisheries.

Boats and Nets

In 1850 a series of articles appeared in the Royal Cornwall Gazette describing in detail the Mounts Bay Fishery (23).

The Mounts Bay seine unit involved the use of three boats and two nets. The seine boat itself was a heavy wooden craft made of Oak or Elm invariably painted black or tarred and weighed about 30 tons. It was able to accommodate a crew of 8 or 9 men, which comprised 6 rowers plus two to "shoot" or feed out the Seine net, (also called the "Stop net"), and a Bowman. Measurements varied slightly but they could be over 30`-40` in length, 7-12` in beam width and from 3` to 3` 6" deep. There was no deck but often a canvas tent or "tilt" could be erected to afford protection from sun and rain and do their cooking.

The seine net was contained in a "net room". The rowlocks, so important a piece of equipment were stored in a locker. A well kept seine boat could last for 50 years.

The second boat is shorter than the seine boat, often called a "Follower" or "Volyer", and carried the "Tuck net or seine". The "Tuck net" with cork floats but no leads had a mesh the same size as the "Stop Seine" but it differed in shape, in having in the middle a hollow bag or bunt into which the fish go when the tucking is commenced.

The remaining boat was a smaller lurker or cock boat. It carried the Master Seiner or Huer and two other men or boys (23). The "Stop net" itself was a massive construction of fine mesh net made of imported twine. It could be over 1200` in length and about 70 ` wide or deep. Cork floats and buoys were attached at regular intervals to the head rope at the top to keep it afloat and lead weights at the bottom, the total probably weighing about 3 ton (1). The "Stop seine" varied in length from 230 -300 fathoms (1400-1800`) and 13-16 fathoms (80`-100`) deep, with meshes of about 2 to the inch or 24 to the foot. These nets cost £300 when bought separately but with the boats complete may cost £600-£800, and if everything was new up to £1200.The hemp nets were all made by hand.

They were tanned or "barked" before use by soaking in an infusion of oak bark stripped off the trees in the spring. The bark was cut into small pieces, put into coppers filled with water and boiled for several hours. This dissolved out the tannic acid and the liquid became fit for tanning the nets, which are then said to be "barked" and fit for use. Later the nets were made by machine from cotton. The advantage was that they did not have to be dried before or after barking which was done after every 5 weeks. The oak bark was later replaced by a dried watery extract material from a tree from the leaves and young shoots of a tree, "*uncaria gambii*", growing in Burma and S.E.Asia. It was called "cutch" and imported from Burma, Borneo, Singapore and SE Asia (24). A properly maintained seine net, regularly and properly dried and barked could last 60-70 years (8).

Wages. In 1850, in general terms, the Huer might be paid a guinea a week, the master seiner 15 shillings / week, the seine shooters 12 shillings / week and the rest of the men 10 shillings / week. There would in addition be a distribution or share of fish amongst the men involved.

Cornish fishermen were in general opposed to fishing on a Sunday. It was rigorously enforced in some localities such as St. Ives, but less so at others (8).

One old Cornish custom was associated with pilchard fishing. After a successful enclosure and payment of their allowance it was common for the women to make a Hevva cake made from plain flour, lard, sugar, and dried fruit, the dough being rolled out in sheets, like pastry, marked in a criss- cross diamond pattern with a knife and baked in the "slab" (8).

Huer

The Huer was probably the most important man in the unit because he would be the first to sight a shoal in the water. In the early 19th century the Huer would look out from sunrise to sunset but it was noted that they would come to the shore more commonly in the afternoons and break up into smaller shoals at night, reuniting again the following day. Only occasionally were nets shot at night.

Fig. 56 A Huer on the cliffs at Gunwalloe signalling to Seine boats with furze bushes. Courtesy of Helston Museum.

The signs included a change in the colour of the water although often the shoal would be seen breaking the surface as it moved along, changing shape and direction in a split second. In some fisheries shoal was trumpeted out by the Huer.

The furze bushes were given the name "Turks Heads" and it was the manipulation of these bushes, along with whistles and shouts, which guided the seine boats to the right position to begin encircling the shoal. On the orders given by the Huer to "shoot the seine" the fishermen would pay out the net which would form a huge open ended circle. It was important then for the circle to be closed. The leading buoy of the seine was thrown overboard and the seine shooters, heaving together throw the whole of the net overboard in 5 or 6 minutes.

In some parts of Cornwall there were over 30 different signals which had to be recognised.

With the net overboard the huer continued signalling until the ends of the net were closely warped one over the other, (a procedure conducted by the "Follower") after which he issued orders for the safe management of boats and fish.

According to the strength of the tide, or depth of water, the seine was moored with, from 4-7 anchors, weighing from 70lbs to 180lbs, and at or near low tide the tucking began (25).

Designated areas of water or "Stems" were allocated to each seine boat to prevent arguments. There were approximately 5 such stems at Mullion.

Johns wrote in 1848, "*Proceeding from Mullion Cove* we *ascend a steep acclivity, and passing a flag staff, the signal station of the coastguard, observe several tall posts fixed in the turf. These are intended as boundary marks for the fishermen in the pilchard season. The shore beneath is sandy and well adapted to shooting the seine, and in order that all parties shall have equal chance of a catch when the pilchards are on the coast, each company takes its station on the best ground for a definite time, and then resigns it to another*" (21). Depth of water, weather conditions, tides and currents all played a big part in getting the nets and fish to shore.

This process didn't always occur immediately due to conditions and volume of fish but involved the use of a Tuck-net being lowered into the seine net with attached ropes. This was then raised to the surface producing a mass of silvery fish which the men scooped from baskets into the boats.

Baulking.

The fish were taken onshore where "blowsers" or carriers removed the fish to the fish cellars in carts or "gurries", boxes with pole handles, holding about 1000 pilchards. *"As soon as the first boat touches land the work begins, boys and men carry up maunds full. Girls hand them in gurries to the bulkers who (ar) range them in their houses with their noses outside , other girls bring up salt for sprinkling between the layers. When the fish are piled up high enough weighted boards will be placed on top, and the oil will begin to run out. The virgin oil is prized far above that which is afterwards squeezed out by stronger pressure"* (26).

Fig.57 An undated photograph described as "Pilchard Tucking at Mullion". Possibly late 1800s Courtesy of Helston Museum

Once ashore the fish were stacked neatly head to tail in layers with salt in between to form a solid wall of fish. These were left for several days or weeks for the oils to drain away. The bulk would then be broken down and the fish packed in the wooden casks. Pressure was applied to the tops of the casks using a large 7" wide wooden lever pivoted on one end in the wall of the cellar and the other by a large pressing stone.

A description published in 1848 said "…. *and now begins a very important part of the process, the curing, which is entrusted principally to women, a large number of which are kept at work, day and night, until all are secured. The floor of the cellar is swept clean, and covered to a distance of 5 or 6 feet from the wall, with a layer of coarse salt, on this is laid a row of fish with their tails touching the wall, outside of these is laid another row with their tails touching the heads of the first, and so on, until a sufficient space is paved with fish. On this foundation layer is placed another, each fish however is surrounded with salt and this process is continued until the pile is several feet high or the supply exhausted. The fish are now said to be in bulk, in which state they are suffered to remain for several weeks during which time they are subjected to heavy pressure. The floor of the cellar slopes from the walls towards the centre where a small channel receives the salt and the water, which leaks away, and afterwards the oil which is expressed, which last is collected and clarified. The process of salting complete, the fish are pressed into barrels, containing about 3000 each, and now are ready for the market. Very few of these remain in the country, the poor having bought their own winters stock, and salted them for themselves. The price when fresh varies from sixpence to two shillings for 120 fish, according to the season … The greater part of the cellared fish is exported to the* Mediterranean *… they are an important food article in Lent. Naples is the principal mart, and here if the market be overstocked, the surplus is stored away until the next year…"* (21).

Pressing would allow more pilchards to be introduced into the cask. Each cask had a capacity of 52 gallons and would contain 2950 pilchards, or 24 hundreds, reckoning 6 score and a cast of three over to each hundred. The pilchards had to be of the same minimum size and quality. The Hogshead weighed 4-5 hundredweight and was marked with the curer`s name, the year, place of curing and the port of destination. In the case of Mullion they were often cured in the Cove but others would be taken to the main port of Newlyn (8).

The pressing of pilchards produced oil which was an additional source of profit and was preserved both when the fish are in bulk and again when taken out and washed.

The water is skimmed of all oily matter and again it is refined by boiling. Different fish give different quantities but averaged 4-5 gallons per hogshead in summer fish and 2 gallons per hogshead in winter fish (27).

The season was short and nets were expensive so there were boat owners net owners and the fishermen all having a share from the catch according to agreed proportions. The Reverend J. Skinner estimated that the initial cost of a seine even in 1798 with all its compliment of boats and nets at approximately £1000 and each seine employed an average of 19 hands. In addition there were thousands of people, many women and children involved. They included rope makers, blacksmiths, shipwrights, sail makers, cask makers, twine spinners and net makers plus many others engaged in such occupations as salting, pressing, washing and cleaning the fish (1).

Wages .

Wages could often be a combination of fish and money and the methods used to calculate payments differed amongst fisheries. In Mullion by the 1870s the following method was used. *"Each Huer received 17 shillings per week and every 20th dozen of fish, the net shooters got 10s 6d per week and the crew 9s per week and these last two divide amongst them ¼ of the whole catch. The two shooters get a share and ½ a share each, the master of the cock boat and the bowman a share and a ¼ each, the remainder of the crew a share each. In addition to this the shooters get 2d each and the master of the cockboat and the bowman, one penny each on every hogshead of the owners share of the fish"* (14). Locally the fish were preserved over winter in salt to be an alternative to meat. The Pilchard season however was short and sometimes few fish were caught. The survival of many Cornish families was dependent upon being able to preserve and store pilchards over the winter period.

"The pilchard, when fresh, is very nice broiled either whole or peppered and salted. Salted it is tough and rancid, but nevertheless highly esteemed by the poor. The usual way of dressing the cured fish, is to boil them in the same saucepan with potatoes, to which they are thought to impart an agreeable flavour" (21).

MULLION CRABS AND LOBSTERS

Crab, Lobster and Crawfish Fishing have for long been part of the history of Mullion Cove and for much of the year a visitor today can still see pots, Dens (long floats on sticks or poles with cork floats and a flag to make them visible at distance in rough weather), gear and of course the boats belonging to the dwindling survivors of this very traditional Cornish industry in the Cove. If you are lucky enough to be allowed to watch these men at work pulling and baiting their pots every couple of days, you will see that they only remove the largest of the breed, thus maintaining the quality and value of the commodity. Today the spawning brown crabs and lobsters are returned to the sea bed. The original willow crab pots were all locally made by the fishermen, some in the Cove, and some around the village. They cost but

a few pence to make back then, using withies grown in willow gardens on the local farms. All the local farms had withy gardens in the valleys.

Fig. 58 Eddie Mundy making withy pots. Photo Courtesy of B. Mundy

New pots were made by the fisherman with skill and patience each season before the fishing started. The willow would need to be soft, and this meant that the wood was cut and most easily shaped before the end of April. They would generally last for only one season and of course caused no pollution. The skill is rarely practiced now but some local fishermen have never lost this important skill. The harbour would be full of pots at the beginning of each season. The pots, which had to be weighted with stones when in use, were durable, practical and cheap to produce. A fisherman who wasn't fit and strong would soon build up strength.

For many years a Smack from Scilly or Lundy would collect the catch, along with that from other fisheries. It would call and be met every 9 or 10 days during the season and take the catch to Southampton.

The Mullion catch was usually reckoned on being 4-5 dozen fish per boat. Payment was made at a market rate which in the early 1870s was Lobsters 14 shillings per dozen, Crabs and Crawfish 26 shillings per dozen, and she-crabs (egg-carrying) 2s 6d per dozen (14).

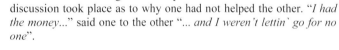

Fig. 59 Right Crab Pot locally made by Eddie Mundy. Much smaller than the ones usually in use and made for the Tourist market. Photo by author 2012.

With it is a local "preen stick", a local name for a spike of wood used to fix bait before the introduction of stretch bands attached to the inside of the opening in the pot.

On top of the pot is an early wooden measuring stick for crabs and lobsters. When the merchant in his Fishing smack called at Mullion for the crabs and lobsters they were all checked for size and if they were considered to be on the small size then they were priced by the merchant as "two for one". The stick was used by the fishermen to ensure that there was no argument and that they were receiving their correct money.

According to a local tale, there were two brothers who took their catch out to the passing Merchant one day in inclement weather and after a short while the exchange was complete and the money safely in the pocket of one of the fishermen. On the way back to the Cove the boat met with difficulties in the weather and capsized throwing the two overboard. Making out for the shore the one with the money kept a close hold on the few shillings in his bag while his partner who apparently was a poor swimmer came close to drowning. Eventually both were rescued but a heated discussion took place as to why one had not helped the other. "*I had the money...*" said one to the other "*... and I weren't lettin` go for no one*".

Fig. 60 Pard Mundy and Eddie Mundy outside the Net Loft. Courtesy B. Mundy

The "crabbers" had about 40-50 pots which cost a shilling (5p) each to make. They were baited through a hole large enough for the crab or lobster to get in ... but not out. All types of fresh fish were used as bait from Turbot to salmon, obtained by trammel nets or bought from passing fishing boats, cut up into pieces and secured in the pots which were sunk on a rope in the chosen location marked with a buoy.

The selected Crabs and Lobsters had their claws immobilised then stored underwater in a large withy store pots, to await collection.

Fishing Fact; In the 1880s Crayfish were also a popular shellfish, in particular in France where 5-6 million were consumed annually in Paris alone. Many came from Germany (28).

The Marine Version of the Crayfish is the "Crawfish", also a favourite of the French and still popular there today.

PHOTOGRAPHS OF EARLY CRABBERS. Both built by Olivers at Porthleven.

Fig. 61 below PZ271 the "*Progress*" a 24` crabber with Eddie Mundy in the early 1960s

Fig. 62 below PZ100 the "*Two Brothers*" a 26` crabber with Joseph and Eddie Mundy in the 1930s

Chapter 9 MULLION COVE FISHING DIARY 1810-1947

The following extracts are taken from old local or national newspapers and provide an insight into the events which made Mullion a Fishery over 200 years ago. The fishery was in operation long before the 19th century but accounts are scarce.

1811 August Letters from Mullion indicated that Pilchards were being sold at Penzance at one shilling for 120 (29).

1814 An advert in the Royal Cornwall Gazette 19 March 1814, reported the sale by Auction "*All that very desirable and extensive concern called The MULLION PILCHARD AND HERRING FISHERY, Carried on at Mullion and Newlyn in Mounts Bay in Cornwall, consisting of 5 Stop seins, 2 Tuck Seins, with Boats Tackle and Materials... also The Remainder of three several terms of 99 years, respectively, determinable by the deaths of two young healthy lives, in all that CELLAR and LOFT, BARKING HOUSE, CAPSTAN, AND Right of Cove, at Mullion aforesaid, and also the ISLAND , called MULLION ISLAND, distant form the Cove about 1 mile, and containing about 3 Acres of Ground. For which purpose (and for selling the materials belonging to the said cellar) a Survey will be held at MULLION COVE on Tuesday the 5th of April next by 2 o`clock in the afternoon precisely... For viewing at Mullion contact Mr Joseph Williams Mullion. Dated 1st March 1814.*"

1816 Part of the "*Mullion Fish Cellars*" in Newlyn were put up for sale (30).

"*To be sold at auction at the Dolphin Tavern on the Quay at Penzance ....1/16th part in the Mullion Fishery Concern ...5 Stop seans, 2 Tuck Seans and 8 Boats, 3000 Bushels of Fishery Salt, now lying in the Cellars at Newlyn. The Purchaser may have 1/16th part of the Mullion Cellars at Newlyn at a fair annual rent if required. For viewing apply Mr Thos. Leah, Merchant, at Newlyn.... Dated April 4[th]1816.*"

In 1803 a successful Pilchard fishery was established at Gunwalloe. In 1805 shares were offered for sale at Newlyn where it was called the "Alert pilchard seine" and had 2 complete seine units' materials a loft and a capstan. It was one of the few places where a seine was operated in an uninhabited cove by temporarily imported labour. The link with Newlyn was strong.

1819 Fires were reported to have been lit on high land near to Gunwalloe and Newlyn to summon boats to fish (8).

1823 September. 3 large shoals of Pilchards were enclosed off Mullion and Gunwalloe. One of the nets burst losing the fishermen 200-300 hogsheads of fish (31).

This was not unusual and in October 1874 a similar thing occurred to the Friends Company, a Mullion concern losing them an estimated 500 hogsheads (32).

1826 September 1826 Mounts Bay appeared full of pilchards, six seines were shot but only two took fish, which turned out to be Horse Mackerel. They were sold to the poor and farmers for manure (33).

1828 Tragedy was not uncommon around the Cornish Coast. September 1828 a seine boat belonging to Mr Marrack of Penzance was returning from Mullion, deeply laden with pilchards which had just been taken from the seine when she took in water and sank. The crew of Mr Marrack, 3 men and 2 boys got into the Jollyboat, which he had in tow, but unfortunately the mizzen boom of the large boat struck the smaller one. Mr Marrack, who left a wife and 5 children, John Curnow, who left a wife and 3 children, and a boy named Pascoe Richards were all drowned (34).

1829 The weather paid a big part in the success or otherwise of the fishing. During heavy gales in August seines were shot which were damaged allowing the fish to escape and the boats had to be taken to Penzance for repair (35).

1830 September Mounts Bay was said to be full of fish. The drift fishermen (Driving Boats) had done well but the seine fishermen had also been favoured. Within 6 days 700 hogsheads had been brought to Penzance Quay from Mullion for curing (36).

1832 At Mullion 800 hogsheads have been taken, and at Gunwalloe large shoals have been taken. All along the south coast seiners have been tolerably successful, but the fish have been of an inferior size, in consequence of which quantities have been sold to the farmers etc for dressing (37).

1833 The season was considered over by early October but around Mounts Bay some boats were left in readiness on the shore. The seine boats at Gunwalloe and Mullion with the exception of one kept afloat were all laid up (38).

Fish Tithes were taxes which required that a man should pay 1/10th of his catch to the Church, and special arrangements had to be made to collect it. In 1836 the Tithe Commutation Acts were passed commuting the tax to a permanent fixed rent charge payable in cash rather than kind. In the ages of faith they were regarded as necessary but gradually they were opposed often because they found their way to landowners and not the church. In pilchard fishing there were two tithes claimed, one from the merchants and one from the fishermen.

List of Fish Tithes 1836 (8)

Town	Tithes claimed from owners	Tithes claimed from Fishermen
Lizard		2s 6d from each fisherman
Coverack		1/10th value of pilchards
St.Anthony, Mawnan, Ruan, Grade - none		none
Porthleven	£1 -1s per seine	£5 altogether per drift boat.
Mullion	As above	As above
Newlyn	Tithes resisted in 1831 and no longer demanded	
Mawnan, Constantine		5s per fisherman... Virtually given up.

1836 Late Oct. a seine was shot at Mullion and 7-800 hogsheads were taken up and sent to Newlyn to be cured (39).

1837 This week the *Sylvia* revenue cutter fell in with a Cawsand boat off Mullion. Attached to it were, upwards of 100 kegs of contraband spirits were attached ready for sinking. The boat was seized together with the spirits were brought to Falmouth and 2 men part of her crew were detained to be dealt with according to the law. Two others are said to have escaped in a punt (40).

1840 On Friday night last, a smuggling vessel attempted to run her cargo at Mullion, when a fight took place between the smugglers and the coastguard in which several persons were wounded on both sides. The goods were sunk and the Dove cutter and her tender are keeping a good look out for them (41).

1841 Census record of Fishermen residing in Mullion Parish- William Mundy, 25 , Church Town , Henry Williams , 30 Church Town, William Williams,40, Church Town, Samuel Hendy, 60, Church Town, Samuel Hitchens, 60, Porth Mellin, Samuel Mundy, 35, Mever Crease, Richard George, 30, Quince.

1843 August A whale, approximately 60 foot long was spotted off the Lizard Coast. It was seen over several days coming inshore within gunshot range and blowing jets of water in the air. It was repeatedly fired at but with no effect. Such a monster could be injurious to the seine fisheries and at Porthleven it was responsible for scattering a shoal of pilchards which had been enclosed (42).

1845 September the Bolitho seine was shot over what appeared to be pilchards, but which turned out to be a shoal of Launce (43).

1850. September A seine boat was being launched down the slope at Mullion Cove when one of the rollers slipped, and struck the temple of Mr Samuel Mundy, killing him. Mr Mundy, Licensee of the Old Inn was a member of one of the oldest families in Mullion (44).

1851 Census Record of Fishermen residing in Mullion Parish- Samuel Plomer, 70, Church Town, Samuel Hendy, 72 , Worn-out Fisherman, Church Town. Fishermen often worked on the land when not at sea. A census taken outside of the fishing season would not include all fishermen and many would give an alternative occupation, which may have been agricultural.

1852 The companies in Mullion Cove included William Thomas (a Share sean), Messrs Bolitho and Co (Newlyn), Messrs Leah and Co (Newlyn). Mr Thomas` sean secured 300 hogsheads of fish (45).

1854 Things didn't always run smoothly. In August, having secured 150 hogsheads, William Thomas`s seine boat was driven from her moorings and became a total wreck. The seine was picked up at Porthleven (46).

1859 The season at Mullion was over by October with all hands paid off, with not a Hogshead of fish taken in the District (47).

1861 Census Record of Fishermen residing in Mullion Parish- Edward Williams 44, Village Vicarage, Henry George 38, Laflowder Village ,Henry George,16, son, John George,14, son. Samuel Plomer , 80, retired Fisherman, Church Village, William Thomas,23, Predannack Wartha, Richard George, 51,Trewoon, Samuel George, 32, Trewoon, William Roberts, 61, Kynance, Lizard Fisherman,

1861 A total of only 14 hogsheads were taken at Mullion by seines in October , while at Mounts Bay, a short distance away, the boats took from 700-2000 hogsheads of fine fish per boat.

1862 Mr Dionysius Williams of Mullion sent to London market 50 lobsters, 200 crabs and 10 crayfish. The above were the first sent up this season from the neighbourhood and were very fine fish (48).

1867 There are 4 seines shot at Mullion. About 600 hogsheads from them have been brought to Newlyn to be cured. This is quite a godsend to the place as many families in Newlyn and Mousehole are in very reduced circumstances from the bad fishing season. The fish are being bulked as they come in, and consequently a good many persons are employed for the time (49).

In November1867 the amount of fish at Newlyn was poor. Early on Monday morning 9 boats arrived with pilchards, 8 from Mullion and one from Gunwalloe with numbers estimated to be 500 hogsheads. Two or three seines at Mullion still had fish in them. 3 or 4 boats had their fish sold at auction at once, fetching 6s 6d per basket. Estimates are for 8 baskets per hogshead (50).

1869 Mr Samuel Mundy the managing huer for Messrs Bolitho, Trehair, and Friends Fishing companies is still making great progress with the pilchards (51).

1870 On Christmas Day there was a fine haul of Pilchards off Mullion. The seine belonging to Mr Trahair of Newlyn enclosed about 1000 hogsheads, the seine of Mr Batten of Penzance 200 hogsheads, and the seine belonging to the Mullion Fishing Company also 200 hogsheads (52).

In the 1870s there were 8 seines employed at Mullion. 5 were the property of Messrs Bolitho Coulson and Co, 1 of Edward Batten, and two of Messrs Trahair and Co of Newlyn. By this time the summer season had been dispensed with, and the autumn season beginning in September was the main season, going through to December (14).

Pilchard Fishing in the 1870s

I have been given the opportunity by a local resident to look at an extract of an undated document entitled "*Extracts from "Man of the Manacles"* manuscript by Jill Newton. Below is a "*resume*". The manuscript provides an excellent opportunity to look at Pilchard Fishing in Mullion Cove in the early 1870s, which of course, was probably the highpoint of Pilchard Fishing in Cornwall. It tells us that Mullion Cove was a very busy place, and each boat had to be hauled up the beach each night. If the weather was fine they may occasionally risk mooring them in the water in the shelter of the Island, while a night-watchman remained on the beach on alert all night, ready to give a warning of a change in the weather. It would take many working hours at night to bring all the seine boats onto shore, and there was no weather forecast available to warn them. It is said that whatever the time of night Mary Mundy would be there to open up the "Old Inn" for them if needed.

The Seine boats were valuable assets and much time, and money would be saved by this process. Within a few hours, however, they might have to relaunch all the boats if the Huer cried "Hevva", and they had to put to sea again.

In the 1870s there were five Huers employed at Mullion, Samuel, the Lifeboat Coxswain, John Mundy, owner of the "Old Inn", John Harvey, Sam Matthews, and Henry George, one of the Laflouder fishermen. Each of the Pilchard concerns employed about twenty men, and early each morning they could be seen walking down to the Cove. On quiet days the fishermen kept themselves busy mending nets and pots, and making net needles from bone or wood.

The problem of an easterly wind was often encountered on the Lizard and ships of all types and sizes, often as many as 100 or more, anchored in or near the Cove and in the Roads until the wind changed. This would render the fishing difficult. It was apparently not uncommon for fishermen to use their guile and enterprise and help themselves to some turnips and cabbages from a nearby field and take to sea in the crab boats to meet, and barter with passing vessels, for coal or a French Boat anxious to do business including take letters to land for posting. Whenever possible it seems that French brandy was part of the deal.

1870 The "Happy Return" seine owners have held their Annual Meeting at Penzance. This company carries on operations at Mullion under the management of Messrs John and Edward Batten of Penzance. The years` operation left £152 in hand. A dividend of £1 a share was declared on 125 shares, leaving £27 in hand (53).

1871 The best Pilchard fishing year recorded was 1871.

Among the Pilchards Part of a Letter written to the Royal Cornwall Gazette 28.10.1871

"*...There are now 25,000 hogsheads under cure, we may reckon the season to be already as successful as the celebrated ones 1850, 1851 and 1863, when the average was about 26,000, and there is no reason... why the amount should not be doubled ... in Cornwall, in the year of grace 1871, the pilchard reigns supreme. P.S. I learn this afternoon that there are immense shoals of pilchards both on the north coast and the south coast. At St. Ives more than 5000 hogsheads of pilchards have been secured, whilst in Mounts Bay, five or six seines are full, and the drift boats are heavily laden. Salt is now scarcer than pilchards. The sea appears to delight in pouring in wealth upon the hard working fishermen.*"

1871 Census Record of Fishermen residing in Mullion Parish - John Gilbert,47,Parkventon, Henry George 51, Laflowder, Samuel George 18, son, Samuel Hitchens , 68 , Mullion Cove , Samuel George , 41 , Trewoon , Francis Harris ,61,ChurchTown, Henry Gilbert,23, Meaver, Richard George,59,Trewoon,Thomas Mercer,60,ChurchTown John Mundy,41, "Old Inn", James Downing,56,Church Town, Henry George,26, Church Town, William Mundy,57, *Rose Cottage*, James Head, 32, Vicarage, Henry Triggs, 43, Vicarage, Richard Gilbert, 45, Vicarage.

In **1871** Messrs Bolitho were tanking pilchards in brine, the old fashioned Pressing Poles were replaced by screw presses (8).

1873 The government were keen to introduce alternative methods of preserving pilchards and canning in oil was experimented with in Cornwall (8).

1874 In October 1874 the Friends concern shot a seine and enclosed a shoal estimated at 500 hogsheads but the seine net immediately burst and the fish lost (55).

By the late 1870s seining was on the decline. In July **1877** shares in the Friends Fishery Company (whose seines had been worked for many years in conjunction with Messrs Bolitho and Coulson at Mullion, St Michaels Mount and Newlyn were offered for sale. It included 2 seine boats, one follower, two cock boats, three seines, two tuck nets, with 70 tons of salt in cellars at Newlyn and 20 tons at Mullion (8).

1881 Census Record of Fishermen residing in Mullion Parish. Henry George, 59, Church Town, William Thomas,65,Church Town, John George 32, Church Town, John Mundy,49, "Old Inn", Samuel Mundy, 33, Church Town, (Ursula Mundy, 62,Fishermans Widow, Church Town,) Hannibal George, 30,Garrow,George Jewell,26, Trewoon, James Pearce 24, Lower Predannack, William George 31, Laflowder, Edward George 17, Trewoon, John Rule, 24, Clahar.

In **1883** Trahair cellar in Newlyn was being converted to "brine curing" involving concrete tanks capable of holding 20 hogsheads of pilchards. Others followed (8) ... dictated by economic circumstances and a need to reduce the cost of labour... but sales of pilchards to Italy declined as a result (56).

1884 Advertisement in the Cornishman for the Sale of Trahair Seines and Gear from the *Union* and *Gull* boats at Mullion.   Fig.63 right Advert

1890 An inventory of Messrs Bolitho Seines at Mullion 6th February 1890-3 seans good (1 barked in 1889)- 1 Ruffle sean (good repair)- 1 Tuck net good (put in thorough repair 1889)- 1 Tuck net wanting repairs & barking- 1 Tuck net small- 1 stop net- ruffle sean-2 sean boats (good)-1 cock boat (good)-1 boat used as a follower-2 dippers,12 good warps, 4 inferior warps, 2 Manilla warps (Ruffle sean), plus ropes, moorings, tarpaulins, launching timbers, washing troughs, water gurry, fish stands, and 20 bucklers (8).

1891 Census Record of Fishermen residing in Mullion Parish - Edward George, 27, Church Town, Francis Harris, 82, Retired Fisherman Church Town, Samuel George 60, Trewoon, William Jewell, 34, Trewoon, Joseph Gilbert 33, Trewoon, John George,43,Nanfrego, Joseph F Mercer, 44, Predannack Wollas, Henry George, 70, Church Town, Samuel Mundy, 40,Church Town, William J Mundy, son,15,ChurchTown, Hannibal George, 40,Trenance Vean, William George,41, Laflowder.

1893 <u>Competition</u>.

In the later stages of the 1800s the rush to the Cove to launch the seines in Mullion following the call of "Heva" was not always a keenly fought battle between the companies of fishermen in Mullion. There were occasions when the cry "*Shot in Mullion*" was met with a different response...a whisper rather than a shout. The news would be sent by a stealthy messenger who would deliver it cautiously to a few friends.

The Owners of the seines at Mullion often required that the Pilchards were brought to Newlyn for processing or "baulking".

During the night fires would be lit on the hillsides and during the day horse riders would be sent with the news. The reward for the fishermen who could get the Pilchards from Mullyon to Newlyn was one fifth of the value of the entire cargo. Risks were run to carry the fish to Newlyn.

In the race to Mullion, however, the increased competition resulted in boats from Porthleven having a big advantage over those from other fisheries in reaching the shoals of fish. The result was the amount paid to the" fish-carriers" was reduced (57).

1897 September, the season had just started and two lots of Pilchards secured.150 hogsheads were taken from Sam Mundy`s seine when the remainder escaped (58). Large schools of pilchards still visit Mullion Cove and 4 seans were shot on Saturday. On account of weather one sean was cleared as soon as possible. The fish were sent to Mevagissey and Looe (59).

1898 Disagreement occurred among the Friends fishing company at Mullion in selecting their huers for the season.

PILCHARD SEINES AT MULLION AND GUNWALLOE, FOR SALE!

TO BE SOLD BY AUCTION, by Mr. A. BERRYMAN, at the "Three Tuns" inn, Newlyn, on SATURDAY, 19th January inst., at Two o'clock p.m., in the following or such other lots as shall be determined on at the sale, all those

PILCHARD SEINES, VIZ.—

AT MULLION:

LOT 1.—The UNION stop seine, tuck seine, seine boat, follower, cock boat, warps, anchors, ropes, tarpaulins, &c.

LOT 2.—The *Gull* stop seine, anchors, warps, ropes, tarpaulins, &c.

AT GUNWALLOE:

LOT 3.—The *Good, Templar* stop seine, tuck seine, seine boat, cock boat, anchors, warps, ropes, tarpaulins, &c.

The whole will be found in good working order. Lots 1 and 2 may be viewed on application to Mr. Samuel Mundy, at Mullion, and lot 3 on application to Mr. William Oats, Gunwalloe.

Further information may be obtained on application to Messrs. TRAHAIR, Newlyn, or to the

AUCTIONEER,

28, Clarence-street, Penzance.

Dated, 10th January, 1884.

William George and John Ride have been appointed to this very important duty, to the satisfaction of all concerned. (60). *"To begin the season, the Mullion Covers have acquired a beautiful modelled seine boat, built by Mr Kitto of Porthleven, and are highly satisfied with this craft, which came to Mullion this Thursday"* (61).

The Covers shot a fine seine on the 15th which proved to be 400 hogsheads. They were sent to Newlyn and Porthleven to be cured and fetched fine prices (62).

On Monday the Newlyn Mackerel Drifter *Onward* towed a new seine boat to Mullion. They were asked to bring the old one back to Newlyn and agreed to do so. After going 2 miles the seine boat began to fill with water and Frank James and a companion got into the punt to try and adjust the hawser. Just as he got back on board onboard the seine boat, however, she sank, the ropes parted and James only got back on board with the assistance of his partner. They then returned immediately to Newlyn. The seine boat was described as being very old and of little use (63).

Catches of pilchards at Mullion did not realise the amount expected. The Rovers and Covers together put on the market about 450 hogsheads, Mundy about 150. The Covers lost a considerable portion of theirs, the flood tide having parted their anchor rope, which resulted in the collapse of the seine. While the Rovers were "Tucking" the fish charged over the Tuck net and seine, when it is understood that about 200 hogsheads escaped. Large schools have been seen breaking water in the twilight, too late to secure them. Britannia and the Friends have not yet shot (64).

On Friday "Heva" was raised at Mullion and the Friends and Mundy shot their seans. The state of the weather made it risky, but good schools of pilchards do not come along every day. Boats were sent for but the bad weather and the approach of Sunday prevented their arrival. On Saturday Rover and Britannia shot; Mundy opened his sean and enclosed another school.

The Covers sean alone remained in the boat, but as they share fates with Rover, all parties were interested and agreed to allow the nets to ride until Monday. During Saturday night a ground sea got up and along with the spring tides, broke away the sean nets and until Monday afternoon, the sea had been too rough to secure them. They are believed to be considerably damaged and in some cases beyond repair and all fish have escaped. There will be heavy calls to repair the damage (65).

A fishing boat the property of Mr T Downing of Mullion was borrowed by neighbours and insecurely moored, the result being that she broke away and was completely wrecked. It will cost him £8 to replace. A small boat belonging to Mr Mitchell of Pollurian House got adrift and was damaged but not so seriously (66).

The last week has been one of further excitement in the cove. The 4 seans in a damaged condition have been brought ashore. On Monday the Covers shot on what appeared to be a fine seine but the fish were small and slipped through the meshes.

About 100 hogsheads were taken with great difficulty and the seans taken up. The following day the fish were again passing through the nets. The Friends, whose boat was damaged and second sean unready joined the Britannia's crew and shot a sean in the twilight. Boats were sent for but buyers wanted samples of fish so the boats were delayed until it was too rough to send them... Rovers and Covers have bought a new sean to replace the one lost. The gear of these united crews is now quite up to its former state and they await a favourable opportunity (67).

1899 In March it was reported that crab and lobster fishing in Mullion Cove had already commenced. The pilchard fishery was likely to expand at Mullion with the Covers intending to get a new boat and more gear. They have so far extended their company from 12 to 20 (68).

An unsuccessful attempt was made by Mullion Covers and Friends to secure a shoal on Friday evening. The failure was due to the shoals entering the greasy water where the sean previously stood, and shot off to the sea too quickly (69).

Mr Sullivan of Newlyn bought the last seine enclosed shoal of Pilchards from Mullion and they were taken to Newlyn to be cured.

Among then was the largest Pilchard ever seen by fishermen there. A good Pilchard would be up to 8inches in length. This one measured 11 and a half inches from nose to tail, over 5 inches round the shoulder and over 3 inches round the tail (70).

The United Seining Companies, Bolitho, Trahair, and Friends shot a fine school at Pollurian yesterday week which turned out about 260 hogsheads, and made a good price. The Covers shot on Monday morning, but ... the amount of fish was not known (71).

Mr Samuel Mundy the Managing Huer for Messrs Bolitho, Trahair and Friends fishing companies is still making great progress with the pilchards (72).

1900 In February Mullion Fish Cellars were put up to auction at Newlyn. There were 171 bids and three main bidders. The under bidders were Mr Dunn of Mevagissy, and Mr Pezzack of Penzance. The buyer was Mr Luxon of Plymouth who paid £510 (73).

1901 In late December storms caused severe damage throughout Cornwall. The lantern of Mullion lighthouse, situated on the end of the west pier in the harbour, was washed away and the Cricket Pavilion was destroyed (74).

Mr John George, Huer, enclosed a nice shoal of pilchards which were sent to Newlyn and fetched a good price. It is hoped that each of the three fishing companies will enclose a shoal between this and Mullion Feast, which comes in another 3 weeks. After that the fishing season will likely be over for 1901 (75).

1902 The Mullion Cove Seining Company was successful in enclosing a large number of pilchards which were sold at Newlyn for 10s 1d per basket. Messrs T Soby and T.H. Downing were the auctioneers (76).

The following report was published in August 1902 by a newspaper correspondent described as "A Cliff Ranger" Part of the column; under the headline "Mullions Wireless Telegraph and Seining" has been recorded here. It was written after the arrival of Senor Marconi and the wonder of the day, Wireless Telegraph, was introduced on the cliffs above Poldhu.

"If like a meteor Mullion has shot into public notice, it is more than likely that it will not fade so suddenly from public view. It will resemble the "fixed" rather than the "falling star" and it promises to increase in importance, and in popularity, as the days go by. But those who know Mullion will be aware that in years remote enough to be lost in the mists of antiquity "wireless telegraphy", or at the very least "wireless" messages have been bound up in the lives of the people of Mullion. Who would venture to guess how far into the past the "huer" from the cliffs, waved his message out to the seiners on the sea, as he saw masses of colour as the masses of pilchards passed the fine old cove... if the Morse system were not used on such occasions, the semaphore telegraphy was effective enough. Out in the seine boat, cock boat or Volyer the crews were scanning the sea, eagerly looking for the pilchards, but equally intent they would be gazing on the cliff to see if the huer was ready with his "bushes" of furze to work the seine round the school of fish which it was hoped to capture. The understanding was complete and the boats crew, obedient to the master hand on the cliff would carry out the drill in a most excellent fashion. Nor did the wireless messages end here. If a good capture was made when night was falling, the fire was at once lighted on the cliff top and its rays were a signal to the dwellers on the western shores of the (Mounts) bay, that boats were wanted to take fish to the Ports of Newlyn or Porthleven. But today the electric spark has taken place of the furze fire. And the "man on horse" who used to ride at breakneck pace when the seines had shot in the day, and fires were indistinguishable in the distance, has now no need to course along the roads, for the little telegraph office at Mullion is equal to all emergencies and soon tells if the seines have been shot... But on the occasion of my visit, how placid the sea, in its glassy smoothness, scarcely rippling on the sandy shore, and made doubly interesting that a seine has been shot. Bearing down upon the great net was a fleet of fine looking boats each racing for the seine eager to be the first in the tuck. Scarce a breeze stirred. The efforts of those on board were not confined to spreading the great jibs and staysails to help the boats along. They rowed as well and quite an exciting scene resulted. But all races end and two boats were ready to load. The tuck net is drawn into small compass, and the imprisoned pilchards boil, and bubble and thrash so that they squeak and the sound of their efforts is heard high up on the cliffs. The silvery finny creatures look lovely from this point of vantage. And boats and men look diminutive under the towering heights of Henscath and the cliffs on which we stand. The fishermen on the boats ready to receive their cargo, now get their oilskins on, and sitting astride the gunwhales, begin to dip into the tuck nets with big baskets , while soon the work of loading goes briskly on. It is a beautiful sight. All is delightfully peaceful and the stately grandeur of the scene most impressive. Mullion will continue to attract visitors, for the enterprising people keep pace with time, the hotels being thoroughly up to date. Bounteous nature has done much- man is loyally assisting" (77).

1903 In a report to the Cornish Sea Fisheries Committee, Mr Sich of Gunwalloe drew attention to Trawling between Porthleven and Mullion often within half a mile of the shore and pointed out that it would cause serious damage to the seine fishing. The pest of crab fishermen, the Spider Crab had much interfered with the fishing. They were so numerous around Mounts Bay that sometimes they filled the crab pots, thus preventing other fish from entering the pots (78).

Mr Thomas Sobey of Sea View House Mullion, while engaged on one of the Covers Fishing boats in Mullion Cove, fell and fractured two of his ribs. Dr Appleton attended and friends will be pleased to know he is making good progress (79). In October 1903, after weeks of waiting, 3 shoals of pilchards were caught by Mullion fishermen. The Friends Company who are amalgamated with the Richards Company of Penzance secured one shoal while the Covers secured two.

200 hogsheads was the estimate, fetching at Newlyn 5s 6d a basket, about 30s per hogshead (80).
1904 On Friday the "Lady of the Isles" brought a number of people to Mullion. A great many walked to the village, and thoroughly enjoyed a good tea after the short sea trip (81).
In September 1904 pilchard fishing was above average. The Trahair Company enclosed a large shoal which was moored overnight and not brought ashore. The following day it was found that the seine boat was almost underwater and the fish gone. The Friends Company shot in the Cove stem but failed to catch. Richards Company shot near the Mullion Island but the fish escaped. The Covers took from their seans which they shot on Monday about 100 hogsheads, this being the third bit of good luck they have had in a fortnight About 350 hogsheads were taken in three takings, eventually being taken to Porthleven and Newlyn. The men shared about £15 each (82).
1905 Pilchards were not the only fish caught in the vicinity of the Harbour. In 1905 a shoal of Mullet was seen off Mullion. In order to get to the location the Cadgwith boats were taken in tow by a Falmouth Tug and a shoal of 11,000 were caught, later to be purchased at Porthleven and sold on to the Paris market (83).
In May a heavy ground sea swept through the harbour. Boats had to be hauled up but much crabbing gear was lost (84). **1905** In August in a southerly gale which broke over the harbour piers. Several boats moored in the centre of the harbour were sunk at their moorings. Local men Edward George and John Bray had their boat, which was only purchased a year earlier, so badly damaged that it was out of use for the season (85).

NEWLYN AND MULLION.

PILCHARD FISHING SEINES AND GEAR, ETC., FOR SALE.

MR. GEORGE E. JENKIN

HAS been instructed by the Executor of the late Mrs. Elizabeth Trahair, deceased, to SELL by AUCTION, the undermentioned

PILCHARD SEINES AND GEAR, ETC.,

viz.:—On FRIDAY, the 7th day of July, 1905, at 2 o'clock p.m., at Fore Street, Newlyn, one pilchard seine, one mackerel seine, one tuck net, two boats, and about twenty tons of salt; and at Mullion Cove, in the Parish of Mullion, on the following day, SATURDAY, the 8th of July, at 2 o'clock p.m., two pilchard seines, tuck net, stop net, set of six warps and anchors, seine boat, cock boat, followers, moorings, etc.

Those at Mullion will first be offered in one lot.

To view apply to Mr. Thomas Trahair, Newlyn, and to Mr. Samuel Mundy, Huer, Mullion; and further particulars may be obtained of the AUCTIONEER, 4, Prince's Street, Penzance.

Dated, 26th June, 1905. 6921

Fig. 64 Advert, Sale of Nets & Boats, 1905(86)

1906 Perseverance has been rewarded. "Heva" was started about 6 in the morning, and the seans were shot, but the fish were shy. About mid day one of the Covers shot between the Pier and the Island and enclosed about 200 hogsheads of fish. Altogether the Covers with two boats shot about 6 times and twice secured 600 hogsheads. The Friends shot three times and secured about 200 hogsheads. The Bolitho seine shot four times, and have about 300 hogsheads. In the evening the Cove was full of fish (87).
In October **1906** local man Mr John Casley, fishing from the pier, caught 4 fine bass, the largest being 11lb. Other smaller fish were taken (88).
1907 In early August it was reported that Pilchard fishing had begun. The Union Fishery had put their sails in the boats and the huers are on the hill looking out for the approaching of the fish (89).
In October local man Hubert Harry, whilst fishing from the Pier caught and landed a large bass weighing 15lb 8oz, a record for Mullion (90). In September large shoals of pilchards had been seen passing Mullion daily but the seines had little success. One shoal was spotted near the "gap" and a boat was launched and even though short -handed managed to catch the shoal which was taken to Newlyn fetching 4s 6d per hogshead (91).
1908. In September visitors to Mullion Cove were treated to a spectacle. Following a long quiet spell the sound of "Hevva" was heard drawing the crews quickly to their seine boats. The Covers quickly launched 2 boats. One net was shot below the Polurrian Hotel but the net could not be closed and the fish escaped. A second net was shot but also failed and the nets had to be returned to harbour to be replaced. Another Covers boat was launched and with their two nets enclosed 2 shoals near the north end of Mullion Island. The Friends shot on a shoal enclosing about 100 hogsheads, the bulk escaping.
The Union and Bolitho Company shot seines and a few were secured. The fish were tucked and immediately despatched (92).In April 1908 Crabbers made a very late start due to the adverse weather (93).
1909 At Mullion on Wednesday the full force of the gale was felt with disastrous results. For several days a heavy ground swell had been running and it blew harder than ever from the SSE. On Thursday the waves were of mammoth proportions and the inhabitants watched the fury of the storm with awe and wonder. The mountainous seas swept the piers from end to end and some of the fishermen who were endeavouring to save their gear had narrow escapes from being carried out to sea, heavy weights were tossed around and crab pots dashed to pieces. The boats had to be drawn up to winter stations to avoid total destruction. It is feared that the Mullion crabbers have lost their entire fleet of pots,

which at this early stage in the season will prove ruinous. The sea dashed madly over Mullion Island and at Poldhu Cove a cliff railway used in the building of the Poldhu Hotel was washed away and carried up the beach (93a).

1910 September. According to the Cornishman Newspaper a seine was shot at Mullion and at the second attempt was successful, though not a great enclosure and the seiners did not get the good price which favoured the Lands End fishermen (Porthgwarra had a spectacular haul about the same time) which was 12 shillings a basket.

1913 A letter to the Cornishman in July gave an insight about problems incurred in the curing of the nets. *"Sir, during the last few years we have heard and read a great deal about the decay of the fishing industry in Mounts Bay, but do the fishermen realise that they themselves are killing their own business by the gross carelessness they exhibit in the use of creosote in curing their nets . This material may be very good as a preservative of the fabric with which the nets are formed but it certainly taints the fish caught in those nets most horribly, and creates a dislike which takes months to wear off...... Formerly it was the custom to cure the nets with cutch, which left no taint on the fish. Unfortunately this practice seems to be abandoned"* (94).

Another letter to the Cornishman in 1913 pointed to the problems created by creosoting fishing nets.*" I think there can be no doubt that even a slight dose of creosote in a great body of water would be sufficient to drive away fish. Creosote is one of the most deadly fish poisons it is possible to find...the old cutch method of preserving nets is infinitely better than the modern innovation. Henry Maddern" (95).*

A seine was shot at Mullion and a large school of fish enclosed (96).

1915 The death was announced of Mr Thomas Bedford Bolitho, son of the late Edward Bolitho associated with the firm of Messrs T Bolitho sons & Co. The family have long been associated with the seine fishing industry (97).

There was considerable concern expressed about the use of creosote to treat nets in Cornwall and Mounts Bay was one of the places affected.

A letter to the newspapers expressed the following,

"During my annual visits to Cornwall I have been much struck by the lessening quantities of fish- especially Pilchards- that visit the shores... I find there is a growing conviction amongst fishermen that it is due to the use of creosote in their nets. I have been told that since it was adopted less and less fish has appeared, and wherever such nets are taken the fishing the locality soon departs. Each night the Mounts Bay pilchard fleet shoots its nets there is a large quantity of creosote left in the water which is of course detected by the fish in the Bay... The nets cured with creosote are never dried, and each time they are shot there is a long train of such substance from each boat seen in the water... and when all is gone the nets are given more. This would undoubtedly tend to drive away all the fish which are there and prevent others from coming in. ONE INTERESTED" (98).

1920 "The Mounts Bay Pilchard Fishery has all the appearance of an abrupt ending. Last week was the poorest one of the season... Years ago Pilchards were scarcely caught until August... but last season and this, a commencement was made towards the close of June, and July contributed nearly the total of the 1920 catch... A peculiarity of this season has been the lack of inshore supplies. Boats have tried in these waters but failed to secure anything like appreciable amounts... consequently the (Drift) fleet has done nearly all its catching in the Wolf (Rock) area. Seiners around the Mounts Bay Coast at Porthgwarra, Mullion, Penberth and Gunwalloe for example used to keep a sharp lookout for such harvests and immediately a shoal was sighted the exciting cry of "Heva" rang through the village or hamlet. But "Heva" has become almost extinct" (99).

1925 CHANGES IN CORNISH FISHERIES

The decline of an old Industry. "As is well known, the fishing industry in Cornwall, like that of other parts of the country, has undergone many changes. Not many years ago all fishing craft were under sail. Now they are either steam or motor driven. Hand capstans were used to get gear on board, now they are done by steam capstan. One significant feature of the Industry is that of late years it has been necessary for fishermen to go further into the ocean to meet with the fish. Formerly the boats fished during the early spring off the Lizard or the Wolf, scarcely ever going into the North Channel, off Trevose or North West of the Longships. Now this is the usual rendezvous of the Mackerel, and rarely off the Lizard as formerly. Then when May came the boats would take off the nets with smaller mesh and put on the larger mesh nets and fish off the Isles of Scilly some hundred miles distant where they would meet Mackerel of a much larger size. There has been a marked decrease in the size of these fish in recent years. Before Steam landings were less frequent on May and June. In calmer weather the sailing boats could not get the fish to shore from longer distances. Now it is the opposite. The use of ice has also made it easier. With ice, Two day old catches can fetch the same price as fresh fish.

Seine fishing for Pilchards has completely fallen through "... St Ives... Mullion, Cadgwith, and Coverack were renowned for their catches" (100).

1930 <u>Report at Cornwall Sea Fishing Committee</u>. There is a very gloomy outlook for the pilchard fishing industry. It was reported that the pilchard fishery had been a complete failure this season. Last year (1929) the curing houses were filled to capacity by the end of August, and the seasons stock of salt was exhausted. The men were forced to abandon the fishery much earlier than usual. Unfortunately higher prices were paid for these fish than the Italian Market warranted and there were still many thousands of casks of last season's fish still in cold storage in that country (101).

1933 The total value of wet and shellfish landed at Westcountry ports in 1932 included the following, Porthleven £7197, Penzance £1263, Cadgwith £2223, and Mullion £1120 (102).

1935 In 1929 this country sent 71,187 cwt of Pilchards valued at £114,405 to Italy. In 1934 36,429cwt valued at £52,830 were sent. There is no other outlet for them... (103).

1935 A part of the Mounts Bay pilchard drifters met with improved fishing on Wolf grounds, a score of boats reporting large meshings. The aggregate proved the best for the season (104).

1935 <u>Industry Facing a Crisis.</u>

Mussolini's Policy of keeping Italian money at home is having an ill effect on the Cornish Pilchard Fishing Industry. This may mean the death knell of the Industry in Cornwall for the quantity of Pilchards consumed in this country is very small. Time was when the Cornish Housewife would salt enough of these fish to last the family through the winter. That time is gone. The closure of the Italian Market means that the Pilchard Fishermen have no one to fish for (105).

1936 There is great interest in the pilchard canning started by Messrs Pawley Bros of Mevagissey, Plymouth, Padstow, and Port Isaac. During the summer they produced 100,000 tins of matured fish in pure olive oil. The average number of fish per tin is 6 and the price is 10d (106).

1938 Despite recent phenomenal catches of pilchards the previous week there were complaints from fish merchants that the catch was tainted by creosote, "...not all of the boats had used creosote on their nets, but as a result of the complaints they will all suffer..." (107).

1939 The Sea Fisheries statistical tables for 1938 showed the returns for value of fish landed at each port in the South West. It included, Newlyn 126,426cwt at £76,797.Porthleven £5056, Penzance £690, Cadgwith £1691 and Mullion £689 (108).

1947 The oldest Mounts Bay Fishermen do not remember such a long spell of inactivity in connection with all branches of the industry owing to prolonged tempestuous weather. A large proportion of the Long-Liners have been confined to moorings for upwards of two months. Not only has there been shortage of bait that jowsters and chip shops have been void of fish for weeks.

Some Old Cornish Fishing Terms;

Beety-To mend nets, *Bolsh*-small rope, *Bowjowler*- place in the fishing boat for (hauling) a foot-line*, Breal*- Mackerel, *Breedy*- To make nets, with needle and pin roller, *Bussa*- salting pot for fish, meat and vegetables, Cabesta – space between the hook and lead on a fishing line, *Caboolen*- a stone used by seiners, and thrown into the sea to keep the enclosed fish in the net, *Caboose*- Portable, fishing boats fireplace, *Capis*- very large meshes in a trammel net, *Cobesta*- a part of fishing tackle, *Cowal* -Fish basket with a band for the head, carried by fishwomen, *Cowel*-Fish bladder, *Croggen*- Limpet shell, Dab- To throw out the nets, *Drethen*- a sandy area beneath the sea, *Enys*- Island, Gijolter- a piece of wood used in Cornish fishing boats, *Gingen*- Twisting wire round a fishing line to make it strong, *Gurry*-A four handled barrow with enclosed sides, *Jouder*- Fish overboiled, *Kanke*r- a small crab, *Kicker*- Fishing boats small mizzen sail, *Laggen*-Fish, to splash in the water, *Lasking*- Fishing term, to keep near the shore, *Ludras*- the name for the *Killick* or stone anchor, *Meanolas*- a fireplace, a square box of stones and clay, made by fishermen, *Pednborbas*- Cods Head, *Shong*- a broken mesh, *Shethen*-a piece of Hake used as bait, *Timmy noggy*- a notched square piece of wood placed on the gunwale of the boat used to support the lower end of the *Vargord*- a spar used as a foresail, bowline on fishing boats, Touser- white apron made of duck and worn by fisherman's wives in Mounts Bay. Trestrem-bait cut up and put on hooks, *Zelli*- a conger eel.

From an essay on the ancient Cornish Language by Bernard Victor (109).

Below, "Superstitions of Mounts Bay" (Herbert Richards 1945).

Easterly Wind is like a Kite. Up by day and down by night.

A North wind is a broom for the Channel

A Saturday Moon is a fisherman's curse

A Rainbow at night is a sailor's delight. A Rainbow in the morning sailors take warning.

A Circle round the Moon said to be a "Cocks Eye", was said to foretell rough weather.
Gulls screaming indicated a coming storm.
Hoar Frost two nights running meant rain on the third night.
Whistling at sea was said to bring on a storm.

Bibliography
See Pages 82-83

Fig. 65 Another hit on the west pier. Photo by author. December 2011

Chapter 10 MULLION FISHING IN THE 20TH CENTURY

<u>Post World War I changes in Fishing.</u>

After the First World War the Pilchard Fishing in the South West of England went through a period of change. There was no pilchard fishing at Mullion and all the boats and nets had been removed and sold. The local Fishermen had some good years and it was mainly these which helped create a change within the Industry. A series of good seasons encouraged and allowed the purchase of bigger, newer boats. The names of *Boy Howard, Peaceful, and Two Brothers* would be seen in the Harbour, along with another major improvement ... engines to power them.

Barry Mundy recalls being told how his grandfather William John Mundy, returned to harbour for the first time in his new engine and sail driven boat. The engine would be a little noisy and would echo around the high cliffs. It was running well and they had had a smooth passage. On reaching the entrance to the Harbour his great grandfather announced in a voice of alarm, *"Now there boy, aren't you going to turn off that engine and row into the Harbour?"* He was asked why, and replied *"Because you ought to show some respect"*.

Fig. 66 Pre- World War II Fishermen of Mullion (Courtesy B. Mundy)
<u>Left to Right;</u> John Bray, Ken Ryan, Jim Downing, Hubert Harry, Herbie Gilbert ("Herbie Dry"), Dick Gilbert ("Dick Wet"), Gilbert Thomas, Joseph Mundy, Jack Pascoe, Glen Pascoe, Pard Mundy, Eddie Mundy, "Admiral" Thomas.

But, with engines, the fishermen could now travel further and faster to new fishing grounds, for example to the Cod Bank 7-8 miles off shore, where they would previously have had difficulty in reaching. The noisy modern age had arrived into a peaceful Mullion Cove, but times were still changing. In the 1920s the boats were bigger and required a crew of three. In the winter local fishermen would join with the bigger boats out of Porthleven and fish for Herring. They would be away for months, beginning at Padstow, following the Herring around the Coast, putting in to sell their catches at local ports and markets. Eventually the Herring found their way along the channel to Plymouth, followed by the Trawlers and then the men would return home by January and resume preparations for the Crab and Lobster season.

The late 1920s and 1930s was the period of the Great Depression, a deep economic downturn. Cornish Boats were unable to get crews as many men went away to find a better living. It was put down to persistent bad luck over a number of seasons but in reality it was partly connected to the volume of foreign steam drifters, fitted with wireless, and in direct communication with each other. They were able to tell each other where the shoals could be located and their methods began to seriously reduce stocks of fish.

Fig. 67 *Asthore.* 1920s Winter Herring fishing out of Porthleven for Mullion men. B. Mundy

In 1907 there were 500 drift boats working out of Newlyn, by 1928 there were only eighty (110). There had been periods of depression in the fishing industry before, but the late 1920s were different. In 1931 views were expressed amongst fishermen of Cornwall that it was time to tackle the declining fishing industry. It was said that one of the reasons for the decline was that local markets were being supplied with fish by a large number of foreign fishing boats. Young men who previously could find other employment could not now do so and there were just no jobs available. The subject of Territorial Limits was now on the agenda. Large Government grants were offered and went some way to improving the situation but the depression was worldwide. It was discussed that the only way to improve the situation was to give the fisherman boats which were able to compete with the European fleets (111).

<u>1939 A new War coming</u>
A torn newspaper article, kept by Barry Mundy, was presented to me for inclusion in this book. It had appeared in the "(*Eve?*)ning Standard" in September 1939, written by a correspondent known only by the initials E.H.V. The full details of the article are not known. It was written in the lead up to the Second World War about an "unnamed" Cornish fishing cove on the Lizard Peninsula. While the names were altered in the article, the place and events were accurate.
Those reading the article now might be forgiven for thinking that this might just be a little Fishing Cove called Mullion. It began "*The little cove was too busy to be dull. There was always something to watch on the quay, boats going out and coming in, fish being unloaded, lobster pots hauled up by rope, bait cut up, nets dried and mended*".
"*Ten days before August ended*", the article continued ... *the fishermen worked as hard as ever, but there was a change in the conversation with the visitors. They discussed matters with a shrewd intelligence and a good grasp of the International situation*". Their views all ended in a general condemnation of Hitler..." "*He've bit off too much of the Lions Tail this time*" said an old naval pensioner known locally as the "Admiral". "*I think t'will blow over*" said another. The Admirals son said "*I don't think it will*". They asked the "Admiral" who replied "*I think there will be a clash. And whats the cause of it all... putting an ignorant man at the head of things. It would be just the same if they put me in charge of the Navy. What should I be like if I really was an Admiral. I'd be just like him, ordering everybody about.*

That`s what folks like him want, authority, for- to order everybody about".

News came that the Territorials had left the area. A local farmer said *"My eldest boy`s gone. Anti -Aircraft. He was called up last September too. And when he went for his training last Whitsuntide, he said we had very different guns now from what we had last September. And I`ve said to my other boy: Your brothers gone, and now it's up to you to think what you`ll do. One`s not more to me than the other- but have you heard any news this morning?"*

The rich man at the Shore-House departed early this morning. His wife followed next day, with a car full of what looked like farm produce. Food supplies might be scarce in London. A few days later a lorry with packing cases arrived and word went round the Cove. *"Mr Smith has sent down all his valuables from London".*

The Admiral came down one morning looking different. He was shaving twice a week. He was on active service. *"We`re to keep watch day and night, on the lookout for hostile aircraft. I was on duty last night, and I`m to go every night 2am -6am. An hour to climb up to the cliff and an hour back. That`s six hours. I have a bit of breakfast and then I`m here in the cove. What must I do if I see an aircraft?. Lots of things it's all strictly confidential."*

One young lady, wife of a fisherman in the Naval Reserve said *"Johnny's got his papers.Wanted for a trawler."* The reply came *"When do `ee go?"* She replied *"Wanted in Penzance in time to catch the afternoon train to Lowestoft. But he`s out at sea, fishing. I`ve phoned to Penzance but he`s got to go first thing in the morning. I must go and get my lad his dinner and iron his collars."* Johnny came back from the sea and helped haul the boats up the beach for spring tides were approaching. *"I`ve made him a Cornish Pasty to take on the train. `Tis a long way to Lowestoft. Yes we`ve been expecting it- but when it comes..."* Johnny visited his relatives and friends before he left. " *I won`t say goodbye. I`ll say cheerio... I was away five years deep sea fishing so I know what it's like to leave home. And it's no use breaking your heart over it, because it won`t do you no good."* A few days later his elder brother went. *"Tommys urgently needed at sea. He`s to report to Devonport at once".* Tommy was a widower with three children. He finished his days work and was driven off to Devonport by midnight.

The serpentine worker who came up from the Lizard to sell his wares said *"We`re ready this time. The Governments been buying up all the best trawlers on the east coast for two months now, and fitting them out. They are needed for mine-sweeping."*

Every day at a set time the little group of Fishermen and visitors gathered around the Harbour masters house. Wireless sets were few in the Cove and the Harbour-master left his window open for the benefit of anyone who wanted to listen. The fishermen said little but their faces became more resolute and they continued their work.

Then came the evacuation order. *"It's bad"* said the harbour Masters wife. *"It's bad"*, echoed everybody else.

Instead of mending nets in the cove it was tidying up. The boats were not moved down into the harbour. A knot of seaman gathered around the window to listen to the wireless. Then the news... Hitler had invaded Poland. *"War"* said the Admiral. The men dispersed in twos and threes and quietly spoke to each other. The serpentine worker said that he had never seen the Cove so quiet. *"Look at the men, nobody's done any work in the Cove today".* Everyone dispersed to search out old blankets, curtains, rugs for the blackout. A few days afterwards the news came on the radio from Prime Minister Mr Chamberlain *"...I have to tell you now that no such undertaking has been received, and that consequently this country is at war with Germany."* (112). Extract from damaged newspaper article written in 1939.

Fig. 68 Local Mullion Fishermen. Courtesy B. Mundy. *Left to right Eddie Mundy, Herbie Gilbert, Dick Gilbert, Pard Mundy.*

The family of Lesley Thomas have long been fishermen in the Cove. His father, William James Thomas was born in 1885. He put an extra year onto his age to get into the Navy and received his training in Plymouth on the *"Wooden Wall"* training ships. His journey from Mullion to Plymouth was a long one, beginning in the horse drawn "bus" from Mullion to Helston, where he caught the train to Plymouth. To get to Plymouth was a day's journey. He spent the First World War as a Signalman aboard HMS Warspite. In 1916 he was aboard the Battleship HMS *Warspite* at Jutland, where she sustained considerable damage. Eventually taking his Pension he returned to Mullion where he fished with Gilbert Thomas. As a Mullion Cove fisherman he went one day into the Billiard Room in Mullion and someone asked him if he had made the rank of Admiral yet?

The name stuck and from then he was known as "Admiral" Thomas. The "family" boat was called *"Boy Howard"* and had been built at Olivers boatyard at Porthleven.

During the War his son Gilbert was called into the Royal Naval Volunteer Reserve and joined the crew of a converted Trawler Minesweeping in the Mediterranean, and sadly, he was badly injured in an air attack on the Harbour at Gibraltar and died of his wounds in Hospital there.

After the war the "Admiral" fished with George Thomas and eventually called it a day at the age of 70. Like all the local fishermen, he always made his own Pots, getting his withies from several miles away near to St. Keverne. They were often brought over by lorry to Tremenhee in the village where he made them up in one of the Barns there.

At the start of the Second World War he was called up to work in the Aux. Coastguard, working a variety of shifts as an observer on the Lizard Coast, near to Vellan Head.

In the war the numbers of boats fishing in the Harbour was reduced.

Also, during the War the "Admiral" became agent for the supply of Twine used in the manufacture of Camouflage nets. These were made by local people around Mullion, as well as in other local villages. The camouflage nets had to be made with a square mesh, and not the diamond mesh used by the fishermen and if they were found to have the wrong mesh they never made it past the Inspectors into the war effort. Fishermans net and rope making skills however came in handy. "Admiral" continued to fish with a man called Chin and Dick Gilbert. Dicks` brother, Herbie, was called up to serve with the barrage balloons in Wales. It is said either 4 or 5 Fishermen went to Wales. Their work was to splice metal cables for the Barrage balloons at sea... Fishermen's skills.

Fig; 69 William John Mundy with 2 local Crawfish. Courtesy B Mundy.

It's said that some experienced fishermen can find his way on the sea as well as a man can find his way on land. Lesley Thomas tells of how he fished with his father one day for crab and lobster beyond the sight of land on the reef known as *Carn Andra*. Now designated as an Inshore Area of Conservation it lies to the south west of Lizard Point and was in sea lanes used by many large ships. Because of the nature of the tides it was necessary to fit what are called "Dans" to the crab pot lines, with long canes or poles with a bright flag on the end, rather than use simple floating buoys. When the fishermen got to the area, unaided by modern radar and other aids, there would be no sign of the "Dans" because they were several feet underwater, to keep them away from the keels and propellers of ships. As the tide slackened and the sea level dropped, suddenly the "Dans" would mysteriously float up to the surface from out of nowhere and the boat would invariably be within yards of the right place to pull up and rebait the pots. Few landmarks would be visible at the time and it was the experience of the fishermen which put them onto the pots. Apart from the Crab and Lobster fishing which continued during the season, the fishermen engaged in net fishing for such fish as Ray and Turbot, but the boat owners had to economise, and crews of three had become a crew of two.

The Mundy family had been engaged in fishing for many generations but in the late 1920s Eddie Mundy, father of Barry Mundy decided to move away and join the Merchant Navy. He travelled the world for 5 years, and when he returned said that he had been to nearly every port in the world. For two years he worked on Oil Tankers, before eventually returned to carry on fishing at Mullion with Joseph Mundy.

Jo was born in 1890 and was destined to fish. He told Barry how at the age of nine he skipped school to go down to the Harbour to where there was, what he called, *"...the last successful seine shot in the Cove"*. He worked all day for *"a quarter of a man's wage"*, running the pilchards in gurries up to the "Run" to be baulked by the women.

He fought in the Trenches in the First World War, alongside another local man Bertie Exelby and eventually returned to Mullion. Just after the war he was working for a short time at RNAS Mullion at Bonython and was unfortunate to have the large doors of a hanger on him trapping him tight. As a result of that accident he was left with one eye, but it didn't stop him from fishing. In the 1920s he would fish with William John Mundy on the *"Two Brothers"*, and in the winter went Herring Drifting.

The Herring Drifting was successful for a few years.

A man known as Captain Rowell had a 44` Herring Trawler called *Asthore* purpose built at Porthleven, and a number of the Mullion men joined the crew during the 1920s. From 1932 until 1938 he fished the "*Two Brothers*" with Eddie Mundy and after the Second World War he left Fishing to work as an agricultural labourer on a local farm.

In 1938 Eddie Mundy had sold his boat the *Two Brothers* and when the war began he was set to work on Trawlers converted for Mine Sweeping duties. He undertook these duties off the Western Approaches, on the routes of the Convoys which were so important to the provision of food and ammunition for the Country. The Germans often laid mines on the routes and so had to be swept on a regular basis.

On one occasion a following trawler struck a Mine and sank. The explosion damaged his hearing and caused Eddie to become partially deaf as a result of which he was discharged. He returned to Mullion where he continued to fish for a time before applying for a job which entailed sailing across the mouth of Falmouth Bay in a war-commandeered yacht, opening and closing it with an anti- submarine mesh as required. After a while the Navy realised that he was partially deaf and decided that he should be discharged, with a warning not to seek further work. Thereafter he returned to Mullion where he again took up his job fishing the Mounts Bay Coastline.

Pard Mundy had spent 22 years in the Navy during and after the First World War and remained fishing in the Cove.

In the Cove an anti tank wall was built, and small areas are still standing on the approach road close to Harbour House. John Pascoe recalls a Spitfire chasing a German bomber inland, up through the Cove, firing his cannons. Some of the bullets hit the roof of the Cafe and Coastguard building, and there were still bullet holes visible in garages nearby a few years ago, but generally action was rare in the Cove.

From the age of about 15 Barry Mundy worked part time for Jim Downing. Jim was about 60 at the time and worked about 60-70 pots. Barry worked the rope to pull up the Pots, a job which Jim was glad to let him do on Wednesdays and holidays for 2/6 (12p) a day. If he worked for 5 days he got 12/6 (62p) and if he worked for 6 days, he got a pound. It was Jim's way of encouraging him to come to work, not that Barry needed much encouraging.

When Barry was 18, Pard Mundy, who had been working with Eddie, retired from fishing. The early 60`s were not good years for the fishermen. Periods of poor fishing were something which happened periodically over the years.

In 1964 Eddie said to Barry that it was about time they became equal partners in the business. He told Barry "*The only way it works is if you own half the boat, and half the gear, and if you do that you`re entitled to half the money*".

Fig. 70 right *Mez Creis*. Barry`s first boat.

Sunday was always a day of rest, to which the fishermen adhered to for many years, but in 1964 Barry decided that it was probably time for a change. Eddie accepted the need to adapt and they decided that it was time. He took some "stick" from a few of the fishermen but it seemed that they weren't really against the move. On the third occasion after they took the decision to go out the Sunday was fine and sunny. Barry and his father left the Cove and began to bait the pots. He looked back and saw that they weren't on their own for the *Patrice* was following them out. The change was made. From 1970 to 1977 Barry Mundy, a Cornish speaker, bought a 38` Breton crabber called *Mez Creis*, which had a 75HP Baudouin engine. She was built in Camaret, and originally named the *St. Ann* by her, then, french owner. Registered in France her size meant that she was only allowed to fish 3 miles off the French Coast, but local fishermen in Cornwall would often see her off the Cornish Coast.

She was sold from France to a fisherman at Marazion who only kept her a short time before Barry bought her. She proved to be a fine boat for crab and lobster fishing, particularly in Carn Andra and the Boa.

Barry took her over to the Scillies to fish the neap tides for Crab and Lobster, but particularly good was the catch of Crawfish. On one day, he recalls catching 107 Crawfish and a 4lb Lobster. The whole catch was taken to Newlyn

Market and would eventually find its way to France. Barry would have a 3-4 day break there to repair his pots, and then off for another trip to the Scillies.

He also fished out of Hayle as well as the Helford, and for a while Looe, and up to Plymouth. He has had some good days fishing ... he suggests ... with the *Mez Creis*.

In April 1979 he completed building the *Flowing Tide*, an 18` boat with 10HP Sabb Marine engine. It was built over an 18 month period in a garage which was once the site of the Rocket Apparatus store on the Nansmellyon Road, adjacent to the Old Vicarage. It is now one of the boats which have become a permanent fixture in the Cove. Barry has continued fishing from there for crab and lobster when the weather and conditions allow and takes visitors on local trips around the coast to see the cliffs, sea caves, the seals or and an occasional Basking Shark or Sunfish. Fig. 71 above left *Flowing Tide.*

Fig. 72 Jimmy Pascoe and Neil Wellum in the Harbour. Photo Courtesy R. Bray

<u>Geoffrey Wellum</u>, DFC, now 91, fished with his father out of Mousehole for 2 years before the Second World War which began in 1939. He recalls the 16lb Pollack which they caught at that time off the Longships. After "another life" involved in the Battle of Britain as a Spitfire Pilot, he eventually left the Royal Air Force in 1961. He worked for a short period in London and then in 1962-3 he returned to Cornwall, which held so many special memories for him, and found his way to Mullion. He said that a friend had told him that it was a good place to be and that was good enough for Geoff. Like so many people before, and since, the peace of the Cove and the tranquillity of the nearby cliffs helped him to regain part of his life which had been taken from him in the war.

He was well liked by the Fishermen in the Cove and he would venture out with the likes of Pard and Eddie Mundy, and "Young boy Barry" while they pulled their crab and lobster pots. They would have strings of about 200, and when Geoff went out with Barry and the others he acted as the deck hand. They would also fish for Turbot, Brill and Ray.

Through the ensuing years Geoff made good friends with the fishermen of the Cove and even made the dizzy heights of Deputy Harbour Master for a few years. The Cove had a working harbour and most people coming into the Cove behaved well, but occasionally a visitor or a few divers took advantage of the hospitality and spoilt things for the others. The fishermen might have a quiet word.

He recalled one fishing boat, belonging to Montague Rosvear going missing from the Harbour one day and it was eventually found floating on the middle of Mounts Bay. It turned out that the person responsible had recently come out of jail and decided to take it, but in taking it had caused the engine to seize up.

Geoff beamed, though, as he said, "*It was an absolutely wonderful community in the Cove and I can still remember the North pier full of Crabs and Lobsters and Pots. Harvey's, the Merchants would send their lorry down and everything would quickly be weighed up and away in those days of the 1970s and 80s.*" He recalled days with the boats of the time, the *Pandora, Progress, Patrice, Diana* and the *White Rose* and his son Neil who spent several years fishing out of the Cove in the *Habascan Moor.* His son had a few Pots off Georges Bay, by Velvet Rock, and said they were always good for a few Lobsters. The weather has always played a big part in the lives of the fishermen and there is nothing more disorientating than fog.

Geoff remembered days when the fog came down thick and they were caught out unexpectedly.

He was out with Barry one day, and the fog came in. He said, "*I was standing right up `forrard`. We saw surf and Barry went right up close and eventually this huge cliff came out. I can hear him now, "Where are we to"? We edged in and I said "I know that, it's Velvet Rock ... and we were in Georges Cove*".

He recalled being caught out one day in thick fog with his son Neil off Pedngwynian.

He said "*I had to bring in a bit of RAF Navigation into it. Neil was really worried. I knew the distance we were approximately from there to the Island, and I reckon we were doing about 4 knots. I said to him, in 17 minutes you turn onto North East and that should bring us back, and in fact it brought us in just off Henscath... it was spot on*".

One day it was noticed that a boat was circling apparently unmanned near to Pedngwinian and realising that it belonged to Barry it was investigated. They found Barry trying to keep afloat in the water having been accidentally knocked off his boat, the *Flowing Tide*. The boat was on rocks nearby with the engine still running. In the swell a wave had carried it up and left it high and dry, still in gear, chugging away. Being water cooled Barry feared that the engine would seize up, but she carried on running. They brought Barry into their boat and as the swell came in, to everyone's amazement it picked up his boat from the rocks, turned it straight round and dropped it in the water, still in gear, disengaging the rudder. It continued, still unmanned, out to sea as straight as a die with no more than a few small holes in the hull. They reminded Barry that it was in fact "*Friday the 13th*" ... but this must have been his lucky day.

He says "*His time hadn't come*".

Geoff recalled that when sailing on the sea, and being in and around the Cove he could get back to nature. Geoff says that he thoroughly enjoyed his time fishing in the Cove with the Fishermen. He could spend the whole day there and loved every minute of it.

Geoff said "*I remember going out with Neil one morning, he wanted to get away a bit early. We put to sea at 5 o`clock in the morning, it was just getting light. It was absolutely out of this world, and I thought, when I die this is heaven. We went to sea that morning and we went out of that harbour. It was idyllic. I can see it now, going out to our pots on Pedngwinian.*

Fig.73 An early start for Kevin in the *Celtic Sunrise*. Photo by author August 2012.

Environmental Disaster.

On the morning of 18th March 1967 there was a dramatic wreck on the Seven Stones Rocks 16 miles West of Lands End which affected the whole of Cornwall. Initially 50,000 tons of crude oil was released on the sea from the Torrey Canyon and after 7 days she broke her back releasing a further 50,000 tons. A further 20,000 tons were burnt when the wreck was bombed. The effect on the coastline and the fishing was devastating. There was huge damage done to the Fishing, the shellfish, lobsters crabs, crawfish and oyster beds. Locally there was damage to the sea floor environment, the beaches and the fishing at all points on the Lizard Coastline. A number of oil slicks came ashore between Marazion and the Lizard. A decision was taken to use solvents and emulsifiers (detergents) for several months. Around Mullion and Gunwalloe the Armed Services sprayed large quantities of detergents on the sea and the shore during daylight hours, and usually on rising tides. Fish Surveys suggested that many fish species were unaffected, but species such as sand eels and breeding grounds were. Dead and dying Crabs and Lobsters were reported. Subsequent dives and examinations between Mullion Harbour and the Island showed minimal damage (113).

The worst problem was the smell of oil. Fishermen reported damage to their boats as a result of the spraying. It was said that there was as much as 3" or 5" of oil covering the beaches which caused great concern for the Tourist Trade in Cornwall. The visual sight of gallons of crude oil along a beach did not go down well. In an effort to minimise the damage to Tourism, the Tourist Board arranged some photo shoots designed to help reduce the adverse effects of the pollution.

One fisherman was photographed near to Henscath, showing his crab pots to two ladies from the Black and White Minstrels Dance Group on one such an occasion in 1967. The photograph as apparently discovered some years later in a shop in Australia where the man in the photograph was recognised.

He is still entertaining visitors to the Cove some 40 years on. Fig. 74 right

The effects of the oil in Mullion Harbour were noticeable. After the spill the tides washed several inches of oil into the Harbour itself, covering the beach and the slipway.

Paul Pearson was another man who came to the Cove and stayed in 1967. As part of the Royal Welch Fusiliers, billeted in Camborne, he was in charge of some of the local spraying operations during the Torrey Canyon disaster. After the Royal Navy delivered the big drums of "detergent" Paul and his men had to haul them up cliffs and along beaches to be dispensed. There wasn't a lot of equipment available, but the job was done and eventually after much anguish and several years the Cove began to return to normal.

One local Mullion businessman recalls travelling over to the Scillies by helicopter in March 1967, and was given a detour over the wreck, not long after it went aground. While he was over in the Scillies he watched on, as the RAF flew over the Islands to the Torrey Canyon and despite direct hits – as well as several near misses with petrol, napalm and rockets – the cargo was reluctant to burn, and several high spring tides put out the flames.

Today there are far fewer boats and far fewer people engaged in Fishing from Mullion Cove than ever before and it is a sign which has to be recognised. From the earliest days the Fishermen have provided food for the community and a livelihood for themselves while their industry has gone through many peaks and troughs. There have been good years and bad years and adjustments have been made, but I suspect that given their time over again they would have wanted to change very little in this tiny fishing community.

Bibliography (Chapters 8-10)

1. Cornwall and its people. A.K. Hamilton Jenkin 1945
2. www.newlyn.info/history/info) Margaret E. Perry 2005
3. Extract of a letter from Caledonian Mercury 20.3.1753
4. Extract of a letter from Caledonian Mercury 16.9.1776
5. Extract of a letter from Caledonian Mercury 27.1.1779
5a Domestic State papers Charles I, June, date missing, quoted at http://www.st-keverne.com/History/Book/curnow.php
6. The History of Helston, H Spencer Toy, 1936
7. www.thepilchardworks.co.uk   22.6.12
8. Cornish Seines and Seiners, Cyril Noall 1972
9. The History of Cornwall. From the earliest records and traditions. Vol II Hitchens and Drew. 1824
10. Mullion Tithe Map & Apportionments, 1840
11. English Heritage.
12. A report for the National Trust , Mullion Harbour Cornwall Archaeological. and Historical Assessment,
    E Ruddle & M Thomas. 2005
13. Natural History of Cornwall 1758, Borlase W.,
14. Rev E.G.Harvey, Mullyon. Its History, Scenery and Antiquities, 1875
15. Cornishman 10.9.1879
16. Cornishman 11.9.1941

70. Cornishman 19.10.1899
71. RCG 20.10.1899
72. Cornishman 26.10.1899
73. RCG 1.3.1900

17. RCG 22.3.1850
18. RCG 6.9.1827
19. RCG 18.9.1835
20. RCG 8.2.1850
21. A week at the Lizard 1848, Rev C A Johns
22. Cornishman 3.9.1908
23. RCG 8.2.1850, 22.2.1850, 1.3.1850, 22.3.1850 et al
24. WMorning News, R. Pearce 11.2.1932
25. RCG 8.2.1850
26. Western Times 2.9.1874
27. RCG 22.2.1850
28. Cornishman 26.2.1880
29. RCG 10.8.1811
30. Extract RCG 13.4.1816
31. RCG 13.9.1823
32. RCG 17.10.1874
33. RCG 2.9.1826
34. Exeter & Plymouth Gazette 6.9.1828
35. Sherborne Mercury 31.8.1829
36. Sherborne Mercury 6.9.1830
37. RCG 25.8.1832
38. RCG 5.10.1833
39. RCG 28.10.1836
40. RCG 2.6.1837
41. RCG 10.4.1840
42. RCG 25.8.1843
43. RCG 5.9.1845
44. RCG 20.9.1850
45. RCG 6.8.1852
46. RCG 18.8.1854
47. RCG 7.10.1859
48. RCG 18.4.1862
49. RCG 7.11.1867
50. RCG 7.11.1867
51. RCG 26.10.1869
52. RCG 1.1.1870
53. West Briton 31.3.1870
54. Extract from RCG 28.10.1871
55. RCG 17.10.1874
56 Cornishman 17.1.1884
57 Cornishman 19.1.1893
58. Cornishman 23.9.1897
59. Cornishman 14.10.1897
60. Cornishman 9.1.1898
61. Cornishman 17.8.1898
62. Cornishman 25.8.1898
63. Cornishman 8.9.1898
64. Cornishman 22.9.1898
65. Cornishman 20 .10.1898
66. Cornishman 20.10.1898
67. Cornishman 27.10.1898
68. RCG 23.3.1899
69. Cornishman 19.10.1897

74. Cornishman 3.1.1901
75. Cornishman 17.10.1901
76. Cornishman 6.11.1902
77. Cornishman Aug 1902
78. Cornishman 3.9.1903
79. Cornishman 24.9.1903
80. Cornishman 1.10.1903
81. Cornishman 18.8.1904
82. Cornishman 22.9.1904
83. Cornishman 20.4.1905
84. Cornishman 25.5.1905
85. Cornishman 10.8.1905
86. Cornishman 6.7.1905
87. Cornishman 13.9.1906
88. Cornishman 11.10.1906
89. Cornishman 8.8.1907
90. West Briton 24.10.1907
91. West Briton 12.9.1907
92. Cornishman 10.9.1908
93. Cornishman 9.4.1908
94. Cornishman 17.7.1913
95. Cornishman 14.8.1913
96. Cornishman 18.9.1913
97. Cornishman 27.5.1915
98. Cornishman 2.9.1915
99. Cornishman 22.9.1920
100. WMN 19.2.1925
101. Cornishman 2.10.1930
102. WMN 19.4.1933
103. Cornishman 7.3.1935
104. WMN 24.7.1935
105. Cornishman 12.9.1935
106. Cornishman 23.1.1936
107. Cornishman 24.11.1938
108. WMN 7.6.1939
109. Cornishman 10.5.1879
110. Western Gazette 29.6.1928
111. Cornishman 7.5. 1931
112. Extract from newspaper 1939. B. Mundy
113. www.cefas.defra.gov.uk
93a Cornishman 29.4.1909

Chapter 11 COPPER MINES...

Less than half a mile from Mullion Mill, situated between Trenance and Predannack lies Vro Farm.(50 00`36.72"N 5 14`52.59"W) On the farm is the site of one of the few Copper mines to be worked on the Lizard Peninsula. The site is now overgrown but it has a very close connection with Mullion Cove. There were two underground shafts, first dug in the 18th century and last worked in 1852.

There has been, and still is, a continuous supply of spring water from the mine for several hundred years and it was at one stage both a domestic and agricultural water supply. It was partly the volume of water which created financial problems for the Adventurers in their early quest to mine deeper ground, and they struggled to build costly underground adits to remove it. Equally they had difficulties in constructing ventilation shafts which were required to be several hundred feet deep.

From the mine adit the water course ran down a small tributary valley for half a mile before joining the main river a matter of yards below Mullion Mill. The main river then ran a further 350 yards to the west before discharging into the Cove. The importance of the Copper mine, however, lay in the fact that it provided some of the purest Copper that could be found.

Native Copper

The earliest stories tell how, in the early 1720s, a man called Peter Hall was riding across Predannack Common when his horse stepped on a rock. On examination this turned out to be a piece of Native Copper. The interest generated by the find and further investigation resulted in the setting up of a Copper mine, called *Ghost Mine*, which operated long enough to raise a quantity of Native Copper Ore also known as *"Virgin"* copper.

The source of the ore was found close to the surface.

Fig. 75 right A piece of Native Copper

It was described in the 18th Century in the following way.
"The most perfect copper is the Malleable, from its purity in Cornwall called the Virgin Ore... It is variously combined and allayed, some with bare crystal, intermixed, some with gossan, some with white gravelly clay, some in ruddle and the rust of iron, in shape very various sometimes thin spread, and shaped like leaves, now like drops and bosses, now branched, fringed or twisted into wires, in hollow filigree in blades and daggers, now in powder little inferior in lustre to that of gold, sometimes blistered, at other times a congeries of combined granules but which is the finest of them all in solid lumps, as the Mullion Copper of several pounds weight, maturated, mixed and highly polished... Its colour is like manufactured copper before it is polished" (1).

Native Copper is the purest form of copper ore and looks like molten metal poured onto rock where it has then set. It is very pure and very rare and since that time a large quantity has been raised.

In the 18th century a piece weighing some 40lbs was recovered, but later much heavier pieces were extracted.

Ghost Mine

There has been much speculation locally about the name *"Ghost Mine"* or *"Ghostcroft Mine"*, but the likely origin surrounds a natural phenomenon called *"ignis fatuus"*, often called *"will o the wisp"*, a ghostly light or luminescence seen over marshes or wet ground, and one which has been described around the world for centuries. Originally it was believed that the glow, or light, sometimes greenish or purplish in colour, drew travellers away from a true path into boggy ground. It is possible that this light is caused by the burning of a small amount of marsh gases (Wikipedia).

One lady living locally recalls how, as a child, she watched a pile of damp logs brought into the house and set beside the fire to dry.

She saw a light emanate from the damp logs, which she could not explain, but from her description it appears to be a similar phenomenon.

Mining- Wheal Providence

The earliest documentary evidence of mining was from a deed dated 20th September 1741, in which the vicar of Mullion, Rev. Hugh Tonkin, and Walter Reed of Stithians were granted liberty "*...to dig for copper and other minerals on a lode called Wheal Providence in Predannack Wartha Common, wherein is an adit already begun.*"

A similar grant was given to Henry Harris of Gwennap and William Passmore of Helston in May 1742 on 70 fathoms (420`) of ground in Goon Vean, above Mullion Cliffs near to Mullion Cove on the run of the lode.

A further lease of Wheal Providence dated May 1748 empowered "*driving a new adit into the said old copper work.*"

There was a final reference dated November 1754 when dues were paid by Rev. Tonkin for copper which was recovered from the "burrows" or spoil heaps in the Mullion Mine (2). It was by then known as *Wheal Providence*. No further known references to copper mining are known to exist in the 18th Century. There was however another mineral being extracted in the locality at the time, often found with the Copper, and that was Soapstone, also called Soaprock, or Steatite, which will be discussed later.

Adits.

By the 1750s it seems that there were at least two adits which drew the water from the mine. One was at 7 fathoms (42`) and another at 20 fathoms (120`). The 7 fathom adit opened to the north and flowed down the valley to join the main river just downstream of Mullion Mill. (The course of this adit may help explain the gulley which appears to cut into the bedrock at the confluence near to Mullion Mill.) The second adit was described in 1807 as being "*driven from the sea*". It is unlikely that such a deep adit was successfully completed, as it would have required a tunnel half a mile in length and a series of ventilation shafts some 200` below ground (2).

Local tradition suggested that it was begun from the "*great cave*" in Porth Pyg, and from inside one could hear the cocks crowing at Predannack Farm (2).

There is no evidence to support this, even though locally some people insist that it is correct.

The largest cave, hidden on the beach and only accessible now at low tide is known as Torchlight Cave. It is on the site of an ancient geological fault line within the Serpentine. The visible fault line inside the cave runs a distance of about 160` and Soapstone was mined from the fault line inside this cave. Some of it still remains in situ.

By 1807 Copper was again mined in the area, this time, a small company, under management of a local man called Joe Vivian and the mine was called Predannack Wartha Mine (2).

While cleaning out a shaft in the deep adit they discovered a vein of Soaprock two feet wide, but 6 months into the venture they still had not reached new copper. Their aim was to cut the lode 16 to 18 fathoms deeper than it had ever previously been seen.

According to A.K. Hamilton Jenkin the early miners were unable to construct the deep adit, but by 1809 did construct a ventilation shaft to deliver air to the adit below, which is some 23 fathoms below the surface.

However they then had to abandon the mine (2). The reasons for the abandonment were likely financial as well as technical.

Wheal Unity (or South Wheal Unity)

Wheal Unity is the name by which many locals know this mine, but it is the same mine with different investors or adventurers. Nearly all mining activities required financial investment to expand, and it was also the case for *Wheal Unity*. A Prospectus was published offering shares to potential investors. At £25 per Share they were made to look good value. Monthly costs were standing at £40.

The information in the Prospectus includes an interesting history of the development of the Mine.

It reads "*This mine was discovered about 60 years since and worked profitably. The Adventurers found a copper lode or vein at 6 fathoms, expending £3000 in driving a deep adit or drain to enable them to cut that lode at a deeper level, but owing to the hardness of the ground and the imperfect mode of working mines at that time they failed in their object; since which period, until within these two years, the mine has lain dormant. Modern ingenuity has surmounted these difficulties, which obstructed the exertions of the original adventurers and has rendered the Wheal Unity Mine, not only a source of present benefit , but also opened the fairest prospect of abundant wealth*".

The adventurers studied the old workings and how it stood when last worked. They discovered the nature and direction of the lode and whether it was possible to extend the line of the deep adit to cut the deepest level possible. However because of foul air in the adit they needed to cut a ventilation shaft. This was eventually completed, but it was an expensive venture.

In January 1809 William Jenkin reported that the adventurers had just now completed an undertaking which they have for a long time had on their hands of boring a hole about 3" in diameter, 14 fathoms (84`) deep to communicate air from a shaft sunk about 9 fathoms deep to the adit below, which is 23 fathoms from the surface (2).

The Prospectus continued, " *The miners are now working the deep adit and it is supposed are not far from cutting the lode of copper at its deeper level. They are also sinking on the lode at its upper end in which they have proceeded to 15 fathoms. The mine is in a productive state, several tons of rich ore have been raised and as the lode becomes richer the further they penetrate it is confidently presumed that when they reach the intersection of the deep adit the produce and consequent profits will be immense"* (3).

There is a handwritten note in pencil at the foot of the Prospectus which says, *"It is intended to have a warf and Harbo to Mounts Bay to operate".* This may indicate that a harbour or wharf was planned as early as 1809 and also that the ore was either moved, or intended to be moved, via the Cove.

Fig. 76 A Piece of native Copper from Wheal Trenance, Mullion now in the National Geology Museum Courtesy of local resident.

"The finest unquestionably ever raised in Europe"

By June 1809 a few large good quality copper pieces were discovered at shallow levels, 5-6 fathoms below the surface, one being 105lbs in weight and valued at over 200 guineas. Another large piece was reported to be in the possession of Lord Falmouth which he reportedly had made into a table but no trace of such an object has been found. By October 1809 no regular copper lode had been found at depth.

In the Royal Cornwall Gazette of January 1810 and advert appeared offering a large number of Native Copper (*Malleable, crystallized and other Mineral*) pieces described as the *"finest unquestionably ever raised in Europe"*.

They had been discovered in the South Wheal Unity mine at Mullion after work had been undertaken costing £3000, and the specimens had shapes similar to the "*Kings Arms mounted on the back of an elephant, a map of England, the figure of a Dolphin, a Fan etc"* When they were put up for sale there was a great interest and high prices were paid. It seems that at least one piece may have found its way back to Mullion because a piece looking very similar to the "*Map of England*" turned up in 1952 back at the mine, found in a Cornish hedge, but has since disappeared (2).

By May 1810 the mine was in danger of closure as the adventurers were running out of money. By 1811 the mine had closed with losses of £1500 (2).

Wheal Trenance

In 1845 adventurers from London reopened the site which they now called Wheal Trenance. By now it was known that in the Lake Superior district of North America there were similar geological conditions producing large quantities of Native Copper. Their objective was to get through the Serpentine to prove that there was copper in the rocks below.

The upper levels of Trenance Mine continued to produce slabs of Native Copper.

In May 1847 a small debt court case (Noel v Verran) indicated that the mine was apparently employing the services of a Dowser to "show the mine" at 3 shillings a month. The plaintiff was claiming *"for agency services in Trenance Mine"* Part of the claim was for the *"...spiritual services of Dowsing"* (4b). Apparently, this was most unusual in mines. Captain William Verran was the Mine Captain at the time.

In 1847 a piece of Native Copper weighing 371lbs was brought up from Trenance Mine. It measured 5` x 2` 9".

A second slab weighing 476lbs was recovered. It was said to be the largest known (4) (4a).

It was found that the former workings did not go below 20 fathoms. A new shaft was sunk 8 fathoms on the lode which ran N-S, underlies E and was about 3` wide with metallic copper on the footwalls and hanging walls. Water had stopped further working until it could be removed by digging a deeper adit. The extent of the Sett was 800 fathoms (4800`) N –S on the course of the lodes and 600 fathoms (3600`) E-W. In June 1848 a large mass of native copper had been discovered weighing 30 cwt (5).

WANTED TO PURCHASE.

A STEAM PUMPING ENGINE, between 30 and 40 inch cylinder, with cylindrical Boilers.

Apply to RICHARD DALTON, Trenance Mine, Mullion, near Helston, stating particulars and lowest ready money price.

Mullion, July 20th, 1848.

Fig. 77 left Advert

In June 1848 a mass of Native Copper weighing over 2 tons was discovered. About 17 cwt was cut from it in lumps of 10-20lbs and subsequently a mass weighing 25cwt was brought up from the 18 fathom level. Large pieces of grey ore weighing 50-100lbs were also brought up. As a result, it being Midsummer's Day, all the miners were given a day's holiday (5a). In July 1848 Richard Dalton, the Director of Trenance Mine, was advertising to buy a 30"-40" pump engine (6).

"The Largest Piece Ever Mined In England"

In the same year a parcel of 15 tons of ore was sold, 9 tons of which fetched £19/ ton, the whole fetching £200. Shortly afterwards another consignment of native copper reached London, one piece weighing 1568lbs, part of a slab 30` long, 4` wide and 6" thick. This was broken from the main mass, which weighed over a ton at a depth of 14 fathoms from the surface and special tackle had to be brought in to raise it.

It has been said locally by people connected to the mine that the slab had to be brought out through the adit which ran out half way down the valley and brought to Mullion Mill before being transported. This was a significant piece of Native Copper and was the largest piece ever mined in England. The severed portion was displayed at the Great Exhibition of 1851. Afterwards it was sent to the Jermyn Street Museum, followed by the Geological Museum. Underground water was a problem.

In 1849 several large slabs of native copper ore of a dendritic or tree like appearance were brought up from the bottom of Trenance Mine. One piece measured 7 foot 6 inches by 4 feet, weighing over 8 hundredweight (cwt) and at the 16 fathom level formed part of a huge mass of native copper weighing at least 25-27 cwt. Other smaller pieces existed and were of a similar high quality. It was the opinion of geologists that the lode was gradually turning into undisturbed grey ore. An engine was due to be erected by the resident director Richard Dalton (7).

During the year 1849 16 tons of copper ore yielding 2 and half tons of metal were sold for £154 (2). In March 1850 the first steam engine, bought with a view to deepening the mine at this time, was started. It had been purchased from Wheal Germoe (2) & (8).

The event was lavishly celebrated in the traditional Cornish mining way, and the whole of the workforce involved in the venture were entertained by Richard Dalton. The meal, which took place at the Count House of the old Vro Farm consisted of good old English Fare of roast beef, and plum pudding, bread and cheese and as much beer and ale as each person could drink. The party sat down at 2pm and were presided over by the Captains of the mines and Mr William Nicholas of Mullion. The health of the adventurers was drunk, along with the Resident Director and the health of the Directors in London given and received. It was good to see the confidence in the venture in Mullion plus the party of principally Cornish adventurers in the adjoining Sett (8) (2).

By 1850 the mine had been sunk to a depth of 41 fathoms (246`) with a lode continuing to grow at depth into grey and yellow ore. After the serpentine has been got through the miners continued to believe it would turn into a lode of undisturbed copper ore. At the 41 fathom depth mundic, steatite, (Soaprock) and portions of iron ore were found.

The Manager, Mr Richard Dalton, and his friends had taken a large number of shares, with Captain Hensley of Marazion, who had begun a new Sett adjacent to the main shaft (9). Hensley was also associated with a nearby smaller copper mine called Wheal Fenwick at Pollurian.

In June 1852 an accident occurred at the mine when a Whim Kibble was ascending the shaft, a large stone weighing over a quarter of a hundredweight fell and hit a young man called Robert Gilbert in the eye causing a large cut.

It was said that he was doing well and it was hoped his sight would be preserved. At the same time it was also announced that the Trenance Mine was due to close the following Saturday (10).

In November 1852 a Case involving Trenance Mine was heard involving two miners. The dispute was between Thomas Nankervis and James Downing over work allegedly carried out by both men on a pitch at the Mine whereby James Downing had been given £2 5s for the work from the purser, and failed to pay the other saying that the money had been a present to him from the purser. The case was adjourned for the purser to attend (10a).

Confidence appeared high. But now, apparently, the spending activities of the "purser" were being brought into question and were described as being extremely lavish. There was concern expressed that too much money was being spent on his personal account and as a result the mining activities were closed down (2).

By December 1852 the mine, the 40" steam engine, mining equipment, materials, tools and property were being advertised for sale in Truro, including the account house furniture, a ten roomed dwelling house with stable and coach house, large walled garden,5 miners cottages, a horse and gig, and an 18` long pleasure boat with oars and sails. The whole covered about 19 and half acres. Included in the sale were 320lbs of Native Copper.

The sale was completed on 4th of January 1853; see over page for details of materials sold.

The Mine was not worked again, but in 1907 the Mining Engineer, Mr Keast, did inspect the mine. The shafts were explored and information was obtained from elderly miners, formerly employed there (11).

Wheal Fenwick.

In the early 1850s there was a second Copper Mine only half a mile away to the north of Mullion Cove which went by the name of Pollurian Mine and later Wheal Fenwick. It was situated on the cliff to the south of Pollurian Cove, on a mass which contained some copper ore, including a small amount of Native Copper. The early adventurer was Capt. W.G. Hensley, but it was not a particularly productive operation and a new company was formed to take over from him.

Up until September 1853 a further £848 was spent in developing the mine and a small engine was purchased.

In October 1853 Hensley was appointed as Mine Agent, and stated that the shaft was now 19 fathoms (114`) below the surface. By December 1853 the engine was operational and the shaft was dug to a depth of 30 fathoms (180`).The adit emptied onto the beach at Pedn-y-ke.

A small amount of Native Copper was found but by June 1854 the operation was suspended. In November 1854, the materials and contents of the mine were put up for auction (2).

The Sale of Materials from the Wheal Fenwick Mine took place on the site on 28th November 1854 and the List of Items in that sale appears overleaf. It included a 24" cylinder pumping engine, plus other pumps, kibbles, whims and tools.

In December 1855 it was restarted, but was unproductive. On 3rd April 1855 a 24" Cylinder engine, 9` stroke, equal beam, with 10 tons of boiler and metallic pistons was put up for auction at the Mine and on April 17th 1855 the balance "Bob" of a 24" Cylinder Engine, 2 Crab winches, Gunpowder, Coal, Brick and slate, wood and all the Account House furniture were auctioned. It seems that the take up for mining equipment here was slow and the cylinder engine was still being offered for auction on 2nd July 1855, but it was finally sold off and the mine closed (12).

The shaft was filled in, but later in 1889 stone from the mine was used in the construction of the Pollurian Hotel.

This ended the Mullion association with Copper Mining in the 19th Century.

Bibliography

1. W.Borlase, Natural History of Cornwall Publ. 1758
2. A.K. Hamilton Jenkin, Mines & Miners of Cornwall Vol. XIII 1967   7. RCG 19.10.1849
3. V127 p68, Royal Institution of Cornwall Courtney, Library.   8. RCG 8.3.1850
4. Manchester Courier 5.5.1847   9. RCG 2.8.1850
4a. RCG 14.5.1847   10.RCG 6.8.1852
4b RCG 14.5.1847   10a.RCG 21.11.1852
5. RCG 16.6.1848   11. West Briton 21.3.1907
5a Cornishman 30.6.1848.   12. RCG 13.4.1855
6. RCG 28.7.1848

Figs.78& 79 Materials and Minerals sold by Auction in at the closure of Trenance Mine and Wheal Fenwick. Trenance Mine closed in 1852, and Wheal Fenwick in 1854 (Royal Cornwall Gazette).

VALUABLE MINING MATERIALS,

Forty-Inch Cylinder Steam Engine, Boiler, &c. The Leasehold Dwelling House and Tenement
FOR SALE

TO be SOLD by PUBLIC AUCTION, by Mr. EDSALL, at TRENANCE MINE, in the parish of Mullion, on Tuesday the 4th day of January next, at Eleven o'clock in the Forenoon precisely, the whole of the valuable

MINING MATERIALS,
CONSISTING OF

A 40-inch Cylinder STEAM ENGINE, 10-feet stroke in cylinder, and 9 feet in shaft, with first piece of Rod ; Boiler about eleven tons ; Balance Bob ; Capstan and Shears.
120 fathoms 9-inch Capstan Rope, quite new.
80 fathoms of Whim Rope.
Horse Whim and Shieves complete.
80 fathoms 7-16ths Chain.
19 10-inch Pumps.
8 9-inch ditto.
1 8-inch ditto.
2 7-inch ditto.
8 6-inch ditto.
1 7-inch, 2 9-inch, 1 11-inch, and 1 12-inch Working Barrels.
1 9-inch, and 1 10-inch Windbore.
1 10-inch Plunger Pole, with Stuffing Box and Glands to match.
1 6-inch ditto and Stock.
1 10-inch Top Door-piece.
1 8-inch Stuffing Box and Gland.
2 5-inch ditto ditto.
1 6-inch, and 1 5-inch H Piece.
1 9-inch Turn-pipe.
1 4-inch Door-piece.
2 3-inch, and 2 4-inch Feed-pipes.
V Bob, 2 Whim Kibbles, 16 Shaft Rollers, 60 fathoms of 7, 8, and 9-inch Rods ; 12 pairs Strapping Plates, 30 fathoms Iron Staved Ladders ; 2 6-inch Treble Blocks, 1 6-inch Head Pulley, 1 set 4-inch treble and single Pulley Blocks, a quantity of Zinc Pipes and Sheet Zinc, Smith's Bellows, Anvil, and Vice ; Smiths' and Miners' Tools, 1 treble Crab Winch, about 2 tons of Wrought Iron Rails 2 × ¼, a quantity of Cast Iron Chairs for ditto, Scale Beam, Scales and Weights, about 320 lbs. NATIVE COPPER, Miner's Dial and Measuring Chain, Assay Scales and Weights, Grindstone, Screw Stocks, Rod and Flanch Bolts and Bars, Turning Lathe, 17 Bars Cast Steel, a quantity of new and old Iron, old Timber, &c. Also, 1 Labour Horse, 2 Carts, Gig and Cart Harnesses, Saddle and Bridle, 2 Horse Rollers and 1 Cloth, and 2 Harness-room Saves.

ACCOUNT-HOUSE FURNITURE,

Consisting of Desk, Stools, Tables, Chairs, Bedstead, Wash-stands, Dresser, Form, &c., &c.

A PLEASURE BOAT, 18 feet keel and 3 feet beam, with Oars, Sails, &c.

And at the same time will be Sold, for the remainder of a term of 99 years, determinable on the deaths of three lives, aged respectively 10, 21, and 22 years, a Leasehold TENEMENT, consisting of a substantially-built ten-roomed Dwelling House, with Stable, Coach House, Harness Room, and domestic offices ; a large well Walled Garden, Five Cottages, and Smiths' and Carpenters' Shops, the whole comprising about 19½ acres of land.

On account of the shortness of the days, the Sale will commence at Eleven o'clock in the Forenoon precisely.

For further particulars application may be made to Mr. STOKES, Solicitor, Truro ; Messrs. GRYLLS and HILL, Solicitors, Helston ; or to
Mr. CHARLES S. EDSALL,
Auctioneer, Truro.

Dated 20th December, 1852.

Valuable Mine Materials for Sale.

TO be SOLD by PUBLIC AUCTION, by Mr. HENRY PENBERTHY, on TUESDAY the 28th of November, 1854, at WHEAL FENWICK MINE, in the parish of Mullion, commencing at 11 o'clock in the Forenoon precisely, the whole of the

MATERIALS
On the said Mine, comprising :—

A 24-inch CYLINDER PUMPING ENGINE (almost new), 9-ft Stroke, equal beam, with 10 Tons of Boiler and Metallic Piston.
4 9-feet 11-inch Pumps.
1 12-feet 9-inch Working.
1 9-feet 9-inch Winbore.
1 9-inch Door Piece.
10 9-feet 7-inch Pumps.
6 6-feet do. do.
1 8-inch H Piece.
1 6-inch Door Piece.
Pole and Stuffing Box complete.
1 6-inch Windbore.
1 9-inch do.
Steel Boyers.
2 Buckets and Iron Rods.
2 Drop Chains.
5 Pair Strapping Plates.
1 Pair Main Cope Cutters and Pins.
1 7-16 Whim Chain.
4 Winze Kibbles, Bolts and Burs, Pump Rings, Staples, and Glands, Rod Pins.
A quantity of New and Old Iron.
A Knocker.
1 Pair large 3 shieves Iron Blocks.
1 Single ditto.
1 Horse Whim and 2 4-ft. Shieves, a Chain Ladder, 4 8-inch Rods, 1 6-inch do., 1 Cistern 5-ft. by 4-ft., 40 fathoms Iron Stave Ladders, 40 fathoms of 5 and 6-inch Launders, 15 fathoms Air Pipes, 2 Winze Trees, Screw Stock, Plates and Taps, Smiths' and Miners' Tools, Smith's Crane and Forge, 40-inch Smith's Bellows, Iron Horse, Anvil, Vice, 2 double Crab Winches, 1 single do., 2 Hand Pumps, a 6-inch Whim Rope, 1 3-inch fall do., 1 Tackle do., Beam, Scales and Weights, a quantity of new Balk, Quartering and Plank, several Wheelbarrows, 2 Stuff Barrows, 2 Water Barrels, 1 Hurl, 1 Centre, Smith's Scoaring Box, several Doors, Sashes and Shutters, Grindstone and Frame, Barrel with 6 cwt. Grease, 5 cwt. Powder, several dozen Candles and Chest, Safety Fuse, a Cask with Olive Oil, Nails, Hemp, Brown Paper, Leather, Pick Hilts, a quantity of Brick, Slate, Carpenter's Bench, numerous lots of Old Timber and various other articles ; also the

ACCOUNT HOUSE FURNITURE.

The whole of the above are entirely new, and of the very best description. Further particulars may be obtained by applying to
Mr. PLOMER,
Solicitor, Helston.

Dated, October 26th, 1854.

... AND SOAPROCK QUARRIES

In the mid-18th century, at a time when tea and coffee drinking was becoming so important, English Ceramic manufacturers could not produce a material capable of withstanding boiling water.

It had been discovered that when crushed Soapstone, "Soaprock" or "Soapy Clay", as it was called, was added to the Porcelain mix, the Porcelain produced was able to withstand "thermal shock". Small Porcelain Factories here could begin to produce a material which could compete with Chinese imports, and hence the English tea and coffee drinking era began to expand.

Fig.80 Soaprock or "Talc", used in the manufacture of Porcelain.

At this time the only known deposits of the mineral were on the west coast of the Lizard Peninsula, and these included Mullion Cliffs in Mullion Cove.

It was quarried at other locations including Gew Graze (Soapy Cove) from 1748, Pentreath and Lizard Downs from 1751 and also at Kynance Cove, Daroose, Wheal Foss at Teneriffe, Penruddock and Mullion Village for over 70 years.

Mainly forgotten about until recently, Soapstone was being quarried from Mullion Cove and around *Wheal Providence* from February 1752 under a 10 year Licence granted by Mary Hunt of Lanhydrock to Nicholas Crisp and John Sanders of the Vauxhall Factory, for quarrying of the cliffs, and inland from the Cove for up to 200 fathoms, taking them close to the Copper Mine at *Wheal Providence*. A total of 29 tons was quarried in the first year.

The sea level was about a foot lower in 1750 and due to adverse weather conditions work took place between April and October with the soaprock firstly weighed off and then sent by sea to ports such as Hayle and then on to Bristol,

London or later to Liverpool, to produce soft paste porcelain. The quarried soapstone from the area was delivered to Porcelain Factories including Worcester, Vauxhall, Liverpool, Caughley in Shropshire, and South Wales via coastal ports until the mid 1820s. One of the exit ports in the area was Mullion Cove (1).

Fig.81 Left, Mullion Cliffs. One of the 18th Century Quarry sites in Mullion Cove.

Soapstone quarrying was an important business in 18th century Mullion Cove, but the Serpentine cliffs here were difficult and dangerous to work.

Only limited amounts of information now survive, with most of the Porcelain Factory records being destroyed.

The London Vauxhall Factory records are limited but some information about the Liverpool Factory in the form of letters sent between the Mine Captain, Gavregan Teppit, and Potter Richard Chaffers existed until 1940 when they were destroyed during the bombing of Liverpool during the World War II.

What we do know from the Letters is that the serpentine of Mullion Cliffs was actively quarried under Licence from the Lanhydrock Estate in the 18th Century on behalf of Nicholas Crisp and John Sanders of Vauxhall.

The 1752 Licence granted them the right to mine for soaprock "*... in the lands of the said Mary Hunt situate and lying and being in the Little Commons or Downs commonly called Goon Vean belonging to an part of the tenements of Predannack Wartha in the Parish of Mullion in the said county of Cornwall to work the said veins and lodes from the extent of the cliff next the sea as far east on the course of the said veins and lodes as 200 fathoms and in extent from a rock called Porth Pyg north as far as Pendenankea ...*"

They paid a Guinea for the first 20 tons and 15 shillings per ton over the 20. A record in the Lords Agents rough book shows that on 14th November 1752, 29 tons and 12 cwt of soapy clay was weighed out from Mullion and a cash payment of £28 3s 6d was made by Nicholas Crisp.

Fig. 82 left, 18th C , horizontal soaprock tunnel or "Drift" in Mullion Cove. Photo by author 2011.

Richard Chaffers, Liverpool. After the failure of the Vauxhall concern due to death of a partner and financial problems, in 1756 a similar Licence was issued to Richard Chaffers of Liverpool.
The story of Richard Chaffers is an intriguing one, in that it is one of few to survive. He rode on horseback from Liverpool to London with £1000, two pistols and some blankets in his saddlebag, in order to obtain permission to search for soapstone from the Lizard land owners, many of whom either lived there or were in Parliament there. On route he obtained letters of introduction to present to the land owners. Having obtained permission he rode to Mullion. On arrival he sought out the Miners, but there were no new soapstone sites available.
He engaged the miners to find him a suitable site and after some time and with his money running out they found him a place to quarry. In order to confirm the legal requirements he had to ride back to London to finalise the Licence. After this journey he became very ill and spent some weeks recovering at an Inn before being deemed fit enough to return to his wife, and the Factory in Liverpool. On the return of the first set of casks filled with soapstone sent to Liverpool by ship from Cornwall it was reported that crowds lined the quay to cheer and flags were flying.
He went on to produce some of the best soft paste porcelain made in the country at this time, and even drew praise from Josiah Wedgwood... who, contrary to some local belief, did not use soapstone in his pottery at all.
On 9th July 1756 Gavregan Teppit wrote of Chaffers recently leaving Mullion and that he hopes the ... "*drawing would answer the charges. He has set some men to work, and paid their wages, and was in good order for raising the clay and had raised 2 tuns or thereabouts*"
On 8th February 1760 he wrote "*I hope we shall raise this summer so much as we did laste. We began in April and gave over in November*"
In March 1761 a letter to Chaffers read, "*I have sent the clay to Hail firmly caskt up. We are obliged to shout night and day and pouder is dear. The cost of everything from 1st March 1760 to March 1761 is £94.*"
The letters include the phrase "*We are shouting (*blasting*) night and day*", which means that there was blasting taking place 24 hours a day at one stage.
Mullion Cove would have been a noisy place indeed with all the gunpowder used at that time. The Cove did not echo to the sound of gunpowder again until the 1890s when the piers were built.

Fig. 83 right Soaprock Mining Level at Sandy Vro. Photo by Author 2011

In 1766 Teppit wrote that the miners were working "levels" but had recently struck copper which was sold for £96/ton. Following the death of Richard Chaffers a Licence was issued to his partner Phillip Christian in 1772 and the area quarried both continued and expanded. By 1775 the Licence was taken over by the Worcester Porcelain Factory, the most successful of all the Porcelain potters who remained in the west coast area quarrying and using soapstone at their Worcester factory until the mid 1820s.

From the Letters sent by Teppit we learn that the Serpentine in Mullion Cliffs was very unstable and dangerous to work. Even today that can be confirmed by looking at the erosion there, but the remains of soapstone veins can still be seen in the face of the cliff.

There were "levels" in other parts of the Cove, and between Tonkens Point and Sandy Vro there are caves cut through the serpentine into sites where soapstone was quarried out.

For many years these Caves were referred to as being widely used by Smugglers. There is little doubt that they were ... but they originated as sites of Soapstone extraction. The Cove at Mullion was one site from which Soapstone was transported for many years. The advert (Fig. 84) in the Royal Cornwall Gazette of 1815 shows a request for a boat to transport 80 tons of clay. Although not a port or even a harbour, Mullion was a trading cove for many years before the Harbour Piers were built (2).

To MASTERS of VESSELS.

WANTED. a VESSEL to remove 80 Tons of CLAY, from *Mullion* to *Penzance*.

For further particulars, apply to *Mr. Jethro Hornblower*, Whitehall, near Redruth, if by letter, post-paid.

Dated April 26. 1815.

It is correct to say that the tea and coffee drinking industry in this country actually started with imported porcelain from China. The extraction of "Soaprock" from Mullion and the neighbouring areas of the coast towards the Lizard, was the important component which allowed quality porcelain to be produced at such locations as Worcester, Bristol, Vauxhall, Liverpool and Caughley in Shropshire.

Its property of preventing the porcelain from cracking and breaking with the introduction of boiling water was paramount. It allowed the production of highly decorated tea and coffee pots, cups, saucers, and dinner services which competed so successfully with the Chinese imports for so many years.

Fig. 85 right; Worcester Porcelain, "*Kempthorne Pattern*" made in the 1760s and named after Renatus Kempthorne, a Mullion Yeoman Farmer who helped provide information which helped Worcester develop a large local Soapstone quarry nearby at Daroose. (Photo by permission from a Private Collector).

Much has been heard about Porcelain produced by William Cookworthy using China Clay from Cornwall but he produced a different type called hard paste porcelain. This was mainly from 1868 when he took out his first Porcelain Patent. Soapstone or soft paste porcelain, therefore, was produced in large quantities at least 20 years before this.

Undoubtedly, Mullion Cove has a strong link to an early industrial revolution in this Country.

Bibliography

1. "Soaprock Coast... the origins of English porcelain" Published in 2011 by R Felce, BSc Hons.
    ISBN 978-0-9569895-0-5
2. Falmouth Packet. 6.5.1815.

Chapter 12   TWO TRAVELLERS FROM AMERICA

In September 1877 in Beverley, New England, some 3000 miles away from Cornwall, two brothers William A. Andrews 35, and Asa Walter Andrews 23, were looking out over the Atlantic Ocean. They had only ever previously been to sea in a small fishing boat, but were planning the greatest, most dangerous and ambitious journey of their lives. They formulated their plan and set about improving both their sailing and navigational skills. After all, they thought, Merchant ships and Mail steamers cross the Atlantic all the year round. In May of the following year they ordered their boat from a Massachusetts Boatyard and named her *Nautilus*.

They were about to attempt to cross the Atlantic Ocean from west to east in a sailing boat made of cedar wood, described as a lap streaked Dory. She was 19` in overall length, 15` on the bottom, 6`- 7" wide and 2`- 3" deep, had only one short mast near the bow, was decked over from stem to stern with two hatchways, and a storm sail. The cedar wood hull was only one half an inch in thickness. She carried a sea anchor, or drogue, plus 50 fathoms of rope for rough weather. The tiny boat carried 60 gallons of water in 6 ten gallon kegs which acted as ballast and provisions for 60 days. After use the water kegs were refilled with sea water.

Equipment.

For cooking they had an alcohol stove and an oil stove, plus canned provisions and stores. There was fuel for lighting and cooking which was 6 gallons of Kerosene Oil. A much reduced provision list for this mammoth voyage may now look somewhat primitive, but food stores included the following *"...60 galls of water in 6 kegs, 100lbs of biscuits in air tight tins, 30 cans of Boston baked beans, 10 cans of tomatoes and peaches, 10 cans of green corn, 10 cans of green peas, 7 cans of St.Louis Corned beef, 1 can condensed milk, 1 can of grapes, 1 can of preserved apples, 1 can of crab apples, 1 can of condensed beef, 1lb of tea, 10lb of coffee, 2lb of salt, 4 oz pepper, 10lb figs, 2lb oatmeal, 2lb of Indian Meal, 2 bottles of horse radish, 1 bottle of Rennes magic oil, 2 bottles of French Mustard, 1 doz lemons, 1 loaf of bread, 1 Ham, 1 gall of cod liver oil (to lay on the sea), 1 jug of molasses, 4 boxes of sardines, 20lb of Tobacco (for smoking and chewing), 2 bottles of Irish Whiskey, 15 bottles of lager beer..."*

William A. Andrews.   Asa Walter Andrews.

Fig. 86 The Andrews Brothers.

The plan.

Their intention was to sail to France to take part in the Great Exhibition held in Paris. They kept a log of their journey. The Atlantic had been crossed before by the great yachts, *America* in 1851, the *Fleetwing, Henrietta* and *Vespa* in the Great Ocean Race of 1866, and the husband and wife team of Captain Crapo in the diminutive *New Bedford* in 1877, but none were as small as the *Nautilus*.

Mullion.

In June 1878 Mullion was a sandy cove, noted as part of the Mounts Bay Pilchard Fishery. It was also known for catches of Crab, Lobster and Crawfish. Seine boats and Crabbers were hauled up onto the foreshore, their pots and nets lining the beach... and fishermen would talk quietly about their catch. The fish cellars would process their catches of pilchards and other fish, while some would be sent to Newlyn to sell. The Lifeboat, the *Daniel J Draper*, had been in place for just over ten years, sitting in the Lifeboat House erected by local builders, and waiting for the call to launch in a storm to help a ship in distress. Coal and other materials were brought into the cove by sailing ships, and farmers would bring their horse and cart to collect and carry away seaweed to put on the fields. The Coastguards looked out onto the Atlantic Ocean and Victorian visitors would come to view the sea caves in the Cove.

And then, one summer day in July 1878, two American sailors called Andrews arrived in a tiny boat... The epic journey of the Andrews Brothers, based on their Log, was recorded in a book published in 1870 and now rarely read, but locally there is a notable part of their important expedition which has sadly drifted from memory... their first landfall was in Mullion.

The Journey begins.

The journey began at 3pm on June 7th when the *Nautilus* started out from Boston Harbour. After a good start she received some early storm damage and they had to return to make repairs on the 9th June and the brothers eventually recommenced the long journey on Friday 14th June. They experienced storms and calms, fog and rain, incidents with larger ships, floating debris and abandoned hulls, with whales, porpoises and flying fish, sunfish, and seabirds, quantities of their namesakes "*Nautilus*", as well as unexplained sightings of sea serpents. There was illness and laughter as they tried to make contact with as many vessels as they could to ensure their position was known to their families and others in Boston.

Fig. 87 Artists impression of the *Nautilus*

But it wasn't just in Boston that their journey was known ... it was broadcast all over the world. Telegraph messages were sent by the ships which they met and they found that many of them already knew of the expedition, and all wished them well. They encountered 14 seperate storms, the first lasting 4 days and the second 5 days, and spoke with 37 vessels on their passage.

An entry in their log gives an impression of how they sometimes struggled to keep the journey together.

The following are extracts taken from their Log and provide a revealing insight into sailing in the 1870s.

Saturday June 15th Morning foggy and cold wind sw. During the gleam of the fog saw a schooner. She saw us and ran down and spoke with us. Proved to be the "Commonwealth of Gloucester, a mackerel catcher 117 miles from Thatchers Island.Got observation. Soon set in foggy. Passed many logs, planks etc Blew Fog Horn occasionaly; sometimes with response. Night very foggy.This keeping your eyes on the compass , and watching for lights, and blowing your foghorn, wet and cold without relief, watching the seas as they follow you, thinking now and again that you may hear a log come crashing through your half inch cedar, is a novelty not to be desired long. We passed to the northward of Georges Stormy Banks in th enight Course E by S, half S. Run 100 miles.Ob. Lat 42.17N"

Sunday June 16th "... saw a ship and schooner to the south ... passed Cunard steamer distance one mile. Spoke fishing schooner Triumph of Maine ... passed a barque to the west Ob Lat 42.21N"

Wednesday June 19th ... "coffee and sardines for two... saw a big smokeand made for it , they saw us ... proved to be the white star steamer Adriatic... they had read of us in the english papers, the departure from Boston had been telegraphed... saw another sail ahead. She passed to the rear of us. Passed another ship bound NW, sighted another steamer..Ob. Lat 42.35NLong 52.20 W."

Wednesday June 26th "Wind SW Passed near to a largebarque painted green bound to the W.(Have since learnt from a lady passenger who saw us that it was a Russian Barque, and was lost soon after, all hands taking to a raft. They were bothered by whales and wondered if the whales bothered us"

Thursday June 27th ... "Everything which is not air tight are completely wet through. Stewed beans for breakfast. Course SE by E. Wind SW. At night a shoal of whales made us feel uncomfortable. .. some rubbed the boat with their sides"

Friday June 28th " A Royal breakfast... coffee with condensed milk, corned beef with hard tack. Plenty of Mother Careys chickens, hagdens and marble headers... passed between two ships one going east and one going west.

This is the first one we have seen going east... Got Ob, difficult 42.29N Longit. Dead Reckoning 53.10W"

Monday July 1st " ... *got under way about 9am, saw 5 flying fish, Walter caught a nautilus in our bucket... one sea swept our lantern overboard. We had to put it behind the mast to keep the wind and waves from putting it out. Lat 43.10N Long. 46.30W"*

Tuesday 2nd July *"Hove to at 6am Remained at drogue all day Wind NW, a gale terrible tide, rips, more rain, fearful waves ... several vessels bound east and west. We allowed one and a half miles an hour drift while at drogue"*

Thursday July 4th " *Drank a bottle of lager that we had been saving for this occasion. Wind NW remained at drogue all day. The most dangerous waves we have had to contend with yet."*

Tuesday July 9th " *ran 90 miles..."*

Wednesday July 10th *"More rain. Ran 190 miles. Thats getting up and on for a small boat...*

Thursday July 11th *"Wind W, foggy. A regular cataract of rain... ran 150 miles more...*
Making up for lost time"

Friday July 12th *"Wind S, stormy foggy. More rain.Run 190 miles.Some of the waves would would come over her stern, burying her completely..."*

Wednesday July 17th *Wind SSW Course E by S Half S, Sea smooth... Just 34 days out. I never took much stock about sea serpents, but I have good reason to believe, after what I saw last evening before dark there are denizens of the deepthat have never been thoroughly explained or illustrated by our zoological societies.It was during a moment of intense calm, and I had been watching some whalessporting and spouting some distance behind me, when,on turningand looking in the opposite direction I was startled to see what what appeared to be part of a huge monster in the shape of a snake. It was about 200` off. I saw 12 or 15` of what appeared to be the tail of a huge black snake from 5 to 15" in diameter, the end being stubby or round and white. It was in the air in a corrugated shape in motion in the act of descending ... I also saw the wake in the water as if more had gone down the whole being in motion in the manner of a snake... Walter was in the cuddy... I told him to pass the hatchet. He heard the splash and saw the form in the water... during the night we heard ... the most horrid noises behind us... we took to be whales.*

Thursday July 18th *"Long 24.30W Invited aboard the English Brig Nellie Crosby from Yarmouth for breakfast"*

Monday July 22nd *Plenty of sails in sight, going E and W.Lat 47.22NLong 18.30W*
(Spoke with 5 ships captains from Britain(Two), Germany, USA, Norway) Run 215 miles

One feature which runs through the Log is the large number of vessels of all types, from many countries, which were crossing the ocean in 1878, vessels ready to provide help and food, which was sometimes exchanged, vessels which ran into trouble of their own, passengers and crew of al denominations. Their trip was known about in the newspapers almost world wide and thanks to Telegraph they were able to meet on their journey people who knew about them, went out of their way to make contact and wished them well. Eventually by 8pm Sunday July 28th they sighted the Bishops Rock Lighthouse- the fastest crossing by any small sailing boat.

By Wednesday July 31st They tried to make the Lizard but the strong current, a spring tide and an easterly wind forced them north along the Lizard coast. They knew little about the English Channel but they were aware of the dangers of this stretch of coastline, the sudden changes in wind direction which drove ships onto the cliffs, the smugglers and the old tales of "*false beacon lights during storms*". They described it as bleak and desolate with numerous caves, but they were looking for a place to land. They spotted a small piece of sandy beach about 40` long and thought it would be a good place for a swim. They wrote ... "[We] *anchored within a few feet of an immense boulder to protect me from the wind, and such a din as the gulls and the wild birds set up I have never heard. It was Mullion Cove, Coastguard and life- saving station. How fortunate we are safe"*. They ate dinner and were then joined by the Falmouth pilot cutter the *Grand Turk* with Captain George Cox and Jacob Harris on board. It was Walter Andrews who went ashore with Jacob Harris for the first time armed with a jug, and a request for fresh water. William remained afloat choosing to complete his log and chart rather than go onshore. Their arrival became known not just locally, but was telegraphed around the world. They visited the "*Grand Turk*" for dinner and spent the first night on board the *Nautilus*.

Thursday August 1st The wind was still blowing an easterly gale and there were many ships anchored in the Mounts Bay. They decided to draw the *Nautilus* up the beach to remove the barnacles from the bottom. These were selected by local people as souvenirs of the occasion. 4000 words of the Log were copied and telegraphed to the New York Herald and the London newspapers, and later they took dinner with Parland Griffiths, the Coastguard man living in the Cove. At the invitation of Rev. Harvey they took supper at the "Old Inn", where they met Miss Mary Mundy

Fig. 88 A Yacht arriving in the Cove at sunset in August 2011 in an easterly breeze. (By author)

The following day the easterly gale had increased and the Bay was full, including with several Steamships. After breakfast they became acquainted with some of the history of the area where they had landed especially the Church where they obtained a souvenir from the font. The houses in Mullion they described as being made of stone and mortar, about a storey and a half high, all whitewashed. Photographs were taken of the *Nautilus*.

By <u>Saturday August 3rd</u> the wind had turned to the NE, but the barometer had not moved so they decided to remain in Mullion in case the wind turned to the SW. They ate a Cornish Pastie for supper and remained on the boat overnight. They contemplated the voyage so far and decided that when they originally set out they wanted to capture a porpoise or a shark as trophies, but decided that this was not appropriate, and that these creatures had become their constant companions through the voyage and they had made no attempt to harm their little boat. They decided to stay for the Church service on Sunday.

On Sunday the wind was west and light. They had breakfast with Parland Griffiths and a Helston Photographer brought them some photographs of the *Nautilus*. They attended the Church Service and then had dinner with Rev Harvey.

The Cove was visited by many people, there to see their boat. They wrote that *"... this was the only event that has happened here outside shipwrecks for many years"*. They put their boat in the water ready to leave the following day.

On <u>Monday August 5th</u> in an easterly wind and rain they departed the Cove watched only by Parland Griffiths on route for Le Havre. Having been feted by many after their arrival, they departed as they arrived in their own company. They passed the Lizard Signal Station where they were signalled, made the English Channel and arrived in France on <u>Thursday August 8th</u> with colours flying.

They wrote that, *"The voyage of the Nautilus is over. We were three days from Lands End to Havre, making our time from Beverley (Boston) to Havre, Paris 48 days.... the smallest boat ever from America to sit in the dry dock there ...weighing only 600lbs."*

On returning to England the "*Nautilus*" was put on display at the Royal Aquarium Westminster, London, and at Brighton. They were honoured at the 1879 Oxford/Cambridge Boat Race and in the autumn of 1879 in Liverpool, before being transported back to America hauled aboard a Cunard Liner. Walter Andrews remained with the boat ... having to work his passage back to the USA. We should remember their brave achievement.

Extracts taken from, "*A Daring Voyage across the Atlantic Ocean by two Americans the Brothers Andrews*". Published in New York by EP Dutton and Co. 1880
http://archive.org/stream/adaringvoyageac00andrgoog#page/n12/mode/2up

Fig. 89 A late- Victorian photograph dated c.1900 looking west showing the Lifeboat House, Winch House and Pilchard Run, Capstan, Seine Boat, Jose Fish Cellar, roof of the Coastguard House, "Porthmellin cafe" site, Casley Refreshment Rooms, Serpentine shop, and nets drying over the wall and on the North Causeway. Photo courtesy B. Mundy.

Fig. 89a below. 1930s photo of the Slipway and a badly damaged South Pier. The photo shows the "*Snike*" which was used in the Dunkirk evacuation and later replaced by the *Pinda*. Photo courtesy B. Mundy..

Chapter 13 VICTORIAN VISITORS

Mullion Cove provided an attractive proposition to the Victorian visitor and tourist. But what was the attraction? The answer was the unique Sea Caves. In 1848 the Rev. C A Johns described Mullion Cove as *"... containing a Mill, which is worked by a stream running down through the valley, some fish cellars and a few humble cottages. Making our way to the beach between the seine boats hauled up beyond the reach of the surf...we find ourselves in one of the most romantic coves on the coast. Mullion Cove should be visited about mid day on the second or third day after a new or full moon. The tide is then low and several interesting spots may be inspected which at other times are inaccessible"* (1). Johns described the rocks as being very beautiful with a natural archway on the left, leading to an open part of the shore and further out with firm sand. He described a projecting mass of serpentine on the far side of which was the entrance to what is by far the most imposing cave on the coast which are accessible by land. He was of the opinion that

this cave was at one time filled with steatite (or soapstone) which had been worn away by the action of the sea.

Fig. 90 Torchlight Cave. Photo by author 2011.

He described the cave as being a huge chink between two sombre rocks, the entrances being partially blocked by a smooth black pillar, curved like the cut-water of a ship *"...a striking object when viewed externally, yet the view from within yet more so-impenetrable gloom above, brilliant light streaming in through the fissures, but revealing nothing behind-the smoothest of all possible sands-little pools of crystal water, so still that not even a sunbeam is seen to dance on them-richly dark rocks, so polished as to reflect light with a splendour scarcely to be endured-the blue sea with its curled edging of snow*

white lace-St. Michaels Mount, the fabled tower n the sea in the extreme distance ...." Johns described the first time he explored this cave in the company of a large group of schoolboys on holiday and how they had not got enough light to see inside, and how one of them had run to the village and brought back 18 candles, which, when lit were not enough to penetrate the gloom. On another visit he described how again he was drawn to the cave and, again, with insufficient light, but found the floor of the cave strewn with apples, sodden with seawater, washed from a ship recently wrecked at Lands End. Johns provided us with an interesting historical record of life in the Cove in the 1840s which he described as containing a Mill, some fish cellars and a few humble cottages on which, due to the ground rising behind them, the sun didn't shine in the winter. In one of the cottages lives an old man who had been blind for many years and *"though at all times contented and amiable, is glad indeed when the month of March is come, for he finds his solitary walk up and down the road in front of his cottage when he feels the blessed sunshine fall on his sightless eyes"* (1).

Census information reveals that the blind man was called William Williams, who was listed as living with the Hichens family. The large cave described by Johns, and later described in a Poem *"Porth Mellin"*, has come to be known as Torchlight Cave.

Rev Harvey, in writing of a visit said *"But here is the entrance to the cave, and here is the old fisherman Sam Hichens with his bundle of furze and tar dipped torch to lighten up its most innermost recesses. As you go in notice that bit of timber high above your head and jammed in so tightly between the rocks... a portion of the barque Chinchas that became a total wreck on the Loe Bar in 1859. It was washed up here and has been firmly held here ever since. But Sam is lighting up. Let us go in. Eh! What does he look like behind the smoke, and the flames flickering and dancing about him, and on the polished sides of this huge cleft. This must be seen to be appreciated. No description could convey its weirdness to the imagination. Stay now and admire it as you please, but take care that you are not caught by the returning tide*" (2).

Fig. 91 Late Victorian Photo of Mary Mundy. Courtesy B. Mundy.

The following was written in 1876 "The Lizard is famous for its cliffs and caverns. Many visitors post along the high road and miss the cliffs, and visit the shore at high water, and miss the caverns. You must time the tide carefully in visiting the Mullion Caves which are the best worth visiting and the least visited of all. The ordinary candles are not enough, better to have a lot of dry furze, to set in a blaze and reveal the height and depth of the great cave. The Mill, the fish-sellers, the few cottages, the island fronting the cave, make up a very pretty picture... Things alter on the line of coast, and the line of coast itself alters. There are grand caverns which have been frequented in their day by smugglers, but smuggling has practically been put down, and no one now is on intimate terms with the caverns (3).

On a tour of Cornwall in September 1881, taking a route by single horse carriage driven by her hired driver, Charles from Falmouth, Dinah Craik and her daughters visited the Lizard Peninsula. The driver said that he was hired about three times a week for such an excursion. Describing the trip she wrote; "*He*, (the horse), *seemed sensible of the attention and what was expected of him and started off as lively as if he had been idle for a week across the Lizard Down and Pradenack Down to the Old Inn at Mullion...I hope Mary Mundy will be at home. Of course you`ve heard of Mary Mundy*".

On arrival they were greeted by Marys` brother who said, "*Marys gone to Helstone Ladies. Her would have been delighted but hers gone marketing to Helstone.I hope her`ll be back soon, for I doesn`t know what to do without she. The house is full, and there's a party of eleven come to tea and actually wanting it sent down to them at the Cove. They won`t get it though. And you shall get your tea ladies, even if they have to go without*"... "*Hers very seldom out, us can`t get on at all without she*"... "*Never mind ladies you`ll get your tea alright. If Mary said she`ll be back at six, back she`ll be. And you`ll find a capital tea waiting for you. There isn`t a more comfortable Inn in all Cornwall.*"

The road from the village to the Cove was rough, which caused the ladies in the party to fear for the horse. "*Not at all Ma`am he`s used to it... often he comes here with picnic parties.. I`ll put him in at the Farm (Trenance) and be down with you at the Cove directly. You`ll find the rocks pretty bad walking, but there`s a cave you ought to see. We`ll try it. And when, after a steep and not too savoury descent-the cove being used as a fish cellar- we found ourselves on the beach shut in by those grand rocks of serpentine with Mullion Island lying ahead, about a ¼ mile off, we felt that we had not come here for nothing*". The great feature of Mullion Cove is its sea caves, of which there are two, one on the beach, and the other round the point, and feeling only accessible at low water. Dinah and her daughters continued through the first cave their way over the stones and seaweed in the dark. Charles, the driver encouraged them to go through into the cove saying "*Don't go back ma`am, you`ll be sorry afterwards. I`ll strike a light and help you. Slow and steady you`ll come to no harm. And it's beautiful when you get to the other end."*

Craik described the cove as follows... "*The most exquisite little nook, where you could have imagined a mermaid came daily to comb her hair. What a charming dressing room she would have, shut in on three sides by those great walls of serpentine, and in front the glittering sea, rolling in upon a floor of silver sand.*

There was an artist and her husband standing painting on an easel in the cove.

She recalled that, "*The tide was rising fast ...and, I remembered that the narrow winding cave was the only way out*"

Returning from the cave the author described how she could still recall the delicious sensation of paddling across the smooth sea sand, and of walking up the bed of a highland burn, the stream running down from the Mill, before climbing the cliff on the north side of the cove and watching the sea and the sky and the whole coastline, St Michaels Mount, Mounts Bay, and Lands End. Charles went on ahead to ready the horse and carriage at the Farm, saying to them *"You can`t miss your way ladies. Just follow the hedges, then cross the cornfield, and take to the hedges again. You`ll be at the Farmyard directly". "...In the field they gathered armfuls of cornflowers before reaching the farm with its old*

fashioned milk maid, sitting among her shining pails, her cows standing around her meekly waiting their turn.

Fig. 92 Source "An unsentimental Journey to Cornwall" 1884.

The cows were sleek, calm creatures, soft skinned and that peculiar grey colour as only seen in Cornwall. The carriage was taken back to the Old Inn, where Mary Mundy greeted them from the carriage. She had come home and everything was right. She was stood at the door to greet them- a brown eyed little faced woman with the reddest of cheeks and the blackest of eyes. She was, so to speak, public property, known and respected far and wide. The party was ushered to a neat little parlour at the back of the Inn where the tea was ready.
On the table were serpentine candlesticks, already lit, a bright teapot, a gigantic home baked loaf which it seemed sacrilegious to turn into toast, a rich yellow butter, and cream so thick the spoon could be almost stood upright in it. There was a quantity of that clotted cream, something which accompanied every meal. The recipe could not be obtained, Mary saying Oh, ma`am it would be of no use to you, Cornish cream can only be made   from Cornish cows."
Every sentence ended with the phrase "Please `m", such as "Yes, I`m glad you came, and I hope you`ll come again, please `m".

Fig. 93 Picture Source; "Mullyon;Its History, Scenery, and Antiquities. E.G Harvey 1875, affectionately known locally as the "Gull Book". Cave at Porth Pyg, Mullyon Cove. From a watercolour by Rev F.C. Jackson. Current location unknown

They left by the dim light of a newly risen moon and everything seemed solitary and ghostly. They crossed Pradenack Down where they saw coming from behind a furze bush a ghostly sight which mysteriously

crossed their path and stood in the middle of the road waiting for them... Was it a ghost? No, it was merely an old grey donkey. Such was the day- trip to Mullion Cove taken by Dinah Craik and her family in the 1880s (4).

Fig. 94 "A reconstruction of the Jackson scene perhaps - 135 years on."
Photo by author 2011.

Each year the tide can take away the sand in the Cove for weeks or even months at a time, and then bring it back again. Occasionally, in the past, it has brought back so much that it built a sand bank from the harbour right across to the Vro.(5)

The little rocky cave which begins opposite the "Black Loft" and runs through to the Cove is responsible for channelling the mass of seaweed which forms in the Harbour but it is the route which was taken 200 years ago by the quarry workers and even the fishermen to store and dry their nets. Today it is rarely used except by the adventurous visitor or those who take advantage of the beach surrounded by the vast arena of Serpentine cliff.

Bibliography

1. A week at the Lizard, Rev. C.A. Johns 1848
2. Rev E. Harvey Mullyon, Its History, Scenery and Antiquities.1875.
3. Manchester Courier and Lancashire General Advertiser 23.8.1876
4. Dinah Craik, An unsentimental journey through Cornwall 1884
5. Anecdotal from local resident.

Chapter 14 MULLION REGATTA

<u>Mullion Regatta</u>. 1896-1928.Thousands of holidaymakers, visitors and local people alike, will have watched, or even taken part in the "Mullion Regatta", an event which was once celebrated annually in the Cove. For many it was a holiday highlight and in the 1890s took place on the Friday before the August Bank Holiday.

Although not occurring every year the event was brought to life with the building of the Harbour Piers between 1890 and 1897.

Many of the names mentioned below will be well known to some local people.

Equally important are the names of the working Fishing Boats because they are the link to the past working life of so many fishermen in the Cove

Fig. 95 right A 1920s Regatta scene.
Courtesy Sue Truscott.

At the Mullion Regatta and Aquatic Sports event in August 1896, one of the first, it was said that there had never been so many people seen at Mullion before and crowds lined the cliffs and harbour in glorious weather. The secretary was Mr G. Williams, and together with the hard working committee they were able to offer a prize list of £30. Entries were so large that the Committee could arrange an embarrassing number of entries, and the 18 events went on into the dusk. It was impossible to complete the whole programme.

The 1896 results were as follows;
Lug Sail Crabbing boats 1.*Cadgwith* J Lambrick 2.*Primrose* W Russell 3.*Secret* Edward George,
Lieutenant Ayres offered a special prize of £1 for the first two boats to race each other again, which Cadgwith won.
Crabbing boats confined to Mullion and Gunwalloe 1.*Morning Star* W George 2 *Secret* E George 3*Surprise* G George.
Crabbing, Centre Keel Boats 1.*Morning Star*, W George 2. *Surprise* J George 3. *Secret* F George
Open Sailing Boats without Centre Keels 1. *Surprise* J George 2.*Britannia* S Mundy 3. *Kate* E George
Mosquito Fleet 1.*Mabel* W H Cox 2. *Lily* R Matthews 3.*Baby Jim* J Casley
Rowing Four Oars 1. *Kate* E George 2.*Ajax* F Downing 3.*Cornish Girl*, S Bray
Two Oars and Two Paddles 1. *Teaser* W George 2.*Boy Jim* E George 3.*Mary,* JH Wearne.
The swimming events were confined to Mullion.
The Silver Cup was won by J H George, presented by Mr J. James, 2. M Edwards, presented with an aneroid barometer by Mr Nankervis, and 3.R.Casley,who was presented with a tea service by Messrs. Matthews.
Lads under sixteen. Won by George Lobb. 2. Hubert Harry.
Professor Seamour Hicks gave an exhibition of ornamental swimming in the Harbour and a realistic example of life saving of someone who had fallen into the sea from the Harbour and a Torchlight procession concluded the Regatta (1).

The 1897 Regatta had been postponed for a week but it took place in early September in front of a good crowd of spectators. The weather created difficult swimming conditions but the competitors braved the elements.
Results were as follows,
The first sailing event was a 6 mile race for Crabbers.1.*Gleaner* John George 2.*Katie* H George 3.*Morning Star* W George. The second race was between Cadgwith and Mullion Crabbers won by Mullions *Morning Star,* W George.
The "Confined to Mullion" event was won by R Casley beating Herbert Harry. The 600 yard swim was won by Edwards beating Broadhurst in to 2nd spot. Both were members of the Royal Navy.
The Lifeboat House was used to supply a Public Tea with the Porthleven Reed and Brass Band on hand to supply the Music. The event was completed with a Torchlight procession to Churchtown. After the event a dispute blew up between W. George of Mullion and Mr Lambrick of Cadgwith resulting in a challenge being issued (2).

The 19th August 1898 saw the Regatta held in good weather and *"the beautiful cliffs being lined with spectators, whilst the new piers were occupied by a goodly crowd"*. A successful catch of pilchards meant that many local fishermen could not take part.

Some working boats participated and the Working Boat Race result was 1. *Grip* W George 2. *Cover* T Downing 3.*Cornish Girl* J Lugg. The veterans swimming race was won by Edwin Mundy from J Casley.

The Presidents Challenge Cup, a 10 mile Race for Crabbing Boats of any length, for the Cup with additional money prizes was won by *Maude* S Mundy, 2.*Morning Star* W George 3. *Gleaner*, J. George (3).

On 4th September 1899 large crowds were on the cliffs overlooking the cove, which was decked out with flags and bunting for the delayed Regatta. The morning's weather was quite rough and the Mark Boat for the sailing was not placed as far out as previously.

Mr William Sich of Halzephron, Gunwalloe was the President , Messrs G Harvey and J Brown RN were the Treasurers, O. Bosustow and J Nankervis were the Secs, George Beringer was the Timekeeper, CM Wood the starter for sailing and rowing and J James the starter for harbour sports. Some results were as follows; The Sailing races were on a triangular course, twice round the "Mark Boat", about 9 miles.

Open Lug sail crabbing u-21 feet 1. *Ettie* T Downing 2.*Glenmer* J. George 3. *Secret* E W George.

Boats belonging to Mullion and Gunwalloe any length without centre keels, for the Presidents Challenge and Money Prizes 1. *Ettie* Downing 2. *Maude* S. Mundy 3. *Secret* E W George Won by 15 seconds on time allowance

Rowing, open to all comers 4 oared race for working boats *1 Mary Sophia* 2. *Kate* 3. *The Covers Seining Co.*

Race for Cutters belonging to HM Coastguard 1. Porthleven 2. Mullion,

Pair of Paddles 1.T Hart The Lizard 2.E George 3. Matthews.

In the gig and punt race there was a dispute and the Committee reserved their decision. The Helston Volunteer band was in attendance and there were fireworks in the evening (4).

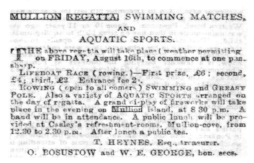

Fig. 96 Advert for 1901 Regatta

The Regattas were well advertised, even if it was at the last minute due to a change in the weather or a good catch of fish. It will be seen from the above advert that the event was followed in the evening by *"a grand display of fireworks on the island"*.

1905 was a bad year for the fishermen of Mullion. Unusually damaging summer storms caused the serious loss of both boats and nets, several of which were lost whilst within the Harbour itself. Monies were sent to the fishermen to help in their recovery, including by Sir Edwin Durning-Lawrence, the Victorian author, who sent 2 guineas through John Casley (5).

It was left to visitors to come to the rescue of the organisers, and in 1905 it was organised by Mr and Mrs Seymour Hicks. Both were famous and popular actors of the Edwardian era, their fame originating from their exploits in the Theatre and Musicals on the London stage. The programme for the event entitled *"The Fisherman`s Sports"*, was autographed by Mrs Hicks, who was more famously known at the time as Elleline Terriss (1871-1971). See Fig. 97 right

She was born in the Falkland Islands and had made her stage debut at Londons Haymarket Theatre at the age of 16, going on to appear in many stage plays and shows. Her career took her into both silent movies from 1913, and the early talkies from 1927. The sale of the signed programme provided much needed funds for the Fishermen of the Cove. The programme also contained a unique set of Rules drawn up by Mr H. Edgar Haines, the well known Victorian author and composer of Musicals.

After an "attic search" a copy recently came to light in the village.

It was a very enterprising early Edwardian event and the contributors were only too keen to support it.

The front page of the programme read as follows "*It has been suggested that the above afternoon should be devoted to Aquatic Sports for competition among the fishermen of Mullion Cove, and the Residents of Mullion, and subscriptions are invited from visitors to the neighbourhood, several of whom have already contributed. These subscriptions may be paid to the Proprietors of the Mullion Cove Hotel, Pollurian Hotel and the Poldhu Hotel or to Samuel Mundy Coxswain of the Mullion Lifeboat.*"

The 1905 Results were,
Sailing Race (1st Prize £2-10s) 1.*Ettie* T Downing 2.*Maud* S Mundy 3.*General Buller* J Gilbert
Rowing Oars & Paddles (1st Prize £1) 1.*Lora* W J Mundy 2.*Boy Jim* J Gilbert, 3.*Kathleen* J Downing Rowing Oars only (1st Prize 10s) 1*Lora* T Downing & W J Mundy 2. *Kathleen* W. Gilbert & J Downing 3.*Boy Jim* J H George and T Gilbert Gig and Punt Race(1st Prize 10s) Punt , J Downing
Swimming 200yds Visitors (1st Prize £1) 1. W Warton, Bristol 2. J Gaskin, Nottingham
Swimming 100 yards 1.George Wilson 2. Hubert Harry 3.W Sobey Swimming U- 16;1.T Green, 2. W Bray
Greasy Pole (Prize, A leg of Mutton) 1. J Sobey and J Downing,
Duck Hunt (Prize, A Duck and 2/6) George Wilson,.
Obstacle Race (1st Prize 10s) 1.George Wilson 2. H. Harry.
At the close Mrs Seymour Hicks (Elleline Terriss) distributed the prizes and after a vote of thanks they received 3 cheers (6). A copy of the 1905 Programme was recently rediscovered in a local loft without the owner realising its significance. Fig.97 below, A rare copy of the 1905 Regatta Event Programme.

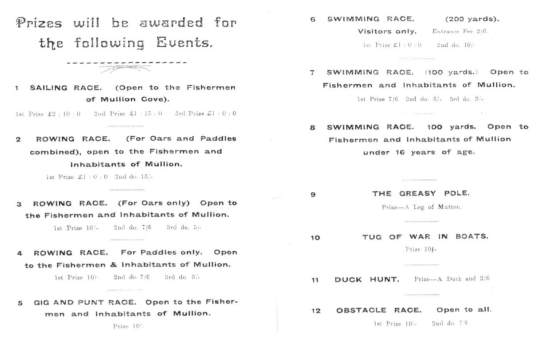

Prizes will be awarded for the following Events.

1 SAILING RACE. (Open to the Fishermen of Mullion Cove).
1st Prize £2 : 10 : 0   2nd Prize £1 : 15 : 0   3rd Prize £1 : 0 : 0

2 ROWING RACE. (For Oars and Paddles combined), open to the Fishermen and Inhabitants of Mullion.
1st Prize £1 : 0 : 0   2nd do. 15/-

3 ROWING RACE. (For Oars only) Open to the Fishermen and Inhabitants of Mullion.
1st Prize 10/-   2nd do. 7/6   3rd do. 5/-

4 ROWING RACE. For Paddles only. Open to the Fishermen & Inhabitants of Mullion.
1st Prize 10/-   2nd do 7/6   3rd do. 5/-

5 GIG AND PUNT RACE. Open to the Fishermen and Inhabitants of Mullion.
Prize 10/-

6 SWIMMING RACE. (200 yards).
Visitors only. Entrance Fee 2/6.
1st Prize £1 : 0 : 0   2nd do. 10/-

7 SWIMMING RACE. (100 yards.) Open to Fishermen and Inhabitants of Mullion.
1st Prize 7/6 2nd do. 5/- 3rd do. 3/-

8 SWIMMING RACE. 100 yards. Open to Fishermen and Inhabitants of Mullion under 16 years of age.

9 THE GREASY POLE.
Prize—A Leg of Mutton.

10 TUG OF WAR IN BOATS.
Prize 10/-

11 DUCK HUNT. Prize—A Duck and 2/6

12 OBSTACLE RACE. Open to all.
1st Prize 10/-   2nd do 7/6

By 1922 Motor Boats had arrived in Mullion and formed part of the entertainments.
The Motor Boat Race was won by J Gilbert, second was Jim Downing and third was John Bray. The Motor Boat Handicap was won by E.C. Montague beating Jim Downing. The Coastguards Paddles was won by W. Minns.
The Boat tug of war was won by Mullion, beating Cadgwith.

In 1924 the Regatta was again held in August, with some modifications to the motor boat races.
The Motor Boat Race, not exceeding 7hp was won by Montague Meyer in *Snipe* second was J Pascoe in *Patrice* and third *Maud* with W J Mundy.

In August 1926 the Regatta was held in flat calm conditions following a postponement of 5 days.
Results included; Motor Boat Race for 7hp boats 1.*5XX* Mr Claridge 2.*Snipe* Master John Meyer 3. *Seeker* R Roberts
Motor Boat Race confined to Crabbers 1.*Peaceful* T Downing 2. *Patrice* J Downing 3.*Two Brothers* Gilbert Brothers
Motor Boat Outboard Motors 1.*Billy* Mr Webster Cadgwith.
Pair Paddles boys u 21for Mullion Challenge Cup W Champion
Pair Paddles Boys u21 J Bray
Pairs Oars Men,1 Mundy & Pascoe 2.Gilbert & Pascoe. Swimming 200yds men 1.S Plomer St Keverne
75Yards Ladies Miss D Palmer Girls
Swimming 50 yards u 16 Miss Paddon
Wrestling on Marine Horses W.R George Mullion
Mullion Ladies Mop Fight, Miss Roberts. Greasy Pole, W A Pascoe, Helston (7).

The events were not without incident and in the 1928 Regatta in August held in front of crowds of people a local boat capsized while leading the other competitors, but the boat and occupants were rescued by a Motor Boat (8).
The Cumberland Challenge Cup Handicap was won by *Happy Dais,* G Claridge of Cadgwith.
The Pair oars, men 1.E Mundy and J Pascoe, 2.G Mitchell and B Stephens. The Ran-Dan was won by Mullion, J Pascoe. 2. *Cadgwith* G Mitchell 3. *Nita* B Stephens,
The Motor and Sail Race Handicap 1. *Boy Howard* W Thomas 2. *Purn* E Cumberland 3. *Tino Brothers* , W J Mundy.
The Motor Boat Race up to 7hp was won by *Snike* Master J Meyer, 2. *Lady Helen* H.Harry 3. *Patrice* Glen Pascoe.

In the years after 1920 there had been an introduction of motor boats to the Regatta and therefore an introduction of motor boats into the fishing way of life.

Regattas were watched by crowds of people but now the events, in particular swimming were often won, for example, by people on holiday from Cheltenham, London, Cheshire, Oxford and Cardiff. Local events were won by people living away from Mullion at Cadgwith, Porthoustock, or St. Mawes (8).

Fig. 98 above Lifeboat at Mullion Regatta and a good crowd in the Cove. Photo by author.

This was no doubt a sign of the coming of modern tourism and an increase in both affluence and mobility.

Although not covered in this book, there followed a gap in the Regatta Festivities which resumed in the 1970s, continuing until the 1990s, and occasionally afterwards. They have always been an entertaining feature for crowds of visiting families and local people alike who have taken away long lasting memories of life in Mullion Cove.

Fig 98a. Left The Lizard Lifeboat, a frequent visitor to the Cove in the late 1900s. Photo by author.

Bibliography

1. Cornishman 3.9.1896
2. Cornishman 9.9.1897
3. RCG 25.8.1898
4. Cornishman 7.9.1899
5. Cornishman 17.8.1905
6. Cornishman 24.8.1905
7. Cornishman 1.9.1926
8. Cornishman 23.81928

Porth Mellin Cove: A-nigh the Rustic Mill!
Had I the language to portray thy charms
How would I paint the emerald of thy waves
A-twinkling `neath the glow of morning sky
How would I hymn the murmurs of the air
The subtle melodies that sooth the ear-
How, raptured, tune my lyre to melody,
Caught from the dulcet tones of tidal tune;
And how hymn on my brain thy rugged cairns
Whose every fissure gleams sun glorified
Alas! `twere vain. Cast aside brush and pen
These rocks, these seas, this witchery of sky
Baffle the pencil and defy the muse.

We catch a glory glimpse and stand enchained
We try to give the pristine picture forth
That other eyes may see, and be made glad.
How futile is the effort! While we gaze
The panoramic wonders shift and change;
Fresh charms reveal them. Lo the swelling tide,
The bounding breakers, or the dancing boat;
With shout of fishermen, made musical,
As rising to these cliffs through fields of air
It tells of spoil within the tiny craft,
And landward hailed, is hauled from out the brine.
Higher, still higher mount we these green cliffs;
Each moment brings revealings -grand, sublime!

On this grey peak, low- seated, will we gaze
And dream a blissful dream, until soul- steeped
With gladness, we low murmur "God is good"!
And our God given earth is very fair.
O, Lord we thank the, thou hast given us eyes to see
And hearts to be made glad with Thy fair works,
Thee would we praise and bless for evermore.

Through the blue ether sail the silvery gulls-
Now perching on the rocks in companies
Now preening wings, now dipping in the wave
Delighted, in their joy they Praise Thee Lord.!

In swift aerial flight the butterfly,
Whose wings prismatic, `tinct with glorious dye,
Dance in the sunbeams, and brown-vested bees,
Who flit from flower to flower, in mazy mirth,
And hum aloud their bliss, they praise Thee Lord!

The cattle, now slow winding up the hill,
That soon will ruminate and low content
Upon the grassy slopes, and these meek sheep
That browse upon the cliffs,they praise Thee, Lord!

Ye all give m*ed of praise. Even these bells,
Those waxen heath-bells, marvels of thy skill
In their fair vesture,- amethystine, white,

And rosy tinted, from the turf look up,.

Ev`n they, in tinkling music, praise Thee, Lord

How boldly rises Henscaths Iron Rock,
And Scoverns Crown, unscaled by foot of man!
How grandly glow their dark titanic ribs-
Naked undecked, save with scant robe of moss
Old ocean fretting ever at their base

Beyond Henscath, the Coastguards rounded bluff
And tiny shelter-house from storms retreat
Behold him- blue frocked gazing o`er the main
Not as of `erst, full dubious of the craft
That nears the strand. No smuggling there,-huge crabs
And long clawed crayfish freight the fisher boats
And note you man, low seated on the verge
Of the green hill awaiting the pilchard- shoals
He is the Huer, and on their approach,
Discerned by ruddy tint upon the wave,
He heralds the glad sight with hue and cry,

From his long sounding trumpet horn, and lo!
`Tis echoed loudly from the hill to coast,
And all the land is soon alive with men;-
Seine boats are manned and launched, and heva shout
Tells the waiting ones "The fish has come"!
Those grand grey shelving stretches of cliff rock
How gleam they in bold contrast, tapestried
With clumps of samphire, green- coronalled
And hiding their black sides `neath mantling grass
From which glossed sea-ferns spring, and laugh in glee
When they are kissed by foam flakes from the brine
Sweet vesturing they make, gold samphire and green moss,
To rocks, that would frown them grim and stern

From this long stretch of rugged cliff we look
Far to the left past Pradannacks head
And many other green-clad, sunny cape
And interlying gully, fringed with foam
There resteth Kynance, Mullyons twin sister,

Enthroned amid her walls of serpentine,-
The peerless princess of the Lizard Coast,
Whose praises ever ring throughout the land.
And still beyond, though undiscernible
The Lighthouses Towers gleam and glow by night –
A blessed beacon for bold mariners
When sailing nigh the treacherous Lizard Coast.

Nearer we gaze down wondrous rifts of rock,
Through narrow creek to Cove of sparkling sand
And from its point delightfully we scan
The famous Gull Rock whose hoar head glows grand,
Yet grandly desolate. Her birds have flown
To lands afar, or nearer Helfords banks
Whose tidal stream affords them sustenance
Their broods are long since fledged, and till the spring
Comes back and wooes them to return, the gulls
And greedy cormorants will rejoice everywhere.
So nigh it lies that from these sunny downs
We bridge the watery pass, and fancy roam

Among those peaks till shudderingly we gaze

Upon its base where waters leap and curl
At dreadful depths defiantly. Anon
We rest our dazzled eyes on Mullion Isle
Like a huge Lion crouching in the sea
With face turned westward to Boleriums coast
Catching the glory of the sunlit skies

Old Enys Pruens Fair, round bosomed isle
Athwart whose sides the waves rest peacefully
And oft give haven to a storm tossed craft
Else rent to fragments by the rocks ashore
Upon her breast the mallow sheds her bloom
And ruddy beet, while at her feet there lie
Fair seaweeds ever at fantastic play
In the translucent pools made animate
With myriad marvel of anemone
And sporting creature of the finny tribe

Long rest we, tranced with witchery of the scene
Mullyons soft beach still bears the crystal waves
That fill her Porths, that guard her corridors
That o`er sands glow as doth malachite,
And clear reveal her underlying rocks,-
Rocks that, when tides are low, stud all the Cove
In polished blocks, fantastic, beautiful!
These massive boulders and these circling heights,
Iron and Hornblende, or red serpentine,
Bossed with green spleenwort,
tressed with sea-drenched grass

Ope to a cave Ah me! How weird and vast,
How beauteous in its rock stained tracery!
`Tis flashed with many-tinted bands of light,
Anear its mouth, where drops pellucid fall
And percolate the stream be-fretted walls,
their impress leaving in the lapse of time.
Blacks frowns its roof; its closing walls of gloom
Gather about one until, half dismayed,
The awe-struck mind, aghast, sinks impotent
Afraid to gaze into its hidden depths,-
Afraid the tide that never long forsakes
May quick return, and cut off our retreat
Unless as oft, old Sam, the fisherman
Appears in sight, when furze fires from the rock
And lighted flambeaux, the grand scene reveal,-
Its gaping fissures and its still rock-pools:
Lost in the dark mysteries are, save in small part,
In dim recesses, where no sunbeams shine;
Away beneath these cliff-downs, this grand cave
And its rock treasures stretch them undiscerned,
Yet legend haunted, as befits the scene.

A summer picture now is ours; The moon,
In its meridian splendour, flashes down
Its shafts of light,and heat. How grateful wafts
The Atlantic sea-breeze,that cool fans the brow.
Ah! What a panorama of fair coast,
Mapped out beyond this twinkling sweep of sea,
A glorious amphitheatre of cliff,
E`en toTol-pedyns heights,ten leagues afar.

Ridge upon Ridge, jagged rock, and rounded carn,

Beaches whose white plains glitter, and wee shores
That lure the fisher-boats; Porth Levens strand;
Tregonnings noble hill, light aureoled:
And distant towans; Marazion strand,
And her peaked isle, crowned with Cornwallias Mount;
Beloved Penzance, shrine of sweet memories!
And Lone Lamorna sleeping twixt her hills.
How bounteous glows each well-remembered spot!
`Tis hard to break the spell, and flee away;
But we must trend the green declivity,
With hurried step, oer thrift and verdant grass.
We gain the Cove. We waft a fond adieu!
And soon Porth Mellin and the sounding sea,
The pretty lifeboat house and fisher-cots
With lazy mill-wheel, and the brattling stream
Are lost in distance; and the hills and dales
Alone, responsive, echo our farewell.

Published in the Cornishman 5.12.1878

Chapter 16   A VIEW FROM ABOVE THE COVE

The Victorian era saw a rapid increase in the number of visitors coming to Cornwall and the introduction of the Railways made travelling easier. Although it was anticipated that the Railway might be extended from Helston or Falmouth to the Lizard Peninsula it did not materialise, but there was an increase in the construction of large hotels in anticipation. 1889 saw the construction of the Pollurian-House Hotel at Pollurian Cove and in 1899 the Poldhu Hotel was opened, but shortly before that came the building of a Hotel in the Cove.

Fig. 99 right Old Cannon overlooking the Cove. Photo by author 2012.

A story exists, recorded in 1824, that above the Cove is a place called the Beacon, in Trenance tenement, from where a Watch was kept during the Civil War, and that there was a large cannon in place. An old man was stationed there to keep guard in case an enemy arrived. One night fishermen arrived unannounced and the watchman shouted "*Who comes here*?" The fishermen replied from their boat below "*Fish and panniers*". The old man, obviously confused, thought he had heard "*French and Spaniards*" and set fire to his beacon, spreading general alarm around the whole coast which took a long time to calm (1).

In 1897 The Mullion Cove Hotel Company announced that they were to begin the process of building a Hotel on the cliffs overlooking Mullion Cove. A road to the site was financed by Lord Robartes and it was declared that the new Hotel would be due to open by Easter 1898 (1a). The contract was won by Messrs. Winn and Son of Helston, and the Hotel was inaugurated in August 1898.

Situated on top of the cliffs overlooking Mullion Cove it commanded a view over a wide area. From the upper rooms it had a view of Constantine and Mabe, while to the north a view of Wendron and Crowan, while to the west Porthleven, St. Michaels Mount, Penzance, Newlyn and on to Tol-pedn Penwith.

Fig. 100 Mullion Cove Hotel.
Photo by author 2012.

It stands in two acres of ground and is built of local stone. It has an 80` frontage bounded by two bays having two windows each, between which had a covered veranda. The main entrance is on the south front with balconies above giving views of the Cove and Mullion Island. Inside it had an elaborate pitch pine staircase, and on the ground floor reading rooms, billiard rooms, rooms for coffee drinking, and 2 large sitting rooms. Ahead was the lavish dining room measuring 34` x 19`. Lighting in the Hotel was provided by 140 electric globes. There were 35 bedrooms on the first and second floors, all electrically lit. The second floor had 18 bedrooms.

On the first floor were 2 drawing rooms one facing west and the other facing south. Each floor was supplied with a modern suite of lavatories and bathrooms. The drain ran down over the cliff on the west side of the hotel and deposited a distance from the hotel into deep water. Other buildings at the hotel included a picnic room, laundry, detached stabling and coach house with provision for cycles. The Picnic Room was a very popular addition to the Hotel and was frequented by many visitors to the area. Not long after inauguration, in August 1898 it was already catering for the many people who attended the local Mullion Cove Regatta.

Furnishings were supplied by Messrs James and son of Helston, one of 13 tenders for the contract. They also won the contract for supplying earthenware, china and glass.

The cutlery and plate was supplied by Elkington of Birmingham and linen by Rapson and Co of Helston. A luggage lift was fitted, and the kitchens and larder together with the servant's dining room were arranged on the north wing with a separate stair service communicating with the cellar in the basement, and the upper floor.

The water supply, financed by Lord Robartes, was piped directly from an adit in the old copper mine to the south, down to a pumping house with double action pumps which were worked by a small water wheel, the power being derived from the Mill stream. It was then forced via a hydraulic Ram Pump through a 2" main up the north slope of the valley into a large concrete reservoir at the top of the ridge which held 12,000 gallons before supplying the Hotel by gravitational feed.

The electricity was provided by a Crossley 7hp oil engine which was worked by a dynamo in a specially built engine house at the rear of the hotel. The engine and dynamo were supplied by electricians Messrs Veale and Co of St. Austell. The formal opening of the hotel was attended by the Committee and table was laid for 65 invited guests. The chairman of directors was Arthur Pearse Jenkin of Redruth. Also present were Rev Scholefield, (Vicar of Mullion), C C Hicking (Mayor of Helston), William George, James Roberts, Alexander Shephard, A.H. Jenkin, Samson Hill (Architect) and W J Winn (Contractor).

The list of those present also included the following; Hedley Thomas, James Roberts and A P Shepherd (Directors), W. Roskruge, George Lory, A. Pengilly, J. W. Tyacke, John James, F.W. Jeffery, R. Joyce, W. J. Winn, S. Hill, R.G Rapson, J Nankervis, W George, Jnr, W. J. Hendy,   J. Jeffrey, J. Guy, R. Dunn, Joseph Hendy, W. Rowe, J. H. Shepherd, Thomas Davey, Franklin Mundy, W Kemp, Thomas Joyce, John Toy,   Mrs C. C. Hocking, Mrs A. Pengilly, Mrs J. Jeffery, Misses Williams, M. Williams and George.

In a speech the Rev Scholefield said that there were three interests in the village of Mullion, Fishing, Farming and the accommodation of strangers, and it seemed that the third interest was going to be first. Mr John Roberts of London, formerly of the Lizard said that he "...*was delighted to see the contractor present. The Mullion Cove Hotel was so substantially built that "Winns" would never blow it away"*.

Mr Hocking said that as far as the situation was concerned they could not possibly get a better site and he considered that they had dropped on the most unique spot they could imagine in Cornwall. The manageress was Mrs Prisk. (2) (3).

Mullion was still primarily a Temperance area and when the Mullion Cove Hotel Company made an application for a Licence for the Hotel they were aware that there may be objections. An application was made by Mr A.H. Jenkin for a Full Licence. He told the Magistrates that if Sunday drinking was a concern then the directors would be happy with a 6 day Licence. There were petitions and objections presented by Mr A.R. Thomas and they came from, Mullion Parish Council, a number of Farmers, businessmen and fishermen, and from the Temperance Society of the Parish, Helston Council of Evangelical Free Churches, including between 40 and.50 Churches, and Mr G.L. Bodilly representing Mr Sobey who had been refused a Licence for a house in the village.

A six day Licence was granted by the bench as long as there was an undertaking that no bar would be opened and no intoxicating drink would be served in the Picnic Room (4).

In April 1899 Veale and Co laid the electric cabling form the Hotel to the pier head from where an electric light would be fitted and it was also said that seven cottages were to be built behind the Hotel for the Coastguard.

In the Cove, Casley Refreshment Rooms were a popular company with a room in a wooden building which later

became The Retreat. It was popular with tourists and the proprietor also made and sold serpentine ornaments. It closed down around 1909 but the Refreshment Rooms were reopened in July 1910 by the Mullion Cove Hotel.

Fig. 101 Left; Fishermen in front of the Refreshment Rooms. Left to Right "Jip" the dog, Eddie Mundy, William Gilbert, William Thomas, Willie Gilbert, William John Mundy, Mrs.William Gilberts. Photo Courtesy B Mundy.

By 1913 the popularity of the Mullion Cove had increased and it became a tourist attraction for many people from London. Newspapers recorded many stories about the Cove, all complimentary.

One unnamed member of a group of visitors described Mullion as "*being a world away*". She wrote that "*For the time they have hung up the receiver of the telephone, and if you want to find them you must hunt the golf links or the cliff sides, or chase them through the sparkling bay.... There is a burly boatman to row you* (to the island)*...one who is a boatman and something more. From his build you would think that skipper* (John) *Casley was always on the water, but in wintertime he is always fashioning the gloriously veined serpentine into beautiful and useful articles to tempt the* *admiring visitor. It is good to be an artistic craftsman and good also to turn from the lathe and the emery paper to the boat and the salt air and the song of the sea amongst the hollows ...We step into the boat, reach the distant strand, shed our trappings of servitude and civilisation, and in a moment are rolling around in a limitless bath with white sand below and an emerald lake sea around us, for the water is as smooth as a polished mirror".* The writer describes climbing the Island where the gulls nest, *"...and see the three maidens having their 1400 yard swim to the Island and back from the Harbour, as if they were sporting mermaids...after tea bathe in the well washed harbour, a magnificent bath between the boats"* and then they are back into the car to London, and Mullion is a dream (7).

The Refreshment Rooms were also used as accommodation and descendants of families who lived there in the 1920s still live in the Cove.

<u>Cove Hotel Bathing Huts</u>

Many visitors may remember that The Mullion Cove Hotel erected 4 bathing huts in the Cove. It is understood that they were in use in the 1950s and possibly 1960s before being removed shortly afterwards. Today, a rustic wooden seat has been erected, in a perfect position to watch the world go by.

One of the finest writers of Cornish History was a man called Alfred Kenneth Hamilton Jenkin (1900-1980). In 1945 he accepted an invitation to join the Directors of the Mullion Cove Hotel Co. Ltd of which his family were one of the main founders (10).

Born in Redruth, his father was Alfred Hamilton Jenkin. A.K. Hamilton-Jenkin was a founder bard of the *Gorseth Kernow* and he was involved in setting up the Cornwall Record Office in Truro.

He was elected president of the Royal Institution of Cornwall in 1958 and 1959 and also President of the Federation of Old Cornwall Societies.

<u>The Huers Hut</u>

On the cliffs directly in front of the Cove Hotel were the remains, now overgrown with vegetation, of an old Huers Hut dating back at least to the 19th Century.

The Huers had an important full time job which they undertook in all weathers. No road existed to this hut until 1898 when the Hotel was being constructed so until then it would have been quite isolated and would have been in a field full of cows. It was a unique structure which was characterised by a stone base constructed in the shape of a boat, with the roof being an upturned boat. The bow pointed north and it was a weatherproof structure. Barry Mundy remembers the Hut and has drawn a representation of this unique structure. He actually says that drawing was his only successful subject at school. See for yourself. (See Appendix D)

<u>Aerial View</u>
Early 1900s aerial photographs are not common. The very Low-Tide photo below, believed to date from between 1927 and 1934 shows there is evidence of serious damage to the seaward end of the South Pier. The Refreshment Rooms have not yet been rebuilt as The Retreat. It appears to have been taken in the mid 1920s.

Fig. 102 Aerial View of the Cove looking towards the NE.
Buildings date the Photo from 1927-1934.

To the east of the "Porthmellin Cafe" site are the small cottages known as "*Gull Rock*" which were initially constructed of wood and later rebuilt. Wooden buildings were not uncommon in the Cove during the early 20th century. On land which originally formed part of the Mullion Mill Farm another building was constructed in the 1920s. It was originally a dwelling called "The Ark", but was also the site of a small Serpentine Turners shop, run by a man called Roberts from the Lizard. Today it is known as the Potter's Wheel.

It was initially of wooden construction but this was knocked down and the current shop and dwelling constructed.

Oscar Hill, 81, remembers how, on a Sunday evening he and a large number of other local teenagers would walk to the Cove from the village, and one of the things which kept them occupied there was singing. They would sit on the wall behind the West Pier and entertain themselves with a song or two, assisted by Basil Williams, husband of Kitty, who had the Cafe upstairs from its present location. Basil would sell them Lemonade and Crisps from the door at the bottom of the stairs, and so began the Porthmellin Cafe.

It was soon afterwards in 1953 that Oscar left the area to join the RAF. How times have changed.

After the War, people wanted the peace and tranquillity afforded them by a life in the Cove and began to move to the locality. In 1946, after many holidays in the area, Archie Camden, principal bassoonist with the BBC Symphony Orchestra, along with his wife, Jan Kerrison, Cellist, Pianist and Composer took a cafe in the Cove for a while in the hope of a different way of life. The Cove was a retreat for many from the everyday bustle.

Ernest Bevin,(1881-1951) a Government Minister, spent many private holidays in the Cove staying at The Retreat.

Film Stars in the Cove.

The Cove has been used as a scenic backdrop for Films which have sometimes have sometimes brought famous stars to the Cove.

Pola Negri.

Pola Negri. In July 1929 the village of Mullion received a visit from a large film crew and an actress who was well known at the time, Hollywood actress Pola Negri (1897-1987).(Fig. 103) Born in 1897 she appeared in films in her native Poland and was the first European actress to be invited to Hollywood where she achieved fame, becoming the richest female actress of her era. She was associated with the likes of Rudolph Valentino, who, it was said, was intending to marry before his untimely death in 1926. Her film, part of which was filmed in Mullion, was at the time called "Seat of the lost" (*but later changed to "The Way of Lost Souls"*). *In the film the heroines` lover had committed a murder and returned to her for shelter, but she refused. A Fishermans wife saw him and informed Police who searched for him in the village.* In the afternoon the film crew went to Mullion Cove and filmed her climbing over the rocks to deliver food to her lighthouse keeper husband. Whilst there, the film crew also filmed the "villain" scrambling over the rocks looking for a hiding place. It was said that

they had great difficulty in tempting a flock of gulls to fly in the background as Miss Negri walked along the pier (12).

Clark Gable and Gene Tierney

In 1953 Mullion entertained the famous duo Clark Gable and Gene Tierney in the making of their film "*Never Let me go*" based on the Cold War romantic drama "*Came the Dawn*" by Roger Bax (aka Paul Winterton).

The supporting cast included Bernard Miles, and Kenneth More. A Moscow based newspaper reporter Philip Sutherland played by Clark Gable was in love with Marya, a ballerina with the Bolshoi Ballet, who he marries. He attempts to get her out of Russia, and accompany him to San Francisco. The Russian authorities are opposed to her leaving and a plan is hatched to get her out of the country on a boat. The plan, set in Russia, almost fails but both are involved in a car chase which eventually results in them both swimming to safety. Part of the chase was conducted and filmed in Mullion Harbour, with the car seen to drive at a fast speed at night along the north and west sections of a pier before going off the end into the sea. They both leapt to safety and swam to a waiting boat (13).

Apparently the actors provided much interest and entertainment in the village during their stay, especially Gable driving his open topped Sports Car through the village. He was known to visit the cafe in the Cove where he would ask for "Scrambled eggs".

Other Film and TV productions were set in the locality, more recently part of an episode of TV Detective show Wycliffe was filmed from the Cove Hotel.

"Voyage of the Dawn Treader"

Not the film itself, but**...** about 7am on 2nd September 2010 dawn in the Cove was greeted by the sight of an overnight visitor, better known for exploits in the film *Chronicles of Narnia; Voyage of the Dawn Treader*. Normally known as the "*Matthew*", a replica ship, she was adapted to promote the film in 2010.

Fig. 104 The converted "*Dawn Treader*" near to "Treguin", Mullion Island in the background. Photo by author 2010.

The ship was on its travels around the coast, escorted by the Lifeboat *Mabel Alice*, which in 1983 was stationed at Penlee and both vessels had moored in the shelter of Mullion Island for an overnight stay. By mid morning she had bid her farewell. A number of films have been made in Mullion Cove over the years related to Tourism, Documentaries and episodes of TV programmes.

Bibliography

1. History of Cornwall Hitchins and Drew 1824
1a. Cornishman 17.6.1897
2. RCG 11.8.1898
3. Cornishman 11.8.1898
4. RCG 8.9.1898
5. Cornishman 20.4.1899
6. Cornishman 1.9.1910
7. Cornishman 28.8.1913
8. Cornishman 5.8.1897
9. www.cornwallartists.org/cornwall-artists/william-casley
10. Cornishman 1.3. 1945
11. Cornishman 24.2.1949.
12. Western Morning News 15.7.1929
13. .http://www.imdb.com/title/tt00461

Chapter 17   THE FUTURE FOR MULLION COVE

Before the future, a little more about the past and the present.
The Campaign for the Protection of Rural England (CPRE) was formed in 1926 in order to limit urban sprawl and ribbon development. It has had an influence on Public Policy relating to Town and Country planning in England, notably in the formation of National Parks and Areas of Outstanding National Beauty.(AONB)

In 1935 the Cornwall Council for the Preservation of Rural England (CPRE) met to discuss the preservation of land from Kynance Cove to the Lizard which had now been passed to the National Trust. As a result of the discussion steps were taken to preserve the coast from Kynance to Mullion Cove. It was said that it would be a disaster if building continued from Mullion towards Kynance Cove and special steps should be taken in collaboration with the National Trust to preserve the area (1). In March 1937 a 2 mile stretch of coast from Mullion Cove to Predannack Head was preserved for the nation. This was due to the benefaction of Mrs Peggy Pollard of St. Mawes, Hon. Secretary of the Cornwall Branch of the Council for the Preservation of Rural England (CPRE). She secured restrictive covenants over 3 headlands, linking them up, which would preserve them as open spaces, accessible to the public, in perpetuity. The three headlands were Laden Ceyn, Men-te-Heul and Pedn Crifton which run from Mullion Cove south towards Predannack.
The area was described as a valuable botanical site, not only with unique plants, but even in the 1930s there had been sightings of the Chough and Peregrine Falcon. The site covered approximately 90 acres. The lands and covenants were handed over to the National Trust (2).
National Trust Records published in the Mullion Harbour Study Report provide some information in connection with damage which has occurred to the Harbour over the years. In the early years up until 1914 maintenance of the Piers was carried out as and when required by a Mullion stonemason James Harry. He is remembered hanging over the edge of the piers in a supporting sling pointing the gaps in the wall.

Mullion Cove was purchased in 1928 by Montague Meyer. During the 1930s there was more damage to the South Pier.
During World War II there were problems in maintaining many small harbours in Cornwall. There was concern expressed at the Cornwall Sea Fisheries Committee Meeting in 1944 that restoration work was needed at Mullion. It was noted that at this time the fishermen were in dispute over fees and this didn't help the situation. It was said that £1000 was required to put the harbour right again. It was decided to write to the District Council and the owner in the hope that matters could be resolved (3).
In May 1945 Mullion Cove and Island was acquired by the National Trust via the munificence of the owner Mr Montague Meyer. About 25 years earlier Mr Meyer had purchased the Harbour, Island and Fish Cellars from Viscount Clifden, and gifted 12 acres to the Trust.
It was said, "*Mullion Cove is one of the show places around the Cornish Coast. It ranks with Kynance Cove, Lands End, and Gurnards Head as one of the finest bits of Cornish Coastal scenery and has for years been the resort of countless visitors who have revelled in its unique setting. The news that it is to become national property will give great satisfaction to inhabitants of Mullion Village and Mullion Cove*" (4).
Fig. 105 Mullion Cove in the 1950s Photo courtesy J. Meyer.

Storm Damage.

Storm damage was always an issue for Harbours in Cornwall especially those exposed to full force of storms and the strong tides. Prior to, and during 1947 the South Pier was further damaged by storms. A total of 15 feet of wall fell from the end of the south pier, and the National Trust which had sole responsibility for the maintenance, launched an appeal for £2000 to safeguard the pier from further damage.

Fig. 106 Damage to a vulnerable section of the South Pier. Photo by Author 2012

The National Trust Representative, Mr Alan Ladner, a Civil Engineer living above the Cove, prepared a report for the Institute of Civil Engineers. He said that if the outer arm fell it would probably block the mouth of the Harbour. A survey was conducted and the Ministry of Works granted approval for a start to be made but the costs were increasing and the National trust feared that the work could not be started until the spring of 1948 (8).

Although the National Trust said that there were only a small number of boats using the Harbour, Mr R Downing, former Harbour Master said that if the outer wall went, boats could only be left on their moorings in fine weather, otherwise they would have to be hauled out at great inconvenience. Mr Edward George, 84 years, said that he remembered the Harbour being constructed and spoke of seas which swept over the Harbour Walls in winter with such violence that they shook the structure (5).

In May 1949 the National Trust London SW1 placed a contract to save Mullion Harbour and appealed for funds which they asked to be sent to the Mullion Appeal Fund (6).

In 1950 the National Trust were suggesting that, though repair was economically unjustifiable, the Trust has felt bound on aesthetic grounds to undertake the costly repairs. (1950 National Trust Guide, Places of natural beauty) & (7).

In 1954 a repair was carried out on the south pier which meant that 12` was cut off at an angle and capped with concrete in order that it could be rebuilt on solid rock. It gave it a substantially different profile from that known today. During the 1950s storm damage to the piers, and occasionally the associated buildings was a regular occurrence.

National Trust Records show damage between 1951- March 1952, September 1953, January and April 1955, October 1959- January1960, December 1994, January and September 1998, October 2004 (8).

An expensive repair was also carried out on the west pier which required steel piles to be driven into the rock, and concrete was added to shore up the wall at the base. The concrete can still be seen around the base of the west pier at very low tide.

In the 1970s general repairs were conducted to the Harbour including grouting and pointing.

In the 1970s cracks began to appear requiring further work to be carried out, and in 1976 repairs were conducted to the wall under the Steps.

In 1971 a Harbour Users Group was established, initially chaired by a local Trust Member, but later by Mr Barry Mundy. The Harbour Users group held meetings and dealt with user issues, with a Harbour Master and deputy who collected fees etc.

In 1978-early1979 further work was necessary and the sloping face of the south pier was removed and rebuilt vertically and metal bolts ("Ties") placed through the whole structure (8).

From 1975 until 1990 the User Group was also involved, in setting up and operating an Annual Harbour Regatta Day assisted by local people. The Regattas, organised by local people from Mullion, which were so popular in the 1890s until about 1928 again proved to be extremely popular, attracting hundreds of adults and children over the years.

In some years donations were made to local charities, with the bulk of the money going to Harbour maintenance.

The angled wall was removed and granite and serpentine was used to rebuild the wall to its original shape at a cost reported to be £35,000.

During the 1990s, specifically in 1992, 1995 and 1998 repairs were reported by the National Trust to cost £1 million were made. In 1995 there was damage to wall stone, and work including the rebuilding the bridges which led from the Net Loft to the South Pier were undertaken (8). Over the years the Harbour was monitored by a committee of local semi professional people connected to the National Trust who liased with the harbour users, took fees and dealt with minor matters including small maintenance requirements. These repairs were carried out by local builders.

The National Trust subsequently decided that the management of the Harbour should be undertaken from Lanhydrock which reduced the requirement for a local group. Storm damage has occurred on a regular basis since and repair work now seems to be a continual, if very slow process.

Fig. 107 Repair work conducted on the South Pier in early 2010 has again been subjected to storms which by December 2011 had resulted in further serious damage. Photo by author April 2010

The need to effect repairs of Mullion Harbour Piers has continued, and the National Trust have spent over a million pounds on repairs since 1990 (9).

To quote from the report, "*The increasing repair and maintenance costs and the limited funds that are available required the development of a sustainable strategic vision for Mullion Harbour. The Mullion Harbour Study was commissioned in 2004.The NT South West Region recognised the key issues and developed a project to ensure the long term future of the Harbour*".

With published scientific study tending to lean towards future sea level rises and climate change, the National Trust has looked at possible future management of the Harbour in Mullion Cove.

They realised the effect that the loss of the harbour would have on the locality as a whole and are trying to manage a solution, anticipating that any change may not be simple. They have suggested some alternative projects as ways to move forward.

a) An Offshore Breakwater. The aim would be to reduce wave height and penetration with an offshore barrier. In 2004 this was regarded as requiring technically challenging engineering works, a multi stage consenting process and full environmental impact assessment.

b) Maintenance and Repair. The aim would be to extend the life of the Piers in their present form by ongoing planned maintenance. The report says that "*The Harbour was assessed to have a good potential lifespan as long as repairs are carried out as needed, at minimum annually*". Problems arose when "*...damage from one storm event couldn't be repaired before the next caused further damage*".

c) Managed retreat, as distinct from unmanaged reactive retreat. It was reported that without maintenance and repair it was likely that the west and south breakwaters would have to be removed within 10-20 years.

d) Maintenance and repair until the harbour suffered major damage and began to fail at which point the managed strategy would change to Managed Retreat.

A study by Halcrow in 2006 identified the "Maintain and Repair" option as the preferred management strategy for Mullion Harbour for the next 100 years and recommended to the National Trust that it be implemented. The Report also outlined areas which would require both structural repair and general maintenance (8).

Although the overall plan is structured to cover the next hundred years, there is no change in the preferred option which means that damaged Piers may not be fully repaired.

Bibliography

1. WMN 17.6.1935
2. WMN 30.3.1937.
3. WMN 10.3.1944
4. WMN 17.5.1945
5. WMN 19.7.1947
6. Western Daily Press 21.5.1949
7. Cornishman 20.7.1950
8. National Trust Mullion Harbour Study Final Report January 2006, Halcrow Group Limited and BSW Ltd..
9. http://www.coastalpartnershipsnetwork.org.uk/core_files/NTra4.pdf
   National Trust June 2010. Bartlett, Cameron, Dyke, Woodall.

CONCLUSION

Many people who visit Mullion Cove do so without knowing anything about its history or true connection with the sea. From before the 1700s to the early1900s it formed part of the Mounts Bay Fishery. Fish, Crabs, Lobsters and Crawfish were plentiful along the coast of the Lizard and the traditional fishing techniques were well practiced. The Industry was directly connected with Newlyn, from where most of the catch was despatched to Italy. Local men in the village of Mullion nearby would form the crew of the seine boats during the season, and women and children would be employed in the local processing which took place in Fish Cellars, but it was still a seasonal occupation and nearly everyone involved worked on local Farms or sought other employment. Pilchards, preserved in salt, along with other locally caught fish also formed a major part of the local winter diet, salted away over the winter.

From the mid 18th Century there was industrial activity in the Cove itself with the mineral Soapstone being quarried for Porcelain manufacture, but also nearby valuable "Native" Copper was mined from what was then known as Ghostcroft Mine, but later was known as Wheal Unity and Trenance Mine, before finally closing on 1852, during a downturn which affected much of the area.

In the Cove itself there were also Mills which took grain, provided flour and feed for Cattle, and also for bread in the local community.

In mid 1700s, despite ongoing wars with France, smuggling or "Free Trade" took place between the two countries on a regular basis, and it was said that "wrecking" was prevalent along the coast. These activities were regulated by soldiers until 1748, and in the early 1800s by the early Coastguard men, but it wasn't until the 1840s and 1850s that some element of control was achieved.

By the early 1800s there was a marked increase in seagoing traffic, but this was tempered by an increase in the number of ships anchoring up for shelter in the "Mullion Roads", unable to pass into the Channel in bad weather and easterly winds.

Many ships were caught out by swift changes in the direction of the wind, along with severe weather conditions and storms which smashed the wooden ships against the cliffs and drowned the crew, many of whom could not swim, and stood little chance in the rocky waters. A lifeboat was obtained in 1867, but it was often difficult to launch. By the time a ship in distress was seen it was often too late to save it from the rocks, and even the Rocket Apparatus which proved so effective on many occasions could not always provide the necessary help in time. The list of casualties was long, and was something which affected the whole community.

The Pilchard Fishing continued throughout the 19th Century but by the early 1900s it was in decline and seine boats were soon to be seen no more. With the introduction of engines and larger Trawlers the methods of fishing began to change, with an emphasis on quantity, an increase in competition and new methods of preservation. The 1920s and 1930s saw more ups and downs in the industry and the Second World War caused further decline. Since that time the number of fishermen has gradually reduced with some making a living, but in general things catches have declined, with only the Crab and Lobster fishing surviving.

There are still many things we do not know about the Harbour. For instance we cannot name the crew of the Lifeboat, or the helpers who were paid for launching the boat, or all the local men who crewed the Rocket Apparatus, and I have not yet named all the fishermen, and I apologise if I have left anyone out. Perhaps in the future we may add to the information.

In the 1850s and 1860s when the shipping was suffering at its worst there were attempts to create a Harbour of Refuge in the Cove, between the Island and the Mainland, and also near to Scovern but despite plans being made, it did not materialise. Only towards the end of the century was a Harbour built in two phases, a West Pier between 1890 and 1892, during the winter of the Great Cornish Blizzard, and a South Pier between 1895 and 1897.

The Harbour has remained standing now for 115 years, and has become an iconic focus for many visiting the Cove. It was well maintained in the early days, but has nearly always suffered from storm and wave damage.

Since 1945 the Harbour has been owned by the National Trust which has spent large sums of money on repairs.

As owners they have spent some time looking forward at the next 100 years. Since 2006, in response to the perceived threat of sea level rises, and continuing costly damage, they have adopted a policy of Managed Retreat leading to total removal. Maybe repair for now, but later...?

The story of the Harbour and Cove has now been told. It is an iconic site, in a beautiful location, with a long history, a story worth telling, and which perhaps is deserved of preservation. Sadly, at the present time, this looks to be an unlikely outcome.

APPENDIX A Copy of Memorial Church Service held in 1872 at Mullion St. Mellanus Church Courtesy B. Mundy.

In Memory

OF

WILLIAM MUNDY,

AGED 58,

Late Coxswain of the *Daniel J. Draper* (Mullyon) Lifeboat,

HIS SONS,

JOEL, aged 25, and HENRY, aged 13,

AND OF

JOHN HENRY WILLIAMS,

AGED 20.

———

MULLYON.
1872.

FATAL ACCIDENT IN MOUNT'S BAY,

CORNWALL.

———

A SAD accident, by which four lives were lost, occurred to a Mullion fishing-boat on Friday, April 19, which, while it has cast a deep gloom over the whole of the little community among whom the unfortunate deceased resided, and while it has rendered desolate the home of one poor woman already a widow, has also deprived another mother with five children of their chief comforter and means of support. William Mundy, a man whose life has been spent in the fishery along this dangerous coast, and therefore an experienced boatman, together with two of his sons and another young man, left Mullion Cove on the Friday morning in his open fishing boat for Porthleven, in order to fetch some nets which were awaiting him there. The morning was fine, with a moderate breeze from N.N.E. ; and the water, therefore, comparatively smooth over the greater part of their course. They had proceeded to within a mile of the pier-head at Porthleven, when, standing in on her last tack, the boat was observed by some persons on the shore suddenly to lose way, and in a few moments to disappear altogether. That those on board were aware of their danger was evident, for they were engaged in lowering the sail when the boat sank. Immediately on the first symptom of disablement three boats were urged out with all speed to the spot, under oars and canvas, reaching the scene of the catastrophe in less than ten minutes ; but, alas ! nothing whatever was to be seen either of the boat or of the men. From the shore, by the aid of a telescope, one poor fellow was seen to struggle on the surface for about two minutes, but all were lost. A hat, a coat, a bag, a pair of oars, and a boat's bucket were found floating about, the last of these being the only thing by which the unhappy craft could be identified. The hat was sent on at once to Mullion by a passing boat, which also brought the sad intelligence that the men were drowned. The hat was recognised as belonging to one of the party, but as a hat might easily have been blown off without further accident, and as the day was so fine, and Mundy such a well-known experienced hand, many at Mullion refused to credit the story of his boat's having sunk. The return of messengers, however, later in the afternoon, confirmed the sad truth of the first report—All were drowned. There are various conjectures as to the cause of the boat's sinking ; but of these the most probable would seem to be that the "step" of the mast giving way, a plank was forced out of the boat's bottom, and thus, without capsizing, she gradually filled and sank, taking with her her unfortunate occupants. The names of the poor fellows deceased are William Mundy, aged 58 ; his sons, Joel, 25, and Henry, 13, and a friend, John Henry Williams, 20. The last named young man, who was a carpenter at Mullion, living with a widowed stepmother, was shortly to have been married—a pitiable case enough ; but poor Mundy's fate is even more distressing. The brave coxswain of the *Daniel J. Draper*, Mullion lifeboat, deservedly respected by all with whom he came in contact, who in his occupation of fisherman along this rugged coast had lived a life of peril, thus suddenly and mysteriously in bright weather finds, together with two of his sons, a watery grave.

REQUIESCANT IN PACE.

THE FAITHFUL DEPARTED.

———o———

*Mullyon Parish Church, 3rd Sunday after Easter,
21st April, 1872.*

———o———

OUR friends and our relations, by the will of God, depart this life and are no more seen by us, and when they have taken their departure the thought which is sometimes uppermost in our mind is—*Where* are they gone? and What is their state? These are questions which the reason alone of man could never answer, and if we had no other light to assist us in the enquiry all our endeavours to solve them would end in doubt, perplexity, and gloomy conjecture. But, Blessed be God ! we are not left to sorrow without hope ; the Gospel has brought Life and Immortality to light, making known to us a future state of endless happiness. The Voice from Heaven which Saint John the Divine records, proclaimed—"Blessed are the dead which die in the Lord"—Rev. xiv, 13 ; and thus we are assured that all who die in the hope and faith of the gospel, though they are no more seen by us, have entered into a state of eternal Rest.

I. This much we know, then, and are assured of *generally* ; but whereof their happiness consists, or by what means it is communicated, we cannot distinctly tell. And the reason of our imperfect knowledge of its nature is that it is too great, too pure, too perfect, for us to comprehend while we remain in the body. It is not that the Gospel which declares their blessedness is wanting in descriptions of it. Sufficient is made known respecting it to animate our hopes and to awaken our diligence ; but when we are told that it consists in endless rest, and enjoyment, and glory, we must remember that not the half has been told us, for "eye hath not seen nor ear heard, neither hath it entered into the heart of man to conceive it," because it surpasses in perfection and duration, the utmost stretch of mortal thought and human knowledge.

II. But while we know but generally we know *certainly*. The gospel of Christ, whose truth is established by miracles and confirmed by demonstrations of the Holy Spirit, everywhere proclaims the blessedness of the Just who are gone before us. Whatever may be obscure in the doctrine of the Redeemer, or in the writings of His Apostles, *this* is not doubtful, nor is it expressed in ambiguous language. The dead in Christ have entered that Rest prepared for them—and they shall rise again to a glorious immortality. This consolatory truth shines forth in the sacred page with a splendour which can never be eclipsed nor diminished —a truth it is which shall stand secure though the earth be destroyed and the heavens flee away. As sure as the Son of God rose from the dead, and, ascending up on high, opened the kingdom of Heaven to all believers, so sure is it that "*Blessed* are the dead which die in the Lord."

Thus the future blessedness of the righteous is certain as truth, and in its perfection beyond all thought. Moreover, the Gospel has, in part, drawn aside the veil which hides its glories from mortal view, and permits us to obtain a distant glance of their transcendent brightness. Accordingly as the Sun in a rough and cloudy day will sometimes appear and gladden us with his beams ; so do the glories of that unseen world penetrate the veil of darkness around us, and, shining from afar, suffer us to obtain a transient view of their celestial splendour. We could not, in our mortal state bear the full view of them, any more than the eye can bear to gaze full and direct upon the brightness of the mid-day Sun. But through the Gospel, as in a glass, darkly, we discover that that happiness consists in a freedom from the evils which assail us in this life, and in a participation of the joys of Heaven which are for evermore.

III. Consider then to what use we should apply this knowledge.

1. It ought to moderate our sorrow after those who have departed.

We may feel—most bitterly feel—the loss we have sustained, in being bereaved of the companions of our earthly pilgrimage. It makes the heart desolate when the object of its affections has been torn away ; it fills the spirit with an anguish which God alone can enable us to endure. How gladly would we restore and bring them back if we were able ! But if there be good reason to hope that they died in the hope and faith of the gospel, that they sought for pardon with true penitence, and placed all their trust in the merits of their Redeemer, then we may indeed hope they have entered into their Rest. And should we wish them back again to this world of trouble and sorrow ? Ought we ? We may bemoan the loss of their company and of their counsel, and feel, for a while, that we are left in the world forlorn and desolate; but so far as *they* are concerned there is no cause for sorrow, but rather for submission and even thankfulness. Had their lives been prolonged and our wishes, in that respect, been gratified, it might have been for them to sorrow, to suffer, and to sin as we do still. But "They are at Rest."

2. This knowledge ought to awaken our diligence in preparing to follow them.

For soon, we know not how soon, it will be our turn. What security have we for a day, or for an hour ? We see with those who have advanced far in life, and in declining years are waiting for their Lord ; the young, the healthy, and the strong, suddenly cut off as at a stroke !

William, the faithful husband, the loving father, the true brother, the steadfast friend ; Joel, the young man in all the strength of youth ; John Henry, with a career of hopeful, useful, manhood, just opening before him ; and Henry, the light-hearted, cheerful, willing boy : gone !—taken from us in a moment !

God's will be done !

"In the midst of life we are in death."

Whose turn next ?

" The souls of the righteous are in the hands of God and there shall no torment touch them. In the sight of the unwise they seemed to die, and their departure is taken for misery, and their going from us utter destruction ; but they are in peace."—Amen.

WHOSE TURN NEXT ?

"Man that is born of a woman hath but a short time to live."

Whose turn next ?

It may be yours. It may be mine. 'Suffer us not, O Lord, at our last hour, for any pains of death, to fall from Thee, and while we live make us in these and all others like daily spectacles of mortality to see how frail and uncertain our condition here is, that we may apply our hearts to that holy and heavenly wisdom that tendeth unto everlasting life.'

This blessed reward let us remember, beloved, is for the faithful only—the crown of life is for those who vanquish only, immortal glory is for those only who diligently seek it " BY PATIENT CONTINUANCE IN WELL DOING."

APPENDIX B; Plans for Harbour at Mullion 1868. From Cornwall Record Office Collections.

Reproduced with Permission from Cornwall Record Office. Ref. QSPDH/12 (1868-1891). (See Chapter 3)

Above; Proposed Plans for a Harbour at Mullion Cove in 1868, between Scovern (Ear Rock) and Henscath.

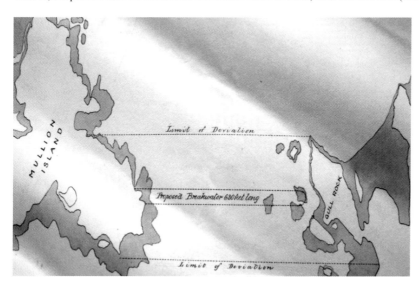

Above; Proposed plan for breakwater between Mullion Island and Gull Rock in 1868.

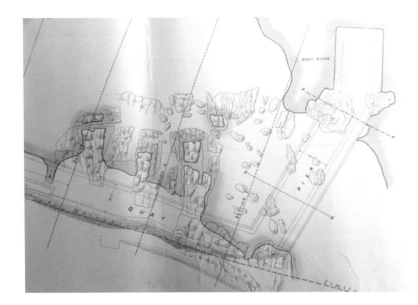

Left; 1890 Harbour Works showing the extent of Rock removed to create a flat Harbour floor.

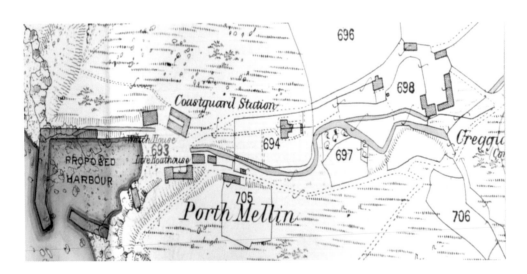

Above; 1880s O.S. Map showing proposed plan of the Harbour under revised plans.

APPENDIX C. 19th CENTURY, VICTORIAN RESIDENTS OF MULLION COVE

1841 Port Mellin. Samuel Hitchens (*Spelling varies to Hichens*) 60yrs, Fisherman Ann Hitchens 60yrs, Prudence Plaister 70yrs, William Pollard 20yrs Mariner, Esther Pollard 20yrs. **Criggian**. John Williams 35, Miller, Ann Williams 30, John Williams 10, Nanny Williams 8, Margaret Williams 7, Andrew Williams 5, William Williams 4, John Gilbert 15, Male Servant, Elizabeth Ford 12, Female Servant, Mary Prows 70, Independant. **1851 Mullion Cove.** Ann Hichens,72, Trinity Pensioner Wife. b Gunwalloe, Samuel Hichens (son) 47 Mariner, b Cadgwith, William Williams 68, Servant b Gunwalloe, Blind. **Mullion Cove**. Thomas Sterling 32,Coast Guard b Swanage, Louisa Sterling,32,b Lymington, Frances Mary Sterling 3, b Mullion, Louisa Sterling 4, b Mullion, James Thomas Sterling 2, b Gunwalloe. **Mullion Mills.** John Williams, 44, Miller and Farmer b. Gulval, Nancy Williams 44 b. Buryan, John Williams 20,b. Buryan, Nancy Williams 18, b Madron, Margaret Williams 16, b Mullion, Margaret Williams 16, b Mullion, Andrew Williams,15, b Mullion, William Williams 13, Scholar, b Mullion, Mary Prows 79, Mother in Law, b Sancreed, Edwin Willey 24, Servant b Mullion, William Rowe 35, lodger, Engineer b St Just **1861 Porthmellow Cove**. Ann Hichens 84, Housekeeper, Samuel Hichens, son, 57 Mariner. **Porthmellow Cove**. William Cotton47,Coastguard R.N. b Paul, Elizabeth Cotton, wife, 50 b Paul **Porthmellow Cove** Thomas Sterling 42, A.B R.N. Coastguard, Lousia Sterling, wife,42, Frances Sterling Dau, Scholar, b. Mullion, Louisa Sterling dau 14 Scholar b Mullion, James T. Sterling ,son, 12 Scholar b. Gunwalloe, Nora Sterling, dau, scholar b .Mullion, Alfred C Sterling, son,2, b Mullion. **Creggian Mill** John Williams 55, Miller & Farmer, Ann Williams 54 Farmers Wife, Nanny Williams 28,Farmers Dau ,Andrew Williams Son, 26, Miller, John Casley 4, Grandson b. Crow. **1871 Mullion Cove** Samuel Hitchens 68, Fisherman b. Grade, Susan Ann Hitchens,wife,25,b Hayle, Samuel A Richard Hitchens, scholar, 7 b Mullion, Harriet Jane Hitchens, dau, 5, b Mullion, Adelaide S Hitchens, dau, 4, b Mullion, Charles Jordan Hitchens, son, 2, b. Mullion, Annie Maria Hitchens, dau, 4 months, b. Mullion. **Coastguard House**. Thomas Ford,32,Boatman Coastguard, b. Kingstown Ireland, Louisa J Ford,wife,33, b. Torrington, Alma Bessie Ford,dau,3, b. Sithney, Harry Ford,son,1, b. Sithney. **Coastguard House**. Richard Woods,35, Coastguard Boatman, b.Plymouth., Maria Woods,Wife,33,b.Bodmin, Elenor Woods,dau,9 scholar, b. Bodmin,Mary Woods dau,7, b. Scholar, b.Isle of Wight, Adelaide Woods, dau,5,scholar b. Bodmin, Kate Woods, dau, 2 b. Mullion, Sophia Woods, dau, 3 months, b. Mullion. **Mill.** John Williams,64, Miller and Farmer of 20 acres Gulval, Ann Williams, Farmers Wife,64,Andrew Williamsson,38,Miller, Ann Williams,dau,37,Dorothy S Wiilliams, Grand-dau, 14, scholar b. St. Keverne, Andrew Casley,Grand-son,12,b.Crowan, Joseph George,14,Servant Indoors, b.Grade. **1881 Mullion Cove** Thomas Rees,43, Coastguard b. Greenhithe, Kent, Charlotte Rees wife, 38, b.Berro Somerset, Florence Rees dau,13 , scholar b. Gosport, William Rees,son,9,scholar b. Ireland, Edward Rees son,7, scholar, b. Ireland, Robert Rees,son,5,scholar, b. Ireland, Joseph Rees son, 4, b. Ireland, Harriet Rees, dau 2,b Mullion, Charlotte Rees,dau,1,b. Mullion. **Mullion Cove** Parland Griffith, Coastguardman, 32, b. Ireland, Matilda Griffith, wife, 24, b Mullion, William Edward Griffith,son,4, b. Mullion, Parland Griffith,son,2, b.Cornwall, Elizabeth M. Griffith,dau,1, b. Mullion, **Mullion Cove** Thomas Rees,43,Coastguardman,b. Greenhithe, Charlotte Rees wife, 38,b. Berro, Somerset. , Florence Rees,dau, 13, scholar. William Rees, son 9, scholar, Edward Rees, son,7, scholar, Robert Rees, son, 5, scholar, Joseph rees,son,4, scholar, Harriet Rees,dau,2,Charlotte Rees,dau,1.**Mullion Mills,** Andrew Williams, 35, Miller, Susan Williams,wife,30.KateTrip,19,Visitor,Dressmaker,b. Gulval, George Casley, Nephew,12,scholar,b. Mullion. **1891 Mullion Cove** John Luxton, 33,Coastguard, b Winkley, Devon. Elizabeth E Luxton wife,33, Ellen B Luxton,dau,5,b.Falmouth,John A Luxton son,3,b.Falmouth,Herbert Luxton,son,3,b Mullion **Mullion Cove** Augustus W Stagg, 34, Coastguard, b.Portsmouth, Grace Stagg,wife,25 b. Sennen Cove, Susanna Stagg,dau,2, b. Sennen Cove, Bertha J Stagg,dau,1.b. Lulworth, Dorset, Elizabeth E Matthews, Domestic Servant,22, Waitress, b.Mullion, Ellen Ede,Servant,25,Waitress,b. St. Pinnock, Cornwall. **Mullion Mills** Andrew Williams, 53,Miller and Farmer, John Williams,son,8,scholar, b Mullion, Jane Combellack 38,Housekeeper, b. Wendron, Mary Moyle,15,Domestic Servant,b.Wendron, Richard Bray,19,General Servant, b. Breage, Tony Bidgood*,Lodger,25,Mason,b. Liskeard, Lilly Bidgood 25, Lodger, b. Bodmin. *(*Bidgood was a stonemason employed by Lang of Liskeard who were the Construction engineers responsible for the building of the Harbour Piers)*

Source Census Records for years stated.

APPENDIX D THE HUERS HUT

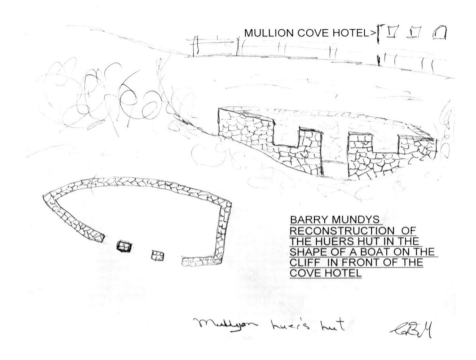

MULLION COVE HOTEL>

BARRY MUNDYS
RECONSTRUCTION OF
THE HUERS HUT IN THE
SHAPE OF A BOAT ON THE
CLIFF IN FRONT OF THE
COVE HOTEL

The Huers Hut. Art lovers and people who know him, may be a little surprised and astounded by the quality of Barrys` artistic talents, which no doubt stem from a misspent childhood messing about in and around Mullion Cove. In school, the Art Teacher could not understand why in every single picture drawn or painted by Barry, whatever the subject matter, he always managed to include a boat. The Fine Art Market, and Collectors will no doubt now be looking for "Originals" of his work.

APPENDIX E Explanation of Tithes as in Tithe Map.

TITHE MAP. *In Saxon times, before the Norman Conquest, 1/10th of all produce was paid to the Church, usually to support the local priest or monastery. With the Dissolution of the Monasteries many rights were acquired by the private Land Lords, but non-conformists began to oppose payment. Some Tithes were later paid in cash by agreement rather than produce following the Land Enclosure Acts. The Tithe Commutation Act of 1836 established a means by which Tithes could be converted to payment by cash.*

This required the drawing up of accurate Maps, which predate Ordnance Survey Maps, & were passed to the Inland Revenue. Many survive in Record Offices. They show field boundaries, rivers, Mills, buildings etc and the Apportionment list, for example, details of rents, owner or leaseholder (Wikipedia).

See next page

APPENDIX E (continued) Extract from MULLION TITHE MAP 1841. From Cornwall Record Office Collections. Reproduced with Permission from Cornwall Record Office. TM/160 (See Chapter 2)

APPORTIONMENT INFORMATION Mullion Tithe Map Apportionments Cornwall Record Office Collections Ref. X585/3
See Page 7.

Landowner	Occupiers	Nos referring to the plan	Name and description of Lands and Premises
			TERE BEAN
Johns, Tremenheare	Foxwell, Thomas	1281	Garden
Esq.Representatives of		1282	ditto
Freeholders (continued)		1283	ditto
		1284	Stitches in Beacon
		1285	ditto
		1286	ditto
		1287	ditto
	William Jose & others	1288	Morrop
	Williams, John	1289	Wastrell
		1290	Meadow
		1291	Mill
		1292	ditto
	Coastguard	1293	Watch House
	Jose & Co.	1294	Fish Cellar
		1295	Part of Cove
			PREDANNACK WARTHA
Leah Thomas Esq. (Lessee)	Leah, Thomas	286	Fish cellar
Shepherd, John	Shepherd, John	287	Fish cellar